Learning Approaches to Therapeutic Behavior Change

CURRENT CONCERNS IN CLINICAL PSYCHOLOGY IV

A series sponsored by the Department of Psychology of the University of Iowa

LEARNING APPROACHES TO THERAPEUTIC BEHAVIOR CHANGE

Edited by DONALD J. LEVIS, *University of Iowa*

Aldine Publishing Company/Chicago

First published 1970 by
Aldine Publishing Company
529 South Wabash Avenue
Chicago, Illinois 60605

Library of Congress Catalog Card Number 71-91721
SBN 202-26020-8
Printed in the United States of America

PREFACE

Learning approaches to psychotherapy indeed reflect an area of current concern in clinical psychology. It is only within the last decade that the learning approach has gained impetus in a field largely dominated for the last sixty years by Freudian and neo-Freudian therapy. Much of the current interest in this area can be attributed to the considerable dissatisfaction with more conventional approaches and to the recent development of new learning techniques of treatment. This marriage with the field of learning has already produced a number of ancillary benefits, the most important being the commitment of individuals associated with this orientation to introduce scientific respectability to a field that has remained relatively untouched by sound experimental data.

Although each of the behavioral or learning therapies has a strong affiliation with basic learning principles, marked differences in the strategy of their treatment techniques are apparent. These differences sometimes result from varying theoretical conceptions and sometimes merely reflect a choice as to which learning principles are selected or emphasized. For one orientation, frequently referred to as the operant conditioning approach, the emphasis has been placed upon the establishment of empirically derived techniques, which are developed relatively independently of any specific theoretical system. Another group is concerned not only with applying their learning orientation directly to the development of new techniques and approaches, but also with advancing theory. This latter group can be subdivided into the approaches of Pavlovian conditioning, systematic desensitization, implosive therapy, and social learning.

The purpose of this volume is to review the main positions developed, how they differ from each other, and the data upon which they are based. From this interchange of ideas it is hopeful that a meaningful foundation for each position's future development will be established. To achieve this objective, each of our distinguished contributors has been assigned the task of reviewing a particular position of behavioral therapy and commenting upon one of the other positions.

In the first chapter, your editor provides an introduction into the history, principles, and theory underlying this important new movement. In Chapters 2 and 3, Bradley Bucher and O. Ivar Lovaas and Leonard Krasner cover the operant conditioning orientation. Bradley and Lovaas review the techniques that apply to children and Krasner covers the token economy approaches used mainly with adult populations. Cyril Franks provides a comprehensive review of the Pavlovian model in Chapter 4, while Peter Lang and Thomas G. Stampfl cover systematic desensitization and implosive therapy, respectively, in Chapters 5 and 6. The social learning approach of Julian Rotter, presented in Chapter 7, completes the theoretical group of contributors. Last, Judson S. Brown keeps our contributors honest by providing an overview in Chapter 8.

Thanks are due to the Department of Psychology of the University of Iowa, who hosted this symposium; to the National Institute of Mental Health, which under Training Grant MH-5062 has made this annual series of lectures possible; to Leonard Eron; and to Karen Larson and Rochelle Holt for their expert secretarial assistance.

DONALD J. LEVIS

CONTRIBUTORS

Donald J. Levis
Department of Psychology
University of Iowa
Iowa City, Iowa 52240

Bradley Bucher and O. Ivar Lovaas
Department of Psychology
University of California
Los Angeles, California 90024

Leonard Krasner
Department of Psychology
State University of New York
Stony Brook, New York 11790

Cyril M. Franks
Psychology Service and Research Center
New Jersey Neuro-Psychiatric Institute
Princeton, New Jersey 08540

Peter J. Lang
Department of Psychology
University of Wisconsin
Madison, Wisconsin 53706

Thomas G. Stampfl
Department of Psychology
University of Wisconsin
Milwaukee, Wisconsin 53201

Julian B. Rotter
Department of Psychology
University of Connecticut
Storrs, Connecticut 06268

Judson S. Brown
Department of Psychology
University of Iowa
Iowa City, Iowa 52240

1

Behavioral Therapy: The Fourth Therapeutic Revolution?

DONALD J. LEVIS

The increasing number of individuals requesting mental health aid, coupled with the heterogeneity of problems brought to psychotherapy, have spurred many writers to stress the need for new and varied theories and techniques of treatment. Yet, a careful review of the literature will indicate that the field of psychotherapy is not without its share of creative ideas and diversified treatment techniques. Over fifty different theories and techniques of treatment can be found. Many of these techniques reportedly are designed to cover a wide variety of psychopathological problems. Some are intended for short-term treatment, and most claim considerable therapeutic effectiveness.

Nor are these positions lacking companions to articulately present their views. The psychoanalytic, Adlerian, Rogerian, existential, and humanistic movements have made an impact upon the field. And there are other choices, such as assertion-structured psychotherapy, au-

The preparation of this manuscript was facilitated by Grant No. MH-16584 from the National Institute of Health.

thoritarian therapy, bibliotherapy, cybernetic therapy, didatic group therapy, directive psychotherapy, family therapy, Gestalt therapy, multiple therapy, psychobiological therapy, psychodrama, rational therapy, reeducative therapy, round-table therapy, sector therapy, vegetotherapy, will therapy, and writing therapy, to mention just a few.

THE CREDIBILITY GAP

With such a vast potpourri of theories and therapeutic strategies available in the treatment arsenal of the therapist, an urgent cry for new approaches would appear unwarranted. Nevertheless, disenchantment with the status quo exists. The concern apparently centers around the unsupported claims of therapeutic efficacy that not only accompany the introduction of each technique but are perpetuated in the literature as accepted fact.

Even a cursory review of the psychotherapy literature attests to the validity of such criticisms. Not only is controlled research almost completely lacking on many techniques, but what research is performed usually falls short of incorporating even a minimum degree of methodological sophistication. This conclusion has been tendentiously and at times cogently presented (Eysenck, 1960, 1966). Unfortunately, the obvious possibility that psychotherapy may not be an effective therapeutic tool has only scratched the defense system of a field that apparently has generated a fetish for psychotherapy.

Professional Organizations. The activities and concerns of the field's professional organizations appear to reflect the above-suggested resistance. Legal, ethical, and other nonresearch issues continue to dominate the agenda of these organizations. Serious attempts to correct general misconceptions about the field's effectiveness or to elicit the aid of the scientific and clinical community to engage in a massive evaluation program are noticeably lacking. The problem of communication between researcher and nonresearcher has become so serious that experimentally oriented clinical psychologists have found it necessary to form a separate group within the clinical division of their national organization (Division 12, Section III). One member of this organization, Leonard Ullmann (1968), stated in his terminal address as chairman:

> More generally, I am worried by the increased pressure for professionalization in Division 12 and by applied psychologists. Application without scientific foundation is witchcraft. The politics I have seen alarm me: just as I think we must fight the medical model in the theory and treatment of people called abnormal, so I think we must fight the medical model in the formulation and treatment of people called psychologists.

Clinical Training Programs. Clinical training programs have also continued to perpetuate the division by teaching the standard techniques and skills as if they were gospel truths. Studies like those conducted by Rioch and her colleagues (1963) and by Albrondo, Dean, and Starkweather (1964) are frequently overlooked. These heretical experiments provide evidence that housewives and other neophyte psychotherapists can function as effectively as more extensively trained therapists. Still other authors, like Eysenck (1952), argue that in many cases no treatment is just as effective as being seen by a trained psychotherapist.

Not only is the concept of the professional clinician being challenged, but a growing number of writers (Ackerknecht, 1959; Rosenthal, 1963; Strupp, 1963; Tourney, 1967) are entertaining the notion that therapeutic achievements, if attainable, may be independent of any theoretical model, valid etiological knowledge, or specific treatment technique. It is possible that favorable results in therapy may be largely dependent on therapist and/or patient expectations, patient-therapists interactions, social learning, or the skill, experience, and emotional attributes of the therapists.

Without appropriate control conditions and without systematic research on these problems, few conclusions about a particular technique can be made. Yet, according to Levy's (1962) data, the median publication output of Ph.D. clinical psychologists sampled was 1.6 with 10 per cent of the group accounting for 45 per cent of the total output. The emphasis of training programs is obviously on producing practitioners, not scientists. Those few programs which do train clinical researchers produce products which are frequently undertrained or who tend to shy away from the more methodologically difficult research areas of psychotherapy.

Those who do attempt to undertake the task of evaluating the effects of psychotherapy are confronted by scores of mental health hospital directors and "humanitarian" psychotherapists who add to the problem by actively making research difficult. The latter frequently assume the a priori premise that existing therapeutic techniques obviously work, and that any introduction of a control nontreated group or unconventional treatment procedure is not only not in the best interest of the patient, but borders on the immoral and unethical. This prevailing attitude is reminiscent of the defenders of bloodletting techniques which dominated the medical profession up to the latter part of the nineteenth century.

The Current Trend. Some conciliation can be obtained, however, from the observation that the strong emotional allegiance characteristic of the early analytic therapies is dwindling. Although "schools" of psychotherapy provide a theoretical framework from which to predict and interpret, they also frequently generate dogmatism, ignorance, selective attention, and derogation of conflicting positions.

The emphasis in recent years has been placed upon short-term treatment procedures with attempts to achieve a rapid rehabilitation of the patient to an acceptable level of functioning. Whether for economical or practical considerations, this trend is in opposition to the objectives of the long-term classical analytic therapies which have dominated most of the verbal therapy world for the first half of this century. Training programs that reflect this change are becoming more eclectic and diversified in their orientation. Students are allowed greater freedom in selecting techniques that reflect their interests. Even the continual increase in available techniques can be viewed as a desire for change.

Despite the increasing signs of change, the need for evaluating psychotherapy has still not been squarely faced. The issue is being sidetracked somewhat by what appears to be a remobilization of the field's energies. The shift is now being made away from individual treatment to involvement in the mammoth program and corporate effort known as community psychiatry or psychology, with its emphasis upon the family, social, and cultural milieu. This latest trend has been hailed (Hobbs, 1964) as the "third psychiatric revolution" (first Pinel, second Freud), or perhaps more appropriately, the "latest therapeutic bandwagon" (Dunham, 1965). Garfield Tourney (1967, p. 794) after reviewing the area concludes:

> As we know, literally millions of dollars are being expended on these programs, with great claims for potential success being raised throughout the nation. The fundamental question remains as to the adequacy of our knowledge to develop such programs in an effective way. Through our fetish for therapy and a political belief that we can legislate away the problems of man, are we only about to enter a second "cult of curability" rather than a "third psychiatric revolution"? Are we to founder in the mire of social application and propaganda before the establishment of a hard basis of fact?

It is very depressing and in many ways alarming that such an important area as the mental health field should take so few precautions. How much more cautious and careful in drawing conclusions is the infrahuman researcher whose work has little immediate bearing on human lives.

THE CASE FOR A LEARNING APPROACH

In recent years, the field of psychotherapy has witnessed a substantial increase in the popularity of yet another new orientation which has frequently been referred to as the behavior, learning, or conditioning approach. This approach, which perhaps represents the development of the "fourth therapeutic revolution," actually encompasses a variety of different theoretical approaches and techniques, although each is based upon the learning literature.

Will this new approach or revolution only add more noise to an already uninterpretable system? Many writers, other than behavior therapists, believe not and have supported its objectives. Greenspoon (1965), for example, sees considerable advantage in the new orientation's emphasis on behavior and its measurement, on its pinpointing of environmental variables, on its attempt to develop precise definitions and specifiable operations, and on its stress of experimental control. Although Ford and Urban (1967) conclude that some of the treatment techniques are not new, they see originality in the emphasis the learning approach places on the systematic and detailed analysis of the presenting problem, the concrete specification of the objectives to be obtained, the selection of procedures in terms of the nature of the problem, the orderly and systematic operation incorporated to implement the desired objectives, and the attempt to obtain an objective verification of the extent to which goals have been achieved.

Nevertheless, critics of the movement, such as Breger and McGaugh (1965), have suggested that this approach, like the other existing clinical orientations, is becoming encapsulated in a dogmatic school. They point to such factors as a lack of adequate validation and the existing deficiencies in establishing a direct relationship between theory and treatment technique. Although Rachman and Eysenck (1966) in their reply to Breger and McGaugh attempt to counter these criticisms (also see Breger and McGaugh's rebuttal, 1966), these warnings should not go unheeded.

Despite the fact that considerable attention has been given to the movement's treatment success, the importance of the learning approach for this writer is independent of the reported rate of 90 per cent effectiveness. Such claims can be found for other techniques as far back as 1890. This so-called effectiveness may well be correlated more with the commitment and enthusiasm of the followers than with the efficacy of the technique per se. Considerably more research on a variety of homogeneous patient populations with long-term follow-ups is needed before any concrete conclusions can be reached. What is exciting, however, is the potential fruitfulness of the philosophy, orientation, and strategy behind this movement, and the possible impact it will have upon the rest of the mental health field. Four of these potential assets particularly stand out and are described below.

Emphasis on a Learning Model. Few investigators would object to the statement that learning plays an important role in the development of both normal and psychopathological behavior. Even the analytically trained Franz Alexander (1965) concluded, after many years of study, that the therapeutic process is best understood in learning terms. The controversy, however, is whether it is feasible to apply existing learning or conditioning laws to complex human behavior. Since the available evidence is insufficient, any strong pro or con statements to the above proposition would be premature. As Kimble (1961, p. 436) appropriately concluded:

> It may, some day, be known whether the laws of conditioning do or do not explain (say) psychopathological behavior. But that day is still far in the future. For the time being all that is possible is to

attempt the explanation of complex phenomena in simpler terms. It is to be expected that the resulting explanations will be incomplete and imperfect. Complex behavior, if it is explainable at all in these terms, certainly involves the simultaneous operation of many principles of conditioning. Unfortunately, these principles are not exactly known, and we know even less about the way in which they combine and function together.

Despite some of the incompleteness of the learning model, data do exist to suggest that some principles developed under laboratory conditions are operating, at least partially, in more complex, less well-defined situations. In Farber's words (1964, p. 37): "I believe a number of behavior theories have proved useful in providing a basis for predicting behavioral phenomena of interest even to those who consider such approaches too simplistic to account for the complexities of personality. Miller's studies of fear and conflict, Skinner's studies of operant conditioning, and the extension of both to the area of psychotherapy are cases in point." It follows then, as Eysenck (1960, p. 5) reasoned:

> If the laws which have been formulated are, not necessarily true, but at least partially correct, then it must follow that we can make deductions from them to cover the type of behavior represented by neurotic patients, construct a model which will duplicate the important and relevant features of the patient and suggest new and possibly helpful methods of treatment along lines laid down by learning theory.

Fortunately, Eysenck's suggestion has materialized. Indeed, a number of new ideas and treatment procedures have been developed.

Nature of Theory Construction. Although faced with the problem of generalizing across species and situational variables, the conditioning laws so far developed do rest upon considerable research data. This state of affairs does not appear to be the case for many nonlearning-based clinical theories. Nor is the strategy of theory construction the same. The usual approach of the learning theorists is to start from the more well-defined and controllable examples of behavior and then systematically and progressively work to build on these. In contrast, the fields of personality and clinical psychology are bombarded with complex, all encompassing theories designed to analyze the whole and complete human organism. Although occasionally riddled with creative and potentially fruitful ideas, the meshing and interlacing of so many surplus meaning concepts makes experimental analysis difficult, if not impossible. Sophistically, these theories provide their followers not only with a comforting set of terminology, but also with an illusory sense of understanding. Inevitably, these objectives have been achieved by sacrificing clarity, precision, and predictability.

This comparison between the strategies of the learning and traditional clinical approach is not intended to minimize the noncomprehensive state of the learning field (or, in fact, any other area of psychology). On the contrary, I want to emphasize how little is known about the laws governing the human organism and what little consolation is all the altruism, humanitarianism, and wishfulness when substituted for the collection of hard-core, reliable data. If we are ever to help people, we must attack the problems systematically.

Alignment with a Basic Research Area. Although the attempt to derive principles and procedures from one of the basic research areas is not necessarily a new maneuver, no other orientation has been so committed to this idea. By having a foundation of basic research to build upon, the behavioral therapists are at a distinct advantage.

Perhaps the slowness of the clinical field to show systematic growth is related to its reluctance to utilize the tools and procedures of basic researchers. Presently, there is little communication between areas. The majority of clinical psychologists are still oblivious to the potential value of the vast amount of human and subhuman data generated. The more advanced applied sciences progressed, in part, because they had learned this lesson. As Ford and Urban (1967, p. 338) suggest:

> One index of the viability and growth potential of a particular therapeutic approach may well be the extent to which it exposes itself to influences from, and attempts to utilize knowledge from, other domains. If the psychotherapy community does not adopt the responsibility for "bridge building," the therapy subject may be the victim.

The lack of integration will be perpetuated as long as the clinician remains deficient in scientific training and unconcerned about the need for a common language to facilitate this communication. The learning approach to clinical problems is an attempt to break down both of the above barriers.

Commitment to Assessment. The last asset to be covered is one of the most important. It is well-known that therapeutic techniques frequently appear to be more effective initially. This historical observation, unfortunately, did not reduce the enthusiastic claims of success generated early in the behavior therapy movement. Many of these claims were based on case histories, nonpatient populations, and experimental studies with patients which fell far short of the rigor required from a discipline striving for scientific respectability.

Despite the fact that even today the behavioral therapists, as a group, still show inadequate methodological sophistication and frequently commit errors of overgeneralization, their strong commitment to the scientific approach, coupled with their identification of psychotherapy as an objective, experimental discipline has resulted in a system of checks and balances. As Franks's book (1969) on assessment and the status of behavior therapies indicates, the policing has become internalized. Such self-correcting procedures are infrequent, if not lacking in other orientations.

Already more sophisticated studies on behavioral therapy are appearing (Paul, 1965). Such studies will eventually illustrate the strength and weakness of the approach. Once these are determined, appropriate modifications can be made. The question of validation, however, cannot be resolved by a few studies and might well take at least another twenty years of systematic work. Wishfulness cannot be substituted for the collection of hard-core data.

Let us now turn to a brief historical analysis of this young field's development.

HISTORICAL DEVELOPMENTS

The systematic application of learning principles to applied areas unfortunately has been a relatively slow development. As Kalish (1965) observed, the important factors contributing to this delay have been the tendency in the field to separate theory and application, a reluctance to use the clinic as a laboratory, and the acceptance of the traditional psychodynamic methods as the model for psychotherapy.

Interestingly, the value of applying the conditioning techniques to practical problems was noted by some of the early behaviorists. For example, Pavlov (1927, 1941) in the latter part of his career gave serious attention to the development and treatment of psychosis and neurosis. This interest influenced both his research efforts, which turned to the development of "neurotic" responses in dogs, and his theoretical endeavors, which touched upon the etiology of such symptoms as hysteria, paranoia, obsessions, and catalepsy. Watson (1925), another early champion of the learning approach, devoted a chapter in his book, *Behaviorism,* to personality. He, along with some of his students, performed the now classic experiments on the establishment of phobic reactions in infants via conditioning principles (Mary Cover Jones, 1924, 1924a; Watson and Rayner, 1920.)

Although a few additional early papers concerned with application can be found in the literature (Bagby, 1922; Brousseau, 1923; Guthrie, 1938; Humphrey, 1922; Mowrer and Mowrer, 1928; Smith and Guthrie, 1922), the field of clinical psychology remained for the most part dominated by the Freudian and neo-Freudian approaches throughout the twenties, thirties, and forties. This domination was partly responsible for the withdrawal of many learning-oriented psychologists from the applied areas.

The next important contributions were not made until the latter forties and early fifties. Dollard and Miller (1950), in their brilliant learning retranslation of Freudian theory, highlighted this period with contributions from Shaw (1946) and Shoben (1949). Although these efforts generated new hypotheses and concepts which illuminate the basic processes and principles essential for behavioral change, the emphasis was placed upon reinterpreting conventional therapeutic stragetegies and goals rather than applying the learning theory orientation directly to the development of new techniques and approaches.

Perhaps it was not until the appearance of Lindsley's paper (1956) on the application of operant conditioning methods to chronic schizophrenia and Wolpe's (1954) paper on reciprocal inhibition therapy that the field of behavior therapy received its real impetus. Both papers applied learning principles directly to the development of new techniques for treatment. Eysenck in 1958, championing Wolpe's approach, labelled the "new" learning approaches to psychopathology "behavior therapy." In that article he described behavior therapy in ten statements:

1. Behavior therapy is based on consistent, properly formulated theory leading to testable deductions.

2. Behavior therapy is derived from experimental studies specifically designed to test basic theory and deductions made therefrom.
3. It considers symptoms as unadaptive conditioned responses.
4. It regards symptoms as evidence of faulty learning.
5. It believes that symtomatology is determined by individual differences in conditionability and autonomic liability, as well as accidental environmental circumstances.
6. All treatment of neurotic disorders is concerned with habits existing at *present;* their historical development is largely irrelevant.
7. Cures are achieved by treating the symptom itself, that is by extinguishing unadaptive conditioned responses (CR's) establishing desirable CR's.
8. Interpretation, even if not completely subjective and erroneous, is irrelevant.
9. Symptomatic treatment leads to permanent recovery provided autonomic as well as skeletal surplus CR's are extinguished.
10. Personal relations are not essential for cures of neurotic disorder, although they may be useful in certain circumstances.

Since that time, the approach has developed considerably, and not all of the conclusions about behavior therapy reached by Eysenck in the fifties would be agreed upon now. The movement also was characterized by a strong anti-Freudian bias (despite Dollard and Miller's influence), and by premature claims of fantastic success.

Currently, the strong tendency by behavior therapists to reject the concepts and rationale of traditional psychodynamic approaches still exists with the emphasis continuing to be placed on the direct treatment of the symptom. Some of the rigidity, however, is giving way, and attempts to incorporate some of Freud's observations and hypotheses are being made. This trend can especially be seen in the approach of Stampfl's implosive therapy (see Chapter 6), Cautela's covert sensitization (1967), and in the work of Weitzman (1967). As concluded elsewhere (Stampfl and Levis, 1968), the adherence to learning or conditioning models of symptom origin and modification should be the sole criterion for labeling a position a "behavioral therapy."

THE IMPACT OF BASIC LEARNING PRINCIPLES AND THEORY

The learning psychologist's retreat to the laboratory was not without its value, because it was here that the groundwork for the principles and theories utilized by behavior theorists were made and well documented. The literature generated on extinction, counterconditioning, discrimination learning, schedules of reinforcement, punishment, and social imitation and reinforcement proved extremely helpful in the development of applied techniques (Bandura, 1961). The theoretical contributions of Pavlov, Hull, Mowrer, Tolman, and others also shed light on the development and treatment of psychopathology. In order to promote a better understanding of the various strategies of the behavior therapist, a review of some of the basic experimental paradigms will be presented, followed by an outline of some of the theoretical positions influencing the field.

The Conditioning Paradigm. Laboratory experiments on classical and instrumental conditioning procedures have had a direct bearing upon the development of most of the behavior therapist's techniques and theories. Descriptively, the classical conditioning paradigm differs from the instrumental procedure in that the sequence of events presented is *independent* of the subject's behavior. This sequence consists of an unconditioned stimulus (UCS), a stimulus known to evoke a regular and measurable response (UCR), and the conditioned stimulus (CS), a stimulus which at the outset of an experiment does not evoke the UCR. The usual order of the sequence is to present the CS followed closely in time by the UCS. The regular and measurable response elicited by the UCS is called an unconditioned response (UCR). If conditioning occurs, the CS presentation will elicit a conditioned response (CR) which resembles the UCR and which occurs prior to or in the absence of UCS presentations. Pavlov's (1927) work with the salivation of dogs illustrates the procedure used in classical conditioning.

Following the work of Bekhterev (1928) and Thorndike (1911), learned responses have also been developed by procedures labeled instrumental or operant conditioning. Here the UCS or reward presentation is made *dependent,* not *independent,* as in the classical procedure, upon the subject's behavior. An essential aspect of this procedure is that the reward follows the subject's response in some systematic manner. For example, every time a rat presses a bar (CR), a food pellet is dispensed (UCS). The instrumental procedures are usually classified into the following four categories: positive reward training, avoidance training, omission training, and punishment training (see Kimble, 1961; Konorski, 1948).

A thorough understanding of each of the classical and instrumental conditioning procedures, the relevant parameters affecting these procedures (such as the length of the CS-UCS interval, type and intensity of the UCS employed; the role of continuous, intermittent, and other schedules of reinforcement), the effects and conditions required to maximize or minimize stimulus and response generalization, and the role of secondary or learned reinforcers is *essential* to adequate and successful application of these principles. To summarize the relevant principles and techniques involved would require a separate chapter, if not a book. A better understanding of the role of the above factors can be obtained by reading Brown, 1961; Ferster and Skinner, 1957; Honig, 1966; Kimble, 1961,

1967; Mostofsky, 1965; Prokasy, 1965; and Wike, 1966.

The Role of Theory. As noted earlier, theory also plays an important role in the development of the behavioral therapy field. A review of the psychological literature can give one the impression that theory construction is the general pastime of the American psychologist. Concerned with this trend, a number of psychologists have questioned the necessity for the development of theories. Before their objections are covered, a short review of the role and value of theory construction may prove helpful. Spence (1951, p. 239) succinctly states the scientist's task in regard to theory construction:

> Briefly, it may be said that the primary aim of the scientist is to develop an understanding or knowledge of a particular realm of events or data. Such scientific understanding consists in formulating relationships between concepts that have reference to the particular event under observation. Thus, beginning with the sense data or events provided by observation, the scientist abstracts out of them certain ones on which he concentrates. To particular descriptive events and pattern of events he assigns, arbitrarily, language symbols (concepts), and then formulates the relationship observed to hold between these events (or concepts) in the form of laws. These observed regularities or laws provide at least partial explanation of the particular event under consideration, for explanation in science basically consists of nothing more than a statement of the relations of a particular event to one or more events.

In other words, theory should lead to a systematic expansion of knowledge mediated by specific empirical propositions, statements, hypotheses, and predictions that are subject to empirical test. As Hall and Lindzey (1957, p. 13) note, it is only the derivations or propositions derived from the theory that are open to empirical test; the theory itself is assumed and acceptance or rejection of it is determined by its *utility,* not by its truth or falsity.

According to Angyal (1941, p. 7), the utility of a theory lies essentially in its ability to serve as a guide for empirical studies. Unguided experimentation frequently can produce an unorganized mass of data.

Although the ordering and interpretation of data is a function of theory, Campbell (1952) reveals its real value when he stresses the importance of theory to predict and explain in advance, laws which were unknown before. He notes that most of the important theories in science have satisfied this test; they have led to the discovery of new laws which were unsuspected before the theory was developed.

Critics of theory construction in psychology do not deny the obvious achievement of theories in the history of science but question whether, at the present stage of the field's development, they are necessary. For example, it is pointed out by Skinner (1950), a most eloquent critic, that a science of behavior must eventually deal with behavior in its relation to certain manipulable variables. According to Skinner, theories in the field generally deal with the intervening steps in these relationships. Instead of prompting us to search for and explore more relevant variables, these intervening steps frequently only serve to provide verbal answers in place of the factual data we might find through further study. This state can easily create a false sense of security. Skinner further argues that research designed with respect to theory is likely to be wasteful since considerable energy and skill are devoted to their defense. This energy, he feels, could be directed toward a more "valuable" area of research.

Skinner's position has influenced many behavior therapists. These individuals, referred to as operant behavior modifiers, are mainly interested in the question of what techniques will shape a patient's behavior to the desired objective, rather than understanding why and how the techniques operate. This strategy has already resulted in the development of some important and interesting techniques (see Bucher and Lovaas's paper in Chapter 2, and Krasner's paper in Chapter 3).

Nevertheless, learning theory has also played a significant role in the development of this new field. The classic theories developed by Pavlov, Hull, Mowrer, and Tolman have had the most influence. A brief review of each system and its effect on the behavior therapy field will now be covered.

Pavlov's Physiological Theory of the Cerebral Cortex. Pavlov viewed conditioning as a function of cortical excitation and inhibition. He reasoned that when a "neutral" stimulus (for example, a tone) is presented to a subject, the afferent stimulation elicited by the tone produces an excitatory process at some definite point on the cortex. At the point of cortical stimulation, the excitatory process is thought to spread gradually over the entire sensory area. The intensity of the spreading effect or "irradiation" of excitation is hypothesized to decrease as the distance from the point of origin increases. With the onset of the UCS (for example, shock) this process is repeated but at a different point on the cortex. Because of its intensity, the irradiation is considered to be greater for the UCS than for the neutral stimulus. With repeated presentation of the neutral stimulus and the UCS (CS-US pairings), the cortical stimulation elicited by the tone should gravitate toward the stronger cortical stimulation of the shock until the locus of the neutral stimulus is of sufficient intensity to elicit a CR.

According to Pavlov, the strength of the response to the CS can be reduced by presenting the CS in the absence of the US (extinction). Under these conditions the cortical process of excitation is changed to inhibition, which like the previous excitation irradiates to the surrounding region of the cortex. The assumption is also made that when the elicitation of either cortical excitation or inhibition occurs, the surrounding areas of the cortex produce concurrently the opposite process, Pavlov, borrowing a term introduced by E. Hering and C. S. Sherrington, called the effect "induction." Excitation, in one area of the cortex, leads to increased inhibition in another area of the cortex (negative induction) while inhibition is believed to lead to increased excitation (positive induction).

When cortical irradiation of the inhibitory process is extreme, the resultant effect should be sleep, while extreme cortical excitation is believed to produce alert, active behavior. With an active clashing of the excitatory and inhibitory processes, or with the presentation of intense stimulation, a functional breakdown leading to psychopathological behavior is postulated. Such excessive cortical excitation or inhibition can then produce such symptoms as hysteria, neurasthenia, depressing mania, and catatonia.

Pavlov's theory of cortical irradiation is not given serious consideration today in many quarters, mainly because of lack of experimental support and because neurophysiologists are committed to synaptic transmission of neural inpulses, which is in opposition to Pavlov's concept of irradiation (Kimble, 1961). Yet his theory has been responsible for stimulating a number of experimental studies, many of which have application to the clinical field. His treatments of language as higher-order conditioned stimuli (second signaling system) and hypnosis as a form of partial sleep are only two of the many available examples.

Pavlov's theory also inspired Salter (1944, 1949, 1965) to develop his conditioned reflex therapy. According to Salter, the neurotic individual is suffering basically from an excess of inhibition, thus blocking his normal output of excitation. By encouraging the patient to directly express his feeling (a technique similar to the "assertive" response approach of Wolpe), Salter believes the neurosis will be overcome with a return to a normal level of excitation. Ban in *Conditioning and Psychiatry* attempts to bring the reader up to date on contemporary "Pavlovian" theory and research and how this literature relates to psychiatric problems. Franks's comprehensive paper in this volume (Chapter 4) also accomplishes this objective.

Hull's Monistic Reinforcement Theory. Hull (1943, 1952) attempted to synthesize the data obtained from Pavlov's classical conditioning procedure and Thorndike's trial and error learning under one, unitary concept of reinforcement, namely drive reduction. Briefly, the theory states that whenever any receptor activity (a stimulus) and effector activity (a response) occur in close temporal contiguity, and this temporal contiguity is closely associated with the diminution of a need (drive reduction), there will result an increment in the tendency for that afferent impulse on later occasions to evoke that reaction. These increments of successive reinforcements summate to yield a combined habit strength ($_{S}H_{R}$) which is hypothesized to be a simple positive growth function of the number of reinforcements received. Although Hull never directly applied his theory to the area of avoidance conditioning, which perhaps has greater clinical relevance, he did assume that the above state of affairs would occur independent of whether the learning was mediated by either the central or autonomic nervous system. For example, it could be deduced from Hull's theory that if a subject is presented with a tone (the neutral stimulus) for a five-second period, and if this period is followed immediately by shock (UCS) that terminates a second later, fear (UCR) elicited by shock onset will be reduced with shock termination. This reinforcing state of affairs (drive reduction) will strengthen any fear reaction anticipated by the occurrence of tone. With repeated trials the tone itself will come to elicit the fear. This new response to tone is called a conditioned or learned response.

Now fear also can be viewed as an acquired drive (Miller, 1948) which can heighten the subject's activity. By making a skeletal response (for example, a rat jumping over a barrier) contingent with CS and UCS offset, the skeletal response motivated by the acquired fear will also be strengthened by drive reduction and like the fear response will eventually be elicited by the CS. By making each skeletal response contingent with CS offset, the resulting drive reduction will reinforce the preceding anticipatory response in the absence of shock. Thus, fear onset serves as a drive, while fear reduction provides the conditions necessary for reinforcement.

To extinguish or weaken the conditioned response (for example, fear or avoidance behavior), Hull, like Pavlov, drew upon an inhibition theory. In brief, the assumption is made that every response of the organism, whether reinforced or not, results in an increment of reactive inhibition (I_R) which according to Hull is a primary negative drive resembling fatigue. The magnitude of I_R is considered to be an increasing function of the rate of response elicitation and the effortfulness of the response. In short, as I_R builds up, the strength of the response just preceding it becomes weakened, a function of the *direct incompatibility* of the two responses. It follows that since I_R (fatigue) is a drive, the reduction of this state is reinforcing and therefore is capable of strengthening any response which precedes it closely in time. Since I_R leads to cessation of activity, a resting response is conditioned, or more appropriately, counter-conditioned to the CS for the active response in the learning situation. Hull referred to this latter process as conditioned inhibition (${}_SI_R$). The total inhibition in the situation results from an additive combination of both I_R and ${}_SI_R$ (Hull, 1943; Kimble, 1961).

The implications of the Hullian counterconditioning model of extinction for psychotherapy has been noted by both Shoben (1949) and Wolpe (1958). According to Shoben the verbal interchange between patient and therapist should center around the symbolic reinstatement of the stimuli which produced and presently maintain the patient's anxiety. By reliving at a symbolic level the stimulus situations originally associated with painful events, the anxiety attached to these stimulus situations will reoccur in the context of the patient-therapist relationship. If the above relationship also generates feelings of pleasure, acceptance, security, and other nonanxious affective reactions, the anxiety stimuli will eventually become counterconditioned by these positive reactions.

Wolpe's interpretation of Hull's notions, however, led to a rather different form of treatment called reciprocal inhibition therapy. Stimulated by Sherrington's (1947) concept of reciprocal inhibition of one spinal reflex by another, Wolpe reasoned that if conditioned inhibition is built up during extinction because traces of the conditioned stimuli are contemporaneous with reactive inhibition of the conditioned response, it is reasonable that any response, not only fatigue, which is directly inhibitory or antagonistic to the conditioned response, will result in the buildup of conditioned inhibition.

Wolpe outlined four responses (assertive, sexual, conditioned avoidance, and relaxation) which he believes can function as reciprocal inhibitors of anxiety. He suggested that assertive responding can be utilized in those situations where anxiety is hypothesized to inhibit the expression of resentment. If the patient can be motivated to express his resentment by verbally asserting himself, the latter response will, according to Wolpe, reciprocally inhibit the anxiety motivating the inhibition. A similar line of reasoning is also applied to those situations in which the anxiety response has been conditioned to various aspects of sexual situations, resulting in partial or complete inhibition of sexual responsiveness. The technique used here is to instruct the patient to wait for or to seek out situations in which pleasurable sexual feelings (the reciprocal inhibitor) are aroused and to "let himself go" in these situations as fully as possible.

A variety of other techniques is suggested by Wolpe which utilize such negative reinforcers as electric shock.

By employing the appropriate contingencies, one can shape new avoidance responses which are designed to provide behavior that can better cope with the anxiety-provoking situations or conditioned behaviors that directly prevent the onset of the anxiety-eliciting stimuli.

Although Wolpe relates each of these techniques to a counterconditioning interpretation of extinction, it is his use of the relaxation technique of Jacobson (1938) in conjunction with the presentation of anxiety-eliciting stimuli that has particular relevance here. This procedure, referred to as systematic desensitization, involves training the patient in deep muscle-relaxation, constructing with the patient a graded list of anxiety-eliciting stimuli, and then pairing the items on the list with relaxation. The list of selected stimuli, referred to as an anxiety hierarchy, is presented from least to most disturbing. The patient is asked to imagine each item for a brief period (3 to 10 seconds) and then to relax after each scene presentation. The complete sequence is to relax, imagine, relax, stop imagining, and relax. When the patient can imagine the item without experiencing anxiety, the next item in the hierarchy is introduced. An attempt is made to keep the anxiety response at a minimum, so the stronger relaxation response can serve as an effective counterconditioning agent (see Lang's paper, Chapter 5).

Mowrer's Two-Factor Theory. Mowrer (1947, 1960) broke away from the monistic reinforcement theory of Hull mainly because of the latter theory's awkwardness in handling problems associated with avoidance learning.[1] Mowrer (1947) maintains that there are two types of learning, one based on the procedure of classical conditioning, which incorporates only a contiguity principle, and one based on instrumental or trial and error learning, which includes both a contiguity and a drive-reduction

1. Eysenck (1963,1963a) also sees the advantage of two-factor theories. He believes this orientation would provide a better framework for Wolpe's techniques.

notion of reinforcement. In Mowrer's system, unlike that of Hull's, a distinction is made between conditioning mediated mainly by the central nervous system and conditioning mediated mainly by the autonomic nervous system. The former is learned by the reduction of a drive, while the latter is learned by drive induction or simply the pairing of a CS with a UCS. For example, if a tone is presented to a subject for a five-second period and followed closely by shock, the necessary and sufficient conditions for the elicitation and reinforcement of the classical or autonomic responses of fear are present. In other words, the conditioning of fear or anxiety responses is simply a result of the above pairing, with a reduction of a drive state playing no part in this learning. With sufficient repetitions, tone will elicit the fear response in the absence of shock. Fear is also considered to have drive properties, and if a response is learned which terminates or reduces the fear-provoking stimuli, the response will be reinforced by a reduction in fear.

Mowrer, in 1960, revised the above two-factor theory so that the theory would be more applicable to appetitive (approach) as well as avoidance learning. He concluded that all learning by implication was a result of classical conditioning of internal states. The theory remained "two-factors" only as to whether the form of reinforcement was incremental (punishment) or decremental (reward). Mowrer's 1947 version, however, still seems to be the preferred interpretation by many theorists (for an updated review of support for this version, see Rescorla and Solomon, 1967).

Extending the two-factor notion to human psychopathology, Stampfl (Stampfl, 1966; Stampfl and Levis, 1967) viewed the conditioning of aversive stimulation in humans as resulting from the simple contiguity of this stimulation in time or space with primary (unconditioned) or other secondary (learned) aversive stimuli. The stimulus patterns correlated with these events are assumed to acquire aversive internal properties labeled fear. Attempts by the patient to minimize or prevent the aversive stimuli from occurring then constitute "symptom" behavior. These avoidance behaviors are believed to be reinforced precisely because they reduce or remove conditioned aversive stimuli. The position that symptoms consist of behaviors designed to avoid anxiety-provoking stimuli is not new and is quite similar to the position taken by Freud (1936) in his last interpretation of the role of the symptom.

The importance of Mowrer's model for Stampfl comes from the two-factor position on extinction. According to Mowrer's theory, to decondition the avoidance response one needs only to extinguish the fear or anxiety associated with the conditioned stimuli. If the drive state motivating a response is not present, stimuli will not be available to elicit the behavior. To extinguish this drive or fear state, one only has to present the total stimulus complex in the absence of the unconditioned stimulus. The extinction process appears to be facilitated in the laboratory when the CS is presented and the avoidance response is blocked to prevent escape from aversive stimuli.

By incorporating the above response prevention notion, Stampfl developed a technique (implosive therapy) in which the patient is "bombarded" with fear-eliciting cues. These cues, which are hypothesized by the therapist, are presented in the form of scenes which the patient is instructed to imagine. Attempts to avoid experiencing these cues are thwarted by the therapist.

Interestingly, many of the hypothesized cues suggested by Stampfl are quite similar to some of the dynamic notions of the Freudian model. Interpretations of early conditioning experiences, in fact, are very similar to those of Dollard and Miller (1950). Unlike other behavior therapy positions, considerable emphasis is given to mediated cues (see Stampfl's paper, Chapter 6).

Tolman's Sign Learning. Tolman (1932) broke away

from the traditional stimulus-response orientation of conditioning in an attempt to develop a theoretical system which would be highly general and applicable to all of psychology. Being dissatisfied with the neater theoretical structures of his time, which he considered to have predictive limitations and oversimplified paradigms, Tolman attempted to integrate into one theory the facts of classical conditioning, trial and error learning, and "inventive" or higher learning processes.

All learning is considered to be sign-gestalt learning or the acquiring of bits of "knowledge" or "cognitions." According to Tolman (1934, pp. 392–393), sign-gestalts can be conceptualized as consisting of three parts: a *sign,* a *significate,* and a *behavior-route leading from sign to significate.* "A sign-gestalt is equivalent to an 'expectation' by the animal that 'this' (that is, the sign), 'if behaved to in such and such a way' (that is, the behavior-route), will lead to 'that' (that is, the significate)."

When signs (certain sets of stimuli) become integrated within the nervous system with certain sign-gestalt expectations, learning occurs. Hypotheses are made and rejected. When one confirms the expectation, it is learned. Therefore, reinforcement in the sense of an S-R position is not an essential ingredient for the learning to occur.

Few behavioral therapists directly ascribe to Tolman theory, although his position has had a definite influence on a number of writers. Breger and McGaugh (1965), for example, suggest that the problem of neurosis can be conceptualized in terms of information storage and retrieval, a concept based on the fundamental idea that what is learned in a neurosis is a set of central strategies which guide the person's adaptation to his environment. The neurosis is therefore not viewed as symptoms. Psychotherapy is conceived by Breger and McGaugh as involving the learning of a new set of strategies via a new language, a new syntax as well as a new vocabulary.

Although influenced by Hull and Lewin, Rotter's "expectancy-reinforcement" theory (1954) which was designed to provide a framework from which the clinician could operate, also definitely shows the impact of Tolman's position. Behavior for Rotter is goal-directed, and the directional aspect of behavior is inferred from the effect of the reinforcing conditions. An individual's behaviors, needs, and goals are viewed as belonging to a functionally related system. The behavior potential is considered to be a function of both the individual's expectancy of the goal and the reinforcement value of the external reinforcement. Emphasis is placed upon a person's social interactions as opposed to his internal feelings as an explanation or criterion for pathology. It is not so much the underlying motivation that needs to be altered or removed according to Rotter, but rather the manner in which the patient has learned to gratify his needs. The question asked is "What is the patient trying to obtain by his behavior rather than what is he trying to avoid?" Once the answer to this question has been ascertained, the assumption is made that the present mode of responding is viewed by the patient as the best way he knows of obtaining his goal. In addition, more efficient behaviors for achieving the same goal are either not available in the patient's repertoire or are believed to lead to punishment or frustration of another need. The task of the therapist then becomes one of manipulating expectancies and reinforcement values in such a way as to bring about new behaviors. These objectives are pursued within the framework of conventional therapy emphasizing the structuring of therapy, the therapeutic relationship and transference, catharsis, interpretations, and insight (see Rotter's paper, Chapter 7).

ANIMAL EXPERIMENTATION

The theories and behavior principles just reviewed are to a large extent supported directly or indirectly by infrahuman research data which frequently utilizes the laboratory rat as subject material. Skepticism naturally arises concerning the applicability of these laws to human behavior, since marked differences are apparent between the rat's and the human's social and verbal development. The argument against the probability of generating the essential laws of human behavior from rat research has been eloquently put forth by Koch (1956), who even questions the possibility of generating adequate laws about rats from rat data that are obtained from different colonies in different laboratories.

Hunt (1964) extends the argument to the data generated by the so-called "experimental neurosis" which is reflected in the work of Liddell (1964), Maier (1939), Miller (1964), Masserman (1943), and Pavlov (1927). Although seductively appealing and full of promise, Hunt believes the animal neurosis experiments have not amplified our knowledge about human psychopathology. He states:

> More characteristically, these experiments receive favorable attention because they illustrate, duplicate, or confirm things already known about the human case. While illustration and confirmation are not trivial contributions, we must ask why this comparative sterility. [p. 28]

The comparative sterility of animal experimentation to provide insight into human psychopathology as compared with that generated by psychoanalytic theory may well be argued. Yet, perhaps this sterility, if it exists, is more a function of the majority of rat runners' lack of clinical training, which may provide the basis for generating stimulating research, than the inherent problem of generalizing from one organism to another. It may also turn out, in the last analysis, that data collected from infrahuman species will prove more useful for generalizing than the vast amount of research presently being conducted on the "sophisticated" college sophomore. If maladaptive behavior is tied, in part, to conditioning of emotional or autonomic responses, and if mediated internal cues such as words, thoughts, images, and memories in the human turn out to follow essentially the same conditioning laws as extroceptive stimuli, the argument for animal research becomes much stronger. Not only does the rat provide a less complex organism which may be more advantageous for deciphering basic laws; it also is equipped with an autonomic nervous system not too unlike that of the human. Furthermore, animals are expendable and subject to experimentation that for ethical reasons cannot be carried out on humans. In fact, if infrahuman experimentation only provides a vehicle for illustration and confirmation of suspected hypotheses about the human, the effort is more than worthwhile.

Despite the various arguments pro and con, and the obvious need for confirmation at the human level, infrahuman research has had a considerable heuristic influence on behavioral therapy development. Both Wolpe and Stampfl's research with animals was instrumental in developing their respective theories, and Skinner's work has had a profound influence on the operant conditioning approach. The influence of these data, whether justified or not, has given impetus to the development of treatment techniques which were previously undeveloped or unhighlighted; and this is certainly no small accomplishment.

CONCLUDING REMARKS

Although the subject matter discussed in this introductory chapter has roamed from such topics as the role of professional organizations to the value of animal experimentation, the main objectives have been twofold—firstly, an attempt has been made to highlight the potential value of a learning based orientation for the clinical field and, secondly, to provide an outline of the theoretical models and principles underlying the therapeutic techniques to be reviewed in the following chapters. It is my belief that the reader will find that the material in this volume more than supports the contention that the learning approach to therapeutic behavior modification has made an excellent start. The ability of the behavior therapists to employ different strategies, to contribute innovative and creative ideas, and to develop new treatment techniques all attest to the field's virility. It should be realized that much more needs to be accomplished. One cannot overemphasize the necessity for continual research both in the laboratory and in the field; the need to bring antiquated theoretical models into the mainstream of contemporary learning literature; and the importance of training students thoroughly in both the areas of learning and psychopathology. If these objectives are met and the virtues of caution, humility, and openness to criticism are mastered, a step will have been made to rescue the mental health field from the Dark Ages. Truly, such a feat would be revolutionary.

REFERENCES

ACKERKNECHT, E. H. *A short history of psychiatry*. New York: Hafner Publishing Co., 1959.

ALBRONDO, H. F., DEAN, R. L., and STARKWEATHER, J. A. Social class and psychotherapy. *Archives of General Psychiatry,* 1964, *10,* 276–83.

ALEXANDER, F. The dynamics of psychotherapy in the light of learning theory. *International Journal of Psychiatry,* 1965, *1,* 189–97.

ANGYAL, A. *Foundations for a science of personality*. New York: Oxford, 1941.

BAGBY, E. The etiology of phobias. *Journal of Abnormal and Social Psychology,* 1922, *17,* 16–18.

BAN, T. *Conditioning and psychiatry*. Chicago: Aldine, 1964.

BANDURA, A. Psychotherapy as a learning process. *Psychological Bulletin,* 1961, *58,* 143–45.

BEKHTEREV, V. M. *General principles of human reflexology,* trans. by E. and W. Murphy. New York: International University Press, 1928.

BREGER, L., and MCGAUGH, J. L. Critique and reformulation of "Learning Theory" approaches to psychotherapy and neurosis. *Psychological Bulletin,* 1965, *63,* 338–58.

BREGER, L., and MCGAUGH, J. L. Learning theory and behavior therapy: A reply to Rachman and Eysenck. *Psychological Bulletin,* 1966, *65,* 170–73.

BROUSSEAU, K. Suggestion on a case of traumatic hysteria. *Journal of Abnormal and Social Psychology,* 1923, *4,* 346–49.

BROWN, J. S. *The motivation of behavior.* New York: McGraw-Hill, 1961.

CAMPBELL, N. *What is science.* New York: Dover Publications, 1952.

CAUTELA, J. R. Covert sensitization. *Psychological Reports,* 1967, *20,* 459–68.

DOLLARD, J. and MILLER, N. E. *Personality and psychotherapy.* New York: McGraw-Hill, 1950.

DUNHAM, H. W. Community psyciatry—the newest therapeutic bandwagon, *Archives of General Psychiatry,* 1965, *12,* 303–13.

EYSENCK, H. J. The effects of psychotherapy: An evaluation. *Journal of Consulting Psychology,* 1952, *16,* 319–24.

EYSENCK, H. J. *The scientific study of personality.* New York: Wiley, 1958.

EYSENCK, H. J. (Ed.) *Behavior therapy and the neuroses.* New York: Pergamon Press, 1960.

EYSENCK, H. J. Behavior therapy, extinction and relapse in neurosis. *British Journal of Psychiatry,* 1963, *109,* 12–18.

EYSENCK, H. J. Behavior therapy, spontaneous remission and transference in neurotics. *American Journal of Psychiatry,* 1963a, *119,* 867–71.

EYSENCK, H. J. *The effects of psychotherapy.* New York: International Science Press, 1966.

FARBER, I. E. A framework for the study of personality as a behavioral science. In P. Worchel and D. Byrne (Eds.), *Personality change.* New York: Wiley, 1964.

FERSTER, C. B., and SKINNER, B. F. *Schedules of reinforcement.* New York: Appleton-Century-Crofts, 1957.

FORD, D. H., and URBAN, H. B. Psychotherapy. *Annual Review of Psychology,* 1967, *17,* 333–72.

FRANKS, C. M. (Ed.) *Behavior therapy: Appraisal and status.* New York: McGraw-Hill, 1969.

FREUD, S. *The problem of anxiety,* trans. by H. A. Bunker. New York: Psychoanalytic Quarterly Press and W. W. Norton, 1936, 85–92.

GREENSPOON, J. Learning theory contributions to psychotherapy. *Psychotherapy: Theory, Research and Practice,* 1965, *2,* 145–46.

GUTHRIE, E. R. *The psychology of human conflict.* New York: Harper and Row, 1938.

HALL, C., and LINDZEY, G. *Theories of personality.* New York: Wiley, 1957.

HOBBS, N. Mental health's third revolution. *American Journal of Orthopsychiatrists,* 1964, *34,* 822–33.

HONIG, W. K. (Ed.) *Operant behavior: Areas of research and application.* New York: Appleton-Century-Crofts, 1966.

HULL, C. L. *Principles of Behavior.* New York: Appleton-Century-Crofts, 1943.

HULL, C. L. *A behavior system: An introduction to behavior theory concerning the individual organism.* New Haven: Yale University Press., 1952.

HUMPHREY, G. The conditional reflex and the elementary social reaction. *Journal of Abnormal and Social Psychology,* 1922, *2,* 113–20.

HUNT, H. F. Problems in the interpretation of experimental neuroses. *Psychological Reports,* 1964, *15,* 27–35.

JACOBSON, E. *Progressive relaxation.* Chicago: University of Chicago Press, 1938.

JONES, MARY C. The elimination of children's fears. *Journal of Experimental Psychology,* 1924, *7,* 383–90.

JONES, MARY C. A laboratory study of fear: the case of Peter. *Pedagogical Seminar,* 1924a, *31,* 308–15.

KALISH, H. I. Behavior therapy. In B. Wolman (Ed.), *Handbook of clinical psychology,* New York: McGraw-Hill, 1965.

KIMBLE, G. A. *Hilgard and Marquis' conditioning and learning.* New York: Appleton-Century-Crofts, 1961.

KIMBLE, G. A. (Ed.) *Foundations of conditioning and learning.* New York: Appleton-Century-Crofts, 1967.

KOCH, S. Behavior as "intrinsically" regulated: Work notes towards a pretheory of phenomena called "motivational." In M. R. Jones (Ed.), *Nebraska symposium on motivation.* Lincoln: University of Nebraska Press, 1956.

KONORSKI, J. *Conditioned reflexes and neuron organization.* New York: Cambridge University Press, 1948.

LEVY, L. H. The skew in clinical psychology. *American Psychologist,* 1962, *17,* 244–52.

LINDSLEY, O. R. Operant conditioning methods applied to research in chronic schizophrenia. *Psychiatric Research Reports,* 1956, *5,* 118–38.

MAIER, N. R. F. *Studies of abnormal behavior in the rat.* New York: Harper and Row, 1939.

MASSERMAN, J. H. *Behavior and neurosis.* Chicago: University of Chicago Press, 1943.

MILLER, N. E. Studies of fear as an acquirable drive: I. Fear as motivation and fear-reduction as reinforcement in the learning of a new response. *Journal of Experimental Psychology,* 1948, *38,* 89–101.

MILLER, N. E. Some implications of modern behavior theory for personality change and psychotherapy. In P. Worchel and D. Byrne (Eds.), *Personality change.* New York: Wiley, 1964.

MOSTOFSKY, D. I. (Ed.) *Stimulus generalization.* Stanford: Stanford University Press, 1965.

MOWRER, O. H. On the dual nature of learning: A reinterpretation of "conditioning" and "problem solving." *Harvard Educational Review,* 1947, *17,* 102–48.

MOWRER, O. H. *Learning theory and behavior.* New York: Wiley, 1960.

MOWRER, O. H., and MOWRER, W. M. Enuresis: A method for its study and treatment. *American Journal of Orthopsychiatry,* 1928, *8,* 346–459.

PAUL, G. L. *Insight versus desensitization in psychotherapy: An experiment in anxiety reduction.* Stanford: Stanford University Press, 1965.

PAVLOV, I. P. *Conditioned reflexes.* London: Oxford University Press, 1927.

PAVLOV, I. P. *Lectures on conditioned reflexes.* New York: International University Press, 1941.

PROKASY, W. F. (Ed.) *Classical conditioning: A symposium.* New York: Appleton-Century-Crofts, 1965.

RACHMAN, S., and EYSENCK, H. J. Reply to a "critique and reformulation" of behavior therapy. *Psychological Bulletin,* 1966, *65,* 165–69.

RESCORLA, R. A., and SOLOMON, R. L. Two-process learning theory: Relationships between Pavlovian conditioning and instrumental learning. *Psychological Review,* 1967, *74,* 151–82.

RIOCH, M. J. , ELKES, C., FLINT, A. A., USDANSKY, B. S., NEWMAN, R. G., and SILBER, E. National Institute of Mental Health pilot study in training mental health counselors. *American Journal of Orthopsychiatry,* 1963, *33,* 678–89.

ROSENTHAL, R. *Experimenter effects in behavioral research.* New York: Appleton-Century-Crofts, 1966.

ROTTER, J. B. *Social learning and clinical psychology.* Englewood Cliffs: Prentice-Hall, 1954.

SALTER, A. *What is hypnosis?* New York: Richard R. Smith, 1944.

SALTER, A. *Conditioned reflex therapy.* New York: Farrar, Straus, 1949.

SALTER, A. The theory and practice of conditioned reflex therapy. In J. Wolpe, A. Salter, and L. J. Reyna (Eds.), *The conditioning therapies.* New York: Holt, Rinehart and Winston, 1965.

SHAW, F. J. A stimulus-response analysis of repression and insight in psychotherapy. *Psychological Review,* 1946, *53,* 36–42.

SHERRINGTON, C. S. *The integrative action of the central nervous system.* Cambridge: Cambridge University Press, 1947.

SHOBEN, E. J. Psychotherapy as a problem in learning theory. *Psychological Bulletin,* 1949, *46,* 366–92.

SKINNER, B. F. Are theories of learning necessary? *Psychological Review,* 1950, *57,* 193–216.

SMITH, S. and GUTHRIE, E. R. Exhibitionism. *Journal of Abnormal and Social Psychology,* 1922, *17,* 206–09.

SPENCE, K. W. Theoretical interpretations of learning. In C. P. Stone (Ed.), *Comparative Psychology.* New York: Prentice-Hall, 1951.

STAMPFL, T. G. Implosive therapy, Part I: The theory. In S. G. Armitage (Ed.), *Behavioral modification techniques in the treatment of emotional disorders,* Battle Creek, Michigan: V. A. Publications, 12–21, 1966.

STAMPFL, T. G., and LEVIS, D. J. The essentials of implosive therapy: A learning theory based on psychodynamic behavioral therapy. *Journal of Abnormal Psychology,* 1967, *72,* 496–503.

STAMPFL, T. G. and LEVIS, D. J. Implosive therapy—a behavioral therapy? *Behaviour Research and Therapy,* 1968, *6,* 31–36.

STRUPP, H. H. The outcome problem in psychotherapy revisited, *Psychotherapy: Theory, Research and Practice,* 1963, *1,* 1–13.

THORNDIKE, E. L. *Animal intelligence.* New York: Macmillan, 1911.

TOLMAN, E. C. *Purposive behavior in animals and men.* New York: Macmillan, 1932.

TOLMAN, E. C. Theories of learning. In F. A. Moss (Ed.), *Comparative psychology.* New York: Prentice-Hall, 1934.

TOURNEY, G. A history of therapeutic fashions in psychiatry, 1800–1966. *American Journal of Psychiatry,* 1967, *124,* 6, 784–96.

ULLMANN, L. Closing address as Chairman of the experimental clinical division of APA. Division 12, Section III, *Business Meeting Report,* 1968.

WATSON, J. B. *Behaviorism.* New York: Horton, 1925.

WATSON, J. B., and RAYNER, R. Conditioned emotional reaction. *Journal of Experimental Psychology,* 1920, *3,* 1–4.

WEITZMAN, B. Behavior therapy and psychotherapy. *Psychological Review,* 1967, *74,* 300–17.

WIKE, E. L. (Ed.) *Secondary reinforcement.* New York: Harper & Row, 1966.

WOLPE, J. Reciprocal inhibition as the main basis of psychotherapeutic effects. *AMA Archives of Neurological Psychiatry,* 1954, *72,* 205–26.

WOLPE, J. *Psychotherapy by reciprocal inhibition.* Stanford: Stanford University Press, 1958.

2

Operant Procedures in Behavior Modification with Children

BRADLEY BUCHER AND O. IVAR LOVAAS

In the past few years behavior modification techniques have been applied to an increasing number of childhood disorders. The growth of operant procedures is especially marked. Reviewing the work then available, Rachman (1962) noted no explicit therapeutic application of operant techniques to problems of childhood. Enough research now exists to warrant a critical evaluation.

We will not attempt a complete survey of the field in this paper; a comprehensive survey with a detailed bibliography is already available (Gelfand and Hartmann, 1968). Rather, we shall attempt to point out some essential elements of operant work with disturbed behavior, using selected studies to illustrate these points. We will begin by outlining some significant conceptual features in behavior therapy work using operant procedures. Then we will review certain procedures for the elimination of psychopathological behaviors, and others designed to help children acquire new behaviors to make them more com-

The preparation of this manuscript was facilitated by Grant No. MH-11440 from the National Institute of Health.

petent in their environment. We will then turn to a discussion of the role of assessment in behavior therapy work, followed by a discussion of the kinds of research designs employed in behavior therapy work. Finally we will comment briefly on some of the implications raised by this research.

THE CONCEPTUAL FRAMEWORK

In attempting to specify the features which distinguish the behavior modification from the more traditional dynamic approaches in therapy, we would probably agree that its emphasis is the concern with experimental-laboratory methodology to analyze the treatment situation. Therefore, behavior therapy is an empirical and manipulative treatment. The empirical emphasis is seen in the concern for exact specification of procedures with a preference for those that are simple and easily described, and the adoption of conspicuous and easily measured behaviors that can be tied to actual experimental manipulations, using change in these behaviors as the basic data of treatment. This concern for discrete and denotable environments and behaviors comes from methodological reasons, and not necessarily because the questions currently being posed at this level are the most interesting that can be raised about people in treatment.

Several other features beyond the concern with experimental manipulations have been presented as distinguishing the behavioral approach. Emphasis on modern learning theory and research has often been cited as its defining characteristic. However, one might entertain some reservations about this point, since it does not seem that the learning field is sufficiently developed to support a technology. There is no comprehensive theory of learning current among psychologists, and the models in use are of quite limited scope. Translation of any specific procedure from the animal or human learning laboratory to the therapy room requires empirical investigation to insure that similar results occur, and for the same reasons. Human learning, particularly, is not obviously analogous to animal learning. Some important variables may be quite different. As examples, the prevalence of verbal and imitative behavior in humans indicates two areas for which analogies from animal research are not well explored. Learning models in current use, then, permit few generalizations without empirical support.

Despite this reservation, it can be argued that the limits of current models for describing pathological behavior have not been fully explored. Limits cannot be determined on the basis of philosophical considerations. Valuable applications of current concepts may yet be made to areas that now seem to have little relevance to learning research, such as the patient-therapist interaction in therapy. Whether such applications can be made, or whether learning theory will have to add dramatically new concepts to handle these data, are matters for careful investigation. A young and viable form of inquiry should not limit itself to a set of problems, techniques, or terminology that might freeze its concepts or its scope.

Independent of any particular theoretical orientations there appear to be two general classes of problems which a therapist must cope with: The patient needs help in overcoming an excess in a certain form of behavior, or he needs help in overcoming a deficiency in some other behavior, or both. For example, the patient experiences too much anxiety, he is self-destructive, or too aggressive. Similarly, the patient may not be sufficiently assertive, may be incompetent to handle interpersonal relationships, and so on. The manner in which a problem is classified will depend in some cases on the criterion behavior specified or on the therapist's understanding of the situation. Aggressiveness in interpersonal behaviors, for example, may be treated by direct training in more adaptive modes of interaction, or by suppression of the aggressive behavior. The criteria for behavior change will vary accordingly.

Granted these two classes of problems, if one turns to operant conditioning or reinforcement theory for guidance, one is faced with two basic alternatives: either to manipulate behavior directly, or to establish stimulus functions. If one decides to center treatment efforts on the direct manipulation of behavior, and if the behavior is an operant, then one can control that operant either by working at the reinforcers which maintain it or the discriminative stimuli that set the occasion for it. The first case, reinforcement control, is the better known and researched form of intervention. If one decides to use reinforcement control to build behavior, then one would expect a reasonably slow change, necessitating considerable shaping on the part of the therapist, as well as the isolation and manipulation of reinforcers that are effective or appropriate. We will review some studies that have attempted to build behavior using positive reinforcers, and pay particular attention to some that involve complex behaviors, such as language. We will also review a number of studies where the main intent has been to weaken behavior through reinforcement withdrawal. We will also examine instances in which noxious stimuli have been used to suppress behavior.

In addition to exercising direct control over behavior through the presentation and removal of reinforcers, one can attempt a similar direct control through the presentation and removal of those stimuli (SD's) that set the occasion for behavior. Most behaviors have a selective reinforcement history and have thus come under stimulus control. This implies that pathology is situational, it occurs in certain environments and not in others, and one may be able to arrange conditions so as to remove the stimulus situations which typically are associated with the occurrence of a particular pathology. In this kind of control one would expect rather immediate changes in behavior without any particular form of shaping occurring in that particular instance. Many times, as one is changing a patient's environment, it is difficult to ascertain whether one is operating on SD or reinforcement control. For example, if one administers noxious stimuli contingent upon self-destructive behavior in psychotic children, then one may be actively suppressing the pathological behavior, or one may be providing the child with stimuli in the presence of which he has been reinforced for normal behavior in the past. Conceivably both processes could be operating. An apparent drawback of such SD control of a behavior is that one would have to assure that the behavior which was evoked was then followed by appropriate reinforcement. Despite the likelihood that there is powerful discriminative stimulus control over pathology, very few people in the field have systematically researched this form of treatment.

We have discussed so far the kinds of interventions where the therapist is addressing behavior directly. One can also conceive of a situation in which the therapist arranges the treatment environment not for a direct manipulation of behavior, but for the manipulation of stimulus functions which, in other environments, would alter behavior. That is, many pathological behaviors probably occur because a person's particular reinforcement hierarchy is deviant, thus allowing the environment to positively reinforce certain behaviors it should discourage, and vice versa. A treatment program centered on the establishment of a normal hierarchy of social and environmental reinforcers would provide tools for external contingencies, and not necessarily for the therapist to build and modify the behaviors necessary for the patient's effective functioning. Thus the therapist does not single out a particular behavior for modification; the environment takes care of that modification, providing that the therapist has appropriately modified its reinforcement function for him. A study by Lovaas, Schaeffer, and Simmons (1965) illustrates this kind of treatment. They worked with two autistic children who, prior to the interventions, were completely unresponsive to any form of social stimulation. The essential feature of the study was to arrange a situation in which people would be associated with pain reduction and thereby acquire positive reinforcing properties. The experimental procedure had the children escape from a noxious situation into the arms of attending adults. Subsequent to this intervention the children would work hard merely to observe the attending adults. The behavior of escaping the noxious situation is not the focus of interest, but the subsequent positive reinforcing properties of people, which can be used to establish socially and personally more meaningful behavior. No doubt many kinds of stimuli acquire a reinforcing function in situations where the therapist is only attempting to systematically manipulate behavior. For example, in the therapy situation where the therapist is addressing himself explicitly to the building of appropriate language, it should also be the case that appropriate language, in being consistently paired with positive reinforcement, should take on conditioned reinforcement properties itself. If this is the case the power of operant procedures over behavior can be extended to areas where the therapist has no specific control. As was the case with SD control, there has been no systematic research into the potentially very therapeutic use of conditioned reinforcement.

REMOVING BEHAVIORS

In this section we review some studies in which the removal of a problem behavior appears to have been of major concern. Studies using direct behavioral control and manipulation of stimulus functions will both be included. These divisions, which we described in the introduction to this paper, cannot always be identified clearly in specific studies. A particular procedure may be viewed as changing behavior either because it deals directly with that behavior, or by the establishment of new stimulus functions, or both. Also, in some cases a new set of behaviors might have been created, even though the therapist dealt specifically with another set. In the absence of detailed assessment it is often difficult to decide which of these alternatives actually occurred.

The controlled use of contingent social reinforcement has been frequent in the past few years. In the studies to be reviewed here the elimination of some undesired response through reinforcement withdrawal was an important if not the only aim of treatment. The treatment had been carried out in a large variety of settings, including the nursery school, the psychiatric ward, the experimental laboratory, the home. A large number of agents, such as parents, psychiatric nursing staff, teachers, and investigators, have served to mediate the controlling or reinforcing stimuli. The general outcome of these studies, although quite reasonable in retrospect, was by no means predicted beforehand: not only did certain behaviors appear to be controlled by functions different from those that were suspected (for example, many behaviors that would have been judged to be emotional turned out to be quite adaptive to their interpersonal environment) but many of the stimuli that maintained these behaviors seemed not to be obvious to those who took care of the child.

There have been several studies of the common problem of excessive crying in infants. In one of the earliest, Williams (1959) reported the successful treatment of an infant by prescribing to the child's parents a procedure by which they effectively extinguished the crying through reinforcement withdrawal. Extinction was rapid. However, at the end of the first week one caretaker delivered reinforcement for a crying spell that was unusually severe. Crying returned at essentially full force before it was again extinguished. The single intervention here was unplanned, but can be interpreted as a test of the variables assumed to be operating. The procedure is eminently practicable. It might be noted that the crying could have been assessed as a specific fear of the bedtime situation, focusing on its respondent qualities, and in this case a desensitization procedure might have been attempted. Under some conditions the application of a desensitization procedure, involving inadvertent reinforcement for crying, might well have made the child worse. Most reasonably, a choice of such procedures should be made on the basis of assessment of the kinds of variables which maintain the behavior. In this case, it appears reasonably obvious that the parents were unfamiliar with the events that maintained the behavior, since they seemed to be reinforcing the behavior they found so annoying.

Hart, Allen, Buell, Harris, and Wolf (1964) eliminated operant crying in two normal boys in a preschool class. Crying occurred at minor frustrations and appeared to be reinforced by adult attention and sympathy. The base rate of crying was observed for a few days in a normal class operation. Treatment was then introduced, in which the teachers ignored crying and attended with encouragement and praise to constructive behavior. The crying dropped out. When conditions were reversed (the teacher attending to the crying and ignoring the constructive behavior) the base rate was recaptured for one child, and partially recaptured for the other. Reinstatement of the treatment contingency brought back the desirable changes. No undesirable side effects were seen, and in fact the children developed satisfactory coping behaviors in the frustrating situations in which they previously had cried. The training here was not entirely reinforcement manipulation, since verbal cues were involved. Social control generally includes these cuing components in addition to the manipulation of reinforcement, and these factors are not usually separated experimentally.

Some more extreme behavioral reactions to stress have been treated using combinations of social, tangible, and edible reinforcers. Wolf, Birnbrauer, Williams, and Lawler

(1965) treated a mentally retarded, brain-damaged girl for frequent vomiting in a classroom for retardates. The vomiting was accompanied by screaming, clothes tearing, and tantrums if the child was not removed from the classroom, which had been the usual teacher response to the onset of these disturbances. During treatment the child was not removed from the class for tantrum behaviors, and was given candy for periods of acceptable behavior. The disturbed behaviors disappeared over a thirty-day period. Return to the original conditions did not succeed in reestablishing the behaviors. It was not clear why the baseline was not recaptured, and this failure weakens, of course, any inference pertaining to therapeutic agents. It is possible that some aspect of the classroom had acquired positive reinforcing property, removing the stimuli for escape. In studies where the baseline is not recaptured, it seems crucial to be able to assess what changes in the pre-experimental conditions control this result.

Gardner (1967) treated a ten-year-old girl who exhibited somatic complaints, tantrums, and seizures, including hair pulling and head rolling. Physiological tests were negative for brain damage. Treatment was carried out at home by the parents under the supervision of the therapist. All behaviors related to seizures were to be ignored, and helpful, happy behaviors were to receive attention and encouragement. Seizures and tantrums disappeared within a month, somatic complaints decreased by half. The parents were then instructed to reinstate the original conditions, providing sympathy and attention for complaints and disturbances. Somatic complaints rose very sharply and a seizure occurred, so that the plan was dropped and the extinction procedure was reintroduced.

In these studies reviewed above and in others not discussed, caretaker and parental attention is seen to provide not only reinforcement for various behaviors, but also, through this reinforcement, to give cues for the behavior that the child can successfully emit. However, the contingencies and cues experimentally manipulated in most of these studies are very complex, involving discriminative verbal statements as well as reinforcement. Although the contingencies adopted appear successful in controlling behavior, the data are not adequate to ascertain what function the various components serve.

Perhaps the most extreme behavioral deviation that can come to the attention of any clinician centers on the intense self-destructive behavior of certain psychotic children. Psychotic as such behavior seems, it is surprising that it can be controlled by the same kinds of operations useful for the milder deviations discussed above. The first report on successful attempts to treat self-injurious behavior by extinction procedures involved isolation from interpersonal contact contingent on self-destructive behavior (Wolf, Risley, and Mees, 1964). They treated the self-injurious behavior of a young psychotic boy. Over a period of two to four months the behavior, which included head banging, hair pulling, and face scratching, gradually decreased and then disappeared.

Further support for the operant nature of self-injurious behavior was reported by Lovaas and Simmons (1968) in a recent study involving three self-destructive retarded children. In two of these cases the behavior was placed on extinction and eventually went to zero (requiring in excess of 10,000 self-destructive responses. In one instance the investigators attended to the self-injurious behavior with statements of sympathy and concern, and gave the child access to the consequences (play, for example) that he appeared to want. The self-destructive behavior very quickly got worse. Thus, both reinforcement and extinction procedures show the operant nature of self-destructive behavior.

Several studies have reported suppression of self-destructive behavior using contingent painful electric shock (cf. Bucher and Lovaas, 1968; and Risley, 1968). The suppression of self-destructive behavior appears to be immediate; a generalized effect of shock across other behaviors gives an increase in socially appropriate behaviors; and if the treatment operations are performed in such a fashion as to allow the child to form a discrimination, he will quickly do so. For example, if the child is punished for self-destructive behavior in one situation, or by one investigator, and not punished in other situations or by other adults, then one can observe a situational and highly differential suppression of the self-destructive behavior.

Three features appear repeatedly in the studies reviewed so far. First, there are frequent reports of the highly discriminative control that various environments acquire over pathology. Several other studies support this point. For example, Browning (1967) treated bragging in an emotionally disturbed boy by instructing attending staff to differ in their response to this behavior. One member ignored bragging, one attended to it positively, and one admonished the boy, when this behavior occurred in their presence. The amount of deviant behavior that each staff member elicited was a function of the kind of contingencies administered. Attending to the boy positively after bragging and admonishing him seemed equally ineffective. Only ignoring bragging appeared to be an effective suppressor. These data on situational control imply that one should not expect to observe generalization of a particular behavior from one setting to another unless the environments operate in a similar manner, delivering similar contingencies for the relevant behaviors.

The second point quite noticeable in the work we have reviewed is the frequent quick change in behavior when new contingencies are introduced. O'Leary and Becker (1967) report a study that also demonstrates this. Working in a class for disturbed children, they attempted to decrease disruptive and overaggressive behavior with seventeen emotionally disturbed children. Preliminary observation indicated that peer reinforcement for misbehavior was operating more effectively than the social reinforcement the teacher provided. A token system with back-up reinforcers was introduced and explained to the students. The teacher awarded tokens to both individual children and to the class as a whole for appropriate behavior. Deviant behaviors were ignored. An extremely abrupt improvement in behavior was seen here, which suggests that the appropriate behavior was already in the children's repertoire and that the reinforcement operations primarily served a cuing function.

The third point concerns the value of even small positive rewards in producing major changes in behavior, when they are used contingently and consistently; and the maladaptive consequences of their use for inappropriate behavior. It is surprising how frequently teachers and professional people have failed to prescribe contingent positive reinforcement. A study by Marwell and Schmitt (1967) may throw some light on this apparent failure. These authors surveyed attitudes of college students toward various means of obtaining compliant behavior in a variety of situations. They found that the use of tangible, positive rewards to obtain compliance from children held an anomalous position being generally regarded as quite effective but undesirable. It is a commonly expressed opinion among teachers and mothers that desired social or educational learning and behaviors should be induced in children by other means. By default, then, an extra burden is probably placed on coercion and aversive control.

The behaviors we have reviewed vary from crying in infants to overaggressive behavior in adolescents to self-destructive behavior in psychotics. Perhaps the most unexpected finding from this work pertains to the very large class of behaviors that can come under reinforcement and discriminative stimulus control. As diverse as these behaviors may seem, they show the same functional relationships to reinforcement operations. The commonly held clinical theories of psychopathology have not led to the expectation that reinforcement was a major variable in maintaining these classes of maladaptive behaviors, but have labeled them as emotional and referred their control to a different set of functions. Similarly, clinical theories have not led to understanding and use of the close discriminative or cue control the environment seems to exercise over these behaviors, and have overemphasized the importance of transsituational variables, viewed as reflections of hypothetical, internalized personality characteristics.

ESTABLISHING BEHAVIOR

The approach to problems generally considered as acquired maladaptive behaviors can also be used to treat behavior deficits. Most clinicians would agree that a patient's problems can often be traced to a failure in development of certain behaviors. Most often, they see a behavioral deficiency as a reflection of some deeper emotional disturbance, and the clinician will choose to address himself to the hypothesized intervening problem, rather than attempting direct rehabilitation. In operant studies the therapeutic plan has almost altogether focused on establishing behavior, rather than attempting to cope with an emotional problem that might be seen to underlie the deficiency.

In apparent contradiction of traditional reservations about direct treatment, there are now a large number of studies showing unambiguously that one can use reinforcement principles to build a variety of skills involved in feeding, continence, dressing, walking, and so on, in children who have not acquired these behaviors in their pretherapy environment. There is reason to believe that such acquisitions benefit the child, rather than harm him through the appearance of maladaptive substitutions as certain clinical theories would lead one to believe. The research on enuresis is a case in point.

Enuresis is the most thoroughly studied of the operant

techniques, at least in the number of research cases treated. The treatment involves use of a special blanket with a bell, buzzer or shock that is activated on the release of urine while the child is in bed. Analyses of the effects of treatment have been offered as due to respondent conditioning (Jones, 1960) and avoidance training (Lovibond, 1963), but operationally the technique involves punishment contingent on a specific response.

The published work on enuresis has been primarily with groups, frequently using control groups to test for effects of no therapy, traditional or counseling therapy, and variations in details of the training procedure (Young and Turner, 1965; Lovibond, 1964). Many hundreds of children have been treated with a high proportion of success, 75 to 90 per cent for original treatment, and also with excellent results for treatment of relapses. Fears over development of substitute symptoms have not been borne out. Instead reports frequently note that desirable new behaviors are much more likely to be seen.

Studies usually conceptualized as involving counterconditioning for treatment of specific fears will not be reviewed here, although it should be noted that it is often difficult to ascertain in these studies the extent to which certain fears are being removed using classical conditioning paradigms, or imcompatible behaviors are being built (overcoming deficiencies) using an operant paradigm. The following study illustrates this problem. Meyerson, Kerr, and Michael (1967) treated an apparent fear of walking and falling in a seven-year-old boy with cerebral palsy. It is left unclear whether the boy had ever walked unaided, but he had at least not done so for a long time. Gradual approaches to a desired criterion, unaided walking, were reinforced with encouragement, praise, and tokens exchangeable for various goods. The boy initially did not walk at all, and expressed fear of standing, and even refused to try. He responded to reinforcement immediately and enthusiastically, demanding to do the acts that could earn tokens. At the end of treatment the subject willingly walked and even fell over on command. A classical counterconditioning explanation is not obviously necessary in accounting for the behavior change observed, although counterconditioning may have occurred as a component of the procedure followed.

The question no longer seems to be whether by the use of operant procedures one can help a person to acquire the fundamental behaviors involved in walking, eating, continence, and so on. Rather, the question is now to determine how and how far one can proceed toward establishing more complex behaviors, such as academic and verbal behaviors, by relying on the operant training paradigm.

There are several extensive programs for the establishment of academic behavior under way. One of the most comprehensive and ambitious was initiated by the "Washington group" (the Rainier School project). One of the reports (Birnbrauer, Wolf, Kidder, and Tague, 1965) describes such a program and deals with the effect of token reinforcement on maintaining intellectual and other kinds of classroom behaviors in retarded children. Several behaviors, such as sight vocabulary, reading comprehension, and elementary arithmetic, were recorded, as well as behavior which would disrupt academic functioning, such as talking out of turn and cursing. After a certain level of appropriate intellectual behavior was reached, the token reinforcement which had been used to build these behaviors was removed. In some children the withdrawal of token reinforcement resulted in major changes, including increase in disrupting behavior which would have resulted in the child being dropped from school under ordinary circumstances. The fact that some children (five out of fifteen) remained unaffected by reinforcement withdrawal raises numerous questions about the function of reinforcement for the maintenance of intellectual behavior, questions pertaining to what stage of the acquisition is most affected by the reinforcement removal, what reinforcers may be implicit in the intellectual material, whether the stimulus functions of academic work had changed during this experience, and so forth. A full discussion of the role of reinforcement in maintaining intellectual behavior would be very comprehensive—it would, for example, deal with recent work in programmed learning—and goes beyond the scope of this paper.

Attempts to teach complex verbal behaviors to retarded and psychotic children illustrate some of the subtleties in the use of the operant paradigm. Consider helping a mute child acquire speech. There are two stages to the program which would try to overcome such a deficiency: first, one has to place a large amount of behavior at the child's disposal; second, one has to teach the appropriate context for the occurrence of that behavior.

Consider the first problem, that of building a large range of complex behaviors. Most therapists seem persuaded that this could not be accomplished through straightforward shaping procedures where the child was reinforced for successively close approximations to the terminal response. Instead procedures have been sought which could catalyze learning of complex behaviors with a minimum of specific training. Imitative behavior may have this capability. There were, however, no procedures available until recently that showed how one might teach imitative behavior to those who needed it most, namely those who did not have it.

The first work that suggested the possibility of establishing imitation was done by Baer and Sherman (1964), who showed the feasibility of viewing imitation as the establishment of a discrimination. Using normal children as subjects, these investigators devised a situation where they could vary the probability that a child would imitate a particular behavior by reinforcing or not reinforcing him for imitation of other behaviors. The authors argued that such training could give matching or similar response both discriminative and reinforcing stimulus properties, and that imitative behavior thus would become more prevalent and apparently autonomous. Subsequently several studies (Metz, 1965; Hewett, 1965; Lovaas, 1967a) appeared, demonstrating a set of procedures that could be used to provide a nonimitative child with imitative behavior, through which novel behaviors could then be taught. The training paradigm in these studies relied on the traditional operant paradigm of prompting, fading of the prompt, and stimulus rotation. It is of interest to examine the nature of this imitative behavior, since a further analysis may throw some light upon a question that is perhaps the most basic one facing all reinforcement theorists: What exactly is being learned under a reinforcement paradigm? In the first place, there appears to be acquisition of a discrimination; the child is learning that a particular behavior in the model is discriminative for reinforcement, should he behave similarly. But also the child apparently acquires a reinforcing function: similarity is discriminative for reinforcement, hence similarity should acquire conditioned reinforcement properties. It is certainly of considerable therapeutic interest if children, after this kind of learning, are able to acquire new behaviors without specific reinforcement. Some findings that support this notion have been reported by Lovaas (1967b, pp. 138–39).

Once the child is capable of manifesting complex behaviors, and will give these behaviors on the basis of mere demonstration, then the training program can focus on placing these behaviors in their appropriate contexts. Several authors (Hewett, 1965; Risley and Wolf, 1967; Lovaas, 1967a) report on work designed to place imitative verbal behavior within the appropriate environmental context so as to facilitate the child's acquisition of meaning or understanding of language. Within the operant conditioning paradigm it has been possible, through shaping procedures, to teach a child both to recognize and to generate meaningful sentences, involving patterns of words that the child has not seen or used before. Programs have also been developed that involve the child's acquisition of very abstract speech, such as terms involving prepositions, pronouns, and time. There are extensive unresolved issues in this work. For example, in both the Risley and Wolf (1967) and Lovaas studies mention is made of the relative ease with which the previously echolalic children proceed through language training as compared with the previously mute—without anyone knowing why. Similarly, we experienced considerable difficulty in helping some children to use the newly acquired verbal behaviors in a conversational, information-seeking manner. Equally puzzling are the large changes in emotional behavior that accompany the acquisition of instrumental behavior. As appropriate behavior is acquired, much of the psychotic, self-stimulatory behavior disappears. Most children take on a very alert appearance, become more affectionate, more "task-oriented," pleased with their successes, and so on. The children seem generally happier. Some completely unpredictable changes take place, as well; for example, a child will stop toe-walking and gain a better appetite. These are very puzzling findings and again raise the questions of the definition of response, response-classes, and basically what is acquired in this kind of learning paradigm.

DISCUSSION

The Generality of Treatment Effect. One can view generalization along two dimensions: generalization across behaviors, and generalization across situations. Let us comment on generalization across behaviors first.

Response generalization is said to exist when operation upon one behavior exerts simultaneous changes in other behaviors, even though these were not explicitly or directly manipulated. Consider self-destructive behavior in psychotic children as an example. A behavior therapist is likely to address himself directly to that behavior by attempting to identify the kinds of conditions that will terminate the behavior. In addition, he is likely to keep an eye on concurrent changes in behaviors other than self-destruction. He wants to know the extent to which socially appropriate behavior, such as physical contact and speech, covary with the self-destruction. He may find that the amount of correlated response change is some function, not just of the magnitude of the self-destructive behavior, but also of the stimulus situation which was used to control the self-destruction. To state this differently, the behavior therapist searches for functionally identifiable behaviors for his treatment efforts, and the apparent shift in larger classes of behavior might be a most important consequence of the treatment he prescribes.

This approach, emphasizing the manipulation of behavior per se, contrasts with the traditional procedures which center treatment on some central construct that is hypothesized to control the behavior. That is, the traditional therapist does not treat self-destruction per se, but rather, he treats the "psychosis" considered to underlie the behavioral disturbances ("symptoms"). Given such a stand, it is appropriate to ask the traditional therapist for a "cure" (from the hypothetical "disease"), while such expectations are inappropriate to place on the behavior therapist. The behavior therapist should hardly be expected to cure a patient of his colleague's inferences. Instead, the behavior therapist should be asked to specify the nature of the behavioral change that he produces, the permanence of these changes, and so on. For example, it appears that one can terminate self-destructive behavior in a very short period of time (a few days). In two years of hard work an echolalic child can be on his way toward the mastery of language. However, we have been unable as yet to isolate the variables that control curiosity and exploration, and have seen little improvement in these areas. Most traditional dimensions for evaluating therapeutic change are inappropriate, at least for behavior therapy work.

The second dimension of generalization pertains to stimulus generalization: the extent to which behavior built in one environment (for example, the hospital) will transfer to other environments (for example, the home). Generalization from a therapeutic setting to the more normal environment is a natural demand to make from a treatment program. If we discuss this question from a behavior therapy viewpoint, we become immediately aware that every person experiences the influence of more than one environment, and displays different behaviors for different environments. A person may be "sick" in one environment, but not necessarily "sick" in another. If this is the case, achievement of appropriate generalization is not necessarily a test of the power of one's variables, but rather a result of the extent to which one has been able to manipulate more than the immediate treatment environment. Repeatedly we have seen that a child may have acquired a large variety of appropriate behaviors in a treatment situation, which will deteriorate upon being transferred to another environment, such as a hospital which cannot implement our procedures. Such deterioration is only a matter of time, requiring a few weeks in some instances, and a few months in others. Brought back into the original treatment environment, the child will recover the lost behavior almost immediately. In other words, generalization across environments is a process that can be manipulated, and it seems pointless to ask about permanence of behavior change unless post-treatment environment is controlled, or somehow assessed. With a different model of psychopathology and health, postulating relatively permanent personality constructs not closely tied to environmental contingencies, as in psychodynamic theories, it seems more reasonable to expect global and permanent change.

The Role of Assessment. A distinguishing feature of

much of the behavior modification literature is relative lack of concern for detailed assessment of the antecedent conditions that produced the pathological behaviors, the environmental contingencies that sustain them, or other aspects of the patient's experiences and learning that may be related. This neglect may be due to the absence of research relating efficiency of behavior-change techniques to the subject's prior learning and his existing behavior repertoire. However, several major classifications of behavior-modification techniques exist, and permit infinite variation in details, so that the choice among alternatives requires some degree of assessment.

If a therapy is to profit from assessment the data collected must be relevant for the conceptual context in which the therapy is conducted. The typical problems one is likely to encounter in behavior therapy are to find effective reinforcers, to find contingencies that operate in the client's environment to maintain a particular pathological behavior, to isolate behaviors that are available to the patient as a basis for adequate functioning, and so forth. The search for adequate reinforcers for an operant procedure is a usual preliminary step in therapy. Individual differences in the values of available reinforcers partly reflect differences in reinforcement histories that may be quite unrelated to the pathological behavior of principal concern. Many of the stimulus functions that control portions of an individual's behavior are also acquired, and may be relevant for choice of therapeutic tactics; however, in many cases these functions may not be part of the pathology. Neglect of such "historical" variables can lead to unexplained individual differences in therapy outcomes in situations where the objective treatment conditions are well controlled.

Risley (1968) explored several alternatives to eliminate inappropriate climbing in an autistic child, including time out, reinforcement for incompatible behaviors, and punishment with shock. Data for each technique were presented in detail. Shock was adopted only after the other methods had been tried unsuccessfully for several weeks. The test of the unsuccessful training methods might be considered as an assessment of reinforcing possibilities for control of the child's behavior. Although the purely pragmatic intention to obtain behavioral control is most clear here, the discovery of the ineffectiveness of some commonly used methods of control is probably of considerable relevance in assessing the child's failure to achieve normal interactions with the environment.

The role of assessment of the details of the pathological behavior itself can be seen using a study by Allen, Hart, Buell, Harris, and Wolf (1964). This is one of many that could be cited. These authors treated a child at a nursery school for excessive isolated play and insufficient interaction with peers. After a period of base level observations under the pre-experimental conditions, they essentially reversed the pretreatment social contingencies by withdrawing adult attention that had been contingent on isolated play and substituted attention contingent on appropriate peer interactions. The child's behavior changed very fast, giving an indication that an adequate repertoire of social behaviors already existed.

Allen *et al.* pointed out that the rapid rate of change had not been specifically anticipated, and that other children exposed to similar treatments did not show such quick change. Under certain circumstances it would seem that the manipulation of attention, as practiced here, would be less successful. One can imagine two such situations. A child may show nonparticipation in peer play due to the possession of an inappropriate or inadequate repertoire of social skills, so that attempts at interaction meet with nonreinforcement or rejection. In such circumstances it is likely that merely shifting reinforcement contingencies without extensive shaping would not bring about the desired behavior, or would do so only very slowly. As another possibility, a child may have acquired an aversion for peer interactions, so that isolated play is maintained as an avoidance or escape response. For this problem many behavior therapists would recommend counter-conditioning procedures of some kind.

In a few studies similar behaviors have in fact received different treatments responsive to the subject's individual repertoires. Etzel and Gewirtz (1967), for example, treated two very young children (six weeks and twenty-one weeks) for operant crying for adult attention. Treatment was done in a carefully controlled setting. In the older child smiling was evoked to counteract crying, using a direct reinforcement procedure. In the younger child partial components of a smile were first evoked using a greater variety of cues and reinforcers, and the full smile was shaped in stages. The diffe.ence in treatment was based on the apparent fact that smiling was an available response in the older child at the start of treatment, but was not in the younger. The assessment was based on initial observations during training. That similar considerations typically influence the skilled researcher in his choice of technique is certain; but the details of the information used are not usually objectively specified, or gathered under objective conditions.

Comments on Research Design. We have argued that the experimental-manipulative feature of behavior therapy work is its most distinguishing characteristic. It seems reasonable, therefore, to discuss briefly the kind of research designs that are most prevalent in behavorial therapy and to center this discussion on the two main objectives of treatment research: to discover effective forms of intervention, and to determine what specific factors control the effects observed. The first question can be conceptualized as a question of applicability, the second is a question pertaining to the analysis of the treatment environment.

Experimental research in behavioral modification has relied heavily on two kinds of designs; the control-group design and the single-subject design. Since the single-subject design is reasonably new in clinical research, it might be useful to describe how it operates. To demonstrate the consequences of a specific operation in a given context, a typical procedure is to measure performance in that context until it stabilizes, then to introduce the therapeutic operation for a time, either briefly as a probe or for longer periods to permit behavior to stabilize again. Then the original conditions are restored and the return of the behavior to its original level completes the demonstration of the controlling effects of the manipulation. The differences between the single-subject design and the case study lies primarily in the reduction in confounding variables that accompany the experimental manipulations, so that a reliable report of what actually happened can be made. Statistical analysis of these data is rare, since the necessary statistical techniques are generally not available, or may be superfluous, since the situation is controlled in such a fashion as to yield inferences of reliable effects by simple inspection of the data. There are certain drawbacks associated with this technique, particularly as this involves instances where the baseline cannot be recaptured; however, these technical problems will not be discussed here.

The single-subject design seems extremely well fitted to clinical research, since it allows for quite exhaustive analysis of the treatment environment for a particular patient over extensive periods of time. This allows the investigator to break down the treatment environment, to present its aspects singly or in new combinations, in a manner that would not be feasible using group designs. There simply are not enough patients or investigator time available to test all the hunches the therapist may have about his treatment of a patient through patient assignments over various experimental groups. Even in the best of group designs, such as Lang, Lazovik, and Reynolds (1965), or Paul (1966) the use of several groups is very costly in patient and experimenter time, and the groups customarily are given treatments that differ along many more dimensions than is usually the case in single-subject manipulations, including various aspects of the physical settings, the interaction of the client with the therapist, and the details of the treatment procedure.

Looking back at the research we have reviewed, it is surprising how much of it has failed to take advantage of the analytic power of the single-subject design. Most frequently, treatment variables involved in these studies are global, and detailed analysis is not attempted. The global nature of these treatment variables involves gross reinforcement stimuli (often combinations of social and tangible reinforcers) administered by personnel whose past interaction with the child is complex; cuing functions are often used in giving instructions or reinforcements, and changes may occur in the total amount of stimulation or attention variables presented to the child. Finally, these variables are generally not quantified; that is, very rarely does the investigator indicate how much or how little of a particular variable was presented. It is not the case, then, that research on operant techniques with children has provided a great deal of analytic information about the treatments they expose their patients to.

Turning to the next objective, that of assessing how effective a particular intervention is, most of the research we reviewed provided unsatisfactory answers to this question. In single-subject designs, usually only scant information is given on the child; a brief description will be presented, such as would appear in a brief case report, based on casual observational data. Humans have highly complex and variable reinforcement histories, and detailed symptomatologies are never identical. Successful or unsuccessful manipulations of a specific variable, such as social reinforcement, may depend on these background factors, which may interact with treatment variables in ways that only exhaustive investigations can detail. The manipulation of an environmental condition to produce a particular result constitutes a demonstration of the effectiveness of the manipulation only for the particular client and circumstances observed, and does not insure generalization or wide applicability.

A large number of successful reports of applications of a given technique in single-subject studies may partially alleviate the difficulty, especially if they came from a single research laboratory from which all pertinent studies are reported. These conditions do not appear to exist at present.

The control-group research design offers a superior alternative for the purpose of assessing applicability. The inclusion of a sizable number of a certain kind of patient, selected according to the more or less well-defined rules followed in the study, and exposed to a given treatment, gives valuable evidence of the degree of success that can be expected. The requirement for clear specification of rules and the procedures followed must still be met, of course. In research in operant methods, the "bell and blanket" conditioning techniques for enuresis is probably the best example. Numerous group studies have been done and a gross set of rules for the application of the procedure can be derived from this work, which gives considerable support for the expectation of favorable results in a new application.

It might be said that if a particular research does not provide detailed analytic data, then its principal justification is in demonstration of its validity as a treatment in a large group of patients. Of course, therapeutic techniques and even schools of therapy have been persuasively advocated without adherence to either criterion. There appears to be little danger that behavior therapy will repeat the past in this respect, although one must entertain some reservation about operant work with children on both these counts.

Finally, we were surprised to find so few reports in

which operant procedures had failed to show desirable results. Consistently favorable outcomes have perhaps produced some sense that behavioral techniques are so powerful that detailed analytical examination of specific situations will not be necessary for achievement of a successful therapeutic armamentarium. To some extent a favorable bias may be due to the filtering processes of publication, with author and editorial selectivity in what is to be published and how it is to be presented. If one adds to this the fact that a few investigators, trained in a limited set of universities, are carrying out most of the work in the field, then it is likely that the future will show several failures in attempts to replicate some of the techniques that have been reported.

REFERENCES

ALLEN, K. E., HART, B. M., BUELL, J. S., HARRIS, F. R., and WOLF, M. M. Effects of social reinforcement on isolate behavior of a nursery school child. *Child Development,* 1964, *35,* 511-18.

BAER, D. M., and SHERMAN, J. A. Reinforcement control of generalized imitation in young children. *Journal of Experimental Child Psychology,* 1964, *1,* 37-49.

BIRNBRAUER, J. S., WOLF, M. M., KIDDER, J. D., and TAGUE, C. E. Classroom behavior of retarded pupils with token reinforcement. *Journal of Experimental Child Psychology,* 1965, *2,* 219-35.

BROWNING, R. M. A same-subject design for simultaneous comparison of three reinforcement contingencies. *Behaviour Research and Therapy,* 1967, *5,* 237-43.

BUCHER, B., and LOVAAS, O. I. Use of aversive stimulation in behavior modification. In M. R. Jones, (Ed.), *Miami symposium on the prediction of behavior 1967: Aversive stimulation.* Coral Gables: University of Miami Press, 1968.

ETZEL, B. C., and GEWIRTZ, J. L. Experimental modification of caretaker-maintained high-rate operant crying in a six and a twenty week old infant *(Infans tyrannotearus):* Extinction of crying with reinforcement of eye contact and smiling. *Journal of Experimental Child Psychology,* 1967, *5,* 303-17.

GARDNER, J. E. Behavior therapy treatment approach to a psychogenic seizure case. *Journal of Consulting Psychology,* 1967, *31,* 209–12.

GELFAND, D. M. and HARTMANN, D. P. Behavior therapy with children. *Psychological Bulletin,* 1968, *69,* 204–15.

HART, B. M., ALLEN, K. E., BUELL, J. S., HARRIS, F. R., and WOLF, M. M. Effects of social reinforcement on operant crying. *Journal of Experimental Child Psychology,* 1964, *1,* 145–53.

HEWETT, F. M. Teaching speech to an autistic child through operant conditioning. *American Journal of Orthopsychiatry,* 1965, *35,* 927–36.

JONES, H. G. The behavioral treatment of enuresis nocturna. In H. J. Eysenck (Ed.), *Behaviour therapy and the neuroses.* New York: Pergamon Press, 1960.

LANG, P. J., LAZOVIK, A. D., and REYNOLDS, D. J. Desensitization, suggestibility, and pseudotherapy. *Journal of Abnormal Psychology,* 1965, *70,* 395–402.

LOVAAS, O. I. Program for establishment of speech in schizophrenic and autistic children. In J. Wing (Ed.), *Childhood autism.* New York: Pergamon Press, 1967a.

LOVAAS, O. I. Behavior therapy approach to treatment of childhood schizophrenia. *Minnesota symposium on child development.* Minneapolis: University of Minnesota Press, 1967b.

LOVAAS, O. I., SCHAEFFER, B., and SIMMONS, J. Q. Experimental studies in childhood schizophrenia: Building social behaviors using electric shock. *Journal of Experimental Research in Personality,* 1965, *1,* 99–109.

LOVAAS, O. I., and SIMMONS, J. Q. Control of self-destruction in institutionalized children. Paper read at American Association of Mental Deficiency, Boston, May, 1968.

LOVIBOND, S. H. Mechanism of conditioning treatment of enuresis. *Behaviour Research and Therapy,* 1963, *1,* 17–21.

LOVIBOND, S. H. *Conditioning and enuresis.* New York: Macmillan, 1964.

MARWELL, G., and SCHMITT, D. R. Attitude toward parental use of promised rewards to control adolescent behavior. *Journal of Marriage and Family,* 1967, *29,* (3), 500–04.

METZ, J. R. Conditioning generalized imitation in autistic children. *Journal of Experimental Child Psychology,* 1965, *2,* 389–99.

MEYERSON, L., KERR, N., and MICHAEL, J. L. Behavior modification in rehabilitation. In S. W. Bijou, and D. M. Baer, (Eds.), *Child development: Readings in experimental analysis*. New York: Appleton-Century-Crofts, 1967.

O'LEARY, K. D., and BECKER, W. C. Behavior modification of an adjustment class: A token reinforcement program. *Exceptional Children,* 1967, *33,* 637-42.

PAUL, G. L. *Insight versus desensitization in psychotherapy.* Stanford: Stanford University Press, 1966.

RACHMAN, S. Learning theory and child psychology, therapeutic possibilities. *Journal of Child Psychology and Psychiatry,* 1962, *3,* 149-63.

RISLEY, T. R. The effects and side effects of punishing the autistic behaviors of a deviant child. *Journal of Applied Behavioral Analysis,* 1968, *1,* 21-34.

RISLEY, T., and WOLF, M. Establishing functional speech in echolalic children. *Behaviour Research and Therapy,* 1967, *5,* 73-88.

WILLIAMS, C. D. The elimination of tantrum behavior by extinction procedures. *Journal of Abnormal and Social Psychology,* 1959, *59,* 269.

WOLF, M. M., BIRNBRAUER, J. S., WILLIAMS, T., and LAWLER, J. A note on apparent extinction of the vomiting behavior of a retarded child. In L. P. Ullmann and L. J. Krasner (Eds.), *Case studies in behavior modification.* New York: Holt, Rinehart and Winston, 1965.

WOLF, M., RISLEY, T., and MEES, H. Application of operant conditioning procedures to the behaviour problems of an autistic child. *Behaviour Research and Therapy,* 1964, *1,* 305-12.

YOUNG, G. C., and TURNER, R. K. CNS stimulant drugs and conditioning treatment of nocturnal enuresis. *Behaviour Research and Therapy,* 1965, *3,* 93-101.

Comment

PETER J. LANG

The current broad application of operant techniques to the treatment of childhood disorders has been admirably reviewed by Bucher and Lovaas (1970). I would like to focus my own comments on those therapeutic methods that employ contingent aversive stimuli to remove maladaptive or socially undesirable behavior. Lovaas's pioneering work with autistic and retarded children illustrates the therapeutic power of this approach. However, there are problems in applying it effectively, as failures of aversive conditioning with other populations illustrate (MacCulloch, M. J., Feldman, M. P., Orford, J. E., and MacCulloch, M. L., 1966). The following discussion is concerned with the special problems of assessment and application that attend the use of aversive conditioning in the treatment of young children.

Two years ago I was asked to assist in the treatment of a nine-month-old infant with chronic, ruminative vomiting.

The preparation of this paper was supported in part by grants to the author from NIMH (MH-35,324) and the Wisconsin Alumni Research Foundation.

This condition had persisted for more than half the child's life. At the time of my initial observation, he was exceedingly malnourished and dehydrated (less than 12 lbs. body weight), and in the medical view life could not long be maintained. A gamut of treatments and diagnostic procedures had been assayed (e.g., exploratory surgery, anti-emetic and antinauseant drugs, physical restraints, "one-to-one care") without palpable result. From the perspective of the hospital and attending physician, behavior modification was a treatment of last resort. As the case has been described in detail elsewhere (Lang and Melamed, 1969), this account will be brief. Our initial step was to analyze the stimulus context in which vomiting occurred and to assess the unique characteristics of the response itself. Emesis always occurred a few minutes after ingestion of a meal (bottle or solids) and continued intermittently until nearly all food had been evacuated from the stomach. The response sequence was initiated by sucking or chewing, sometimes with finger pressure on the soft palate, followed by actual emesis. In order to explore this sequence more carefully, electromyographic recordings were undertaken during this period. Muscle potentials from the chin and esophagus area clearly distinguished sucking behavior from emesis, and permitted us to detect the first and subsequent waves of reverse peristalsis, which precipitated vomiting. The child's appearance during emisis suggested total concentration on that act, and he could not be distracted by normal means once the process had started.

The treatment finally selected was based on avoidance conditioning, in which a brief, intense electric shock was applied to the leg,[1] coincident with the first wave of reverse peristalsis. Shocks were repeated at approximately one-second intervals until vomiting ceased. Success in inhibiting vomiting was achieved in the first treatment

1. The shock was applied by a Harvard Inductorium at an intensity the experimenters judged to be quite painful, and was accompanied by a loud, 3,000 H^z tone.

session, and aversive stimuli were administered on only five treatment days. The child increased body weight by over 20 per cent in the two weeks following the first session, and was at this point discharged from the hospital. Six-month, one-year, and two-year followups indicated that the child is now of average weight and apparently developing normally, both physiologically and psychologically.

This case parallels in many respects the work reported by Lovaas, Schaeffer, and Simmons (1965) and Bucher and Lovaas (1968). A self-destructive behavior was treated by aversive conditioning. Positive results were achieved in a relatively brief time period, without generating any "symptom substitute" or unwanted consequent of the shock stimulus. In point of fact, as with the cases reported by Bucher and Lovaas, reduction in the treated response's frequency was associated with an increase in positive social behaviors. Thus, whereas this infant had shown only minimal interactions with people and little spontaneous play with toys prior to treatment, these latter behaviors increased markedly as the ruminative vomiting dropped out of the infant's repetory.

The present case differs from Lovaas' work in that these results were achieved with a much younger subject who is apparently neither autistic nor retarded. Furthermore, the nature of the response required a careful psychophysiological diagnostic stage, which might not be demanded with more typical striate, motor acts. These considerations prompt the question: What problems are most likely to profit from aversive conditioning and where might it be contraindicated? In partial response, it was illuminating for me to follow a second infant with ruminative vomiting who recently was seen in the same treatment setting as the previous child. Aversive conditioning was not employed in this instance. Instead the vomiting diminished as a function of the persistent ministrations of two nurses, exclusively assigned to this infant. They alternated in representing a constant, loving social being who, during periods when emesis was likely, distracted the child from this response with games and affectionate displays. The effectiveness of this method depended on the fact that vomiting was not maintained by social reinforcement. M. S. Sibinga (1967) has noted that some ruminators persist in this behavior because of the attention and interest it provokes in parents and other adults. He advocates the use of an extinction procedure in these cases, of the sort discussed by Bucher and Lovaas (1970), rather than the "one-to-one" care usually suggested by advocates of dynamic, interpretive therapies (Richmond, Eddy, and Green, 1958). It should be pointed out that these socially maintained ruminators are generally not malnourished and are at least two or three years old. Thus, they represent a very different picture from the infants described here, physiologically as well as psychologically.

The difference between the two infants being considered here does not appear to lie in the antecedents of the response. For both, vomiting seemed to be its own reward—a disposition acquired very early in development and of unknown origin. The essential difference was one of severity. Distraction by social stimuli was simply unavailing in the initial case. The first infant was apparently locked in a self-reinforcing behavioral loop that could only be disrupted by massive external input. Perhaps because of this, the infant treated by aversive conditioning was initially more debilitated physiologically, and less time remained for slower procedures involving distraction and positive reinforcement. It would appear then, that an important advantage of shock is its intensity and novelty and its consequent power to disrupt even well-integrated behavior sequences.

However, powerful tools must be employed with care. Although no cases have yet been reported, animal research suggests that the misapplication of aversive shock in the treatment setting could lead to neurotic effects of the sort described by Liddell (1964) and recently referred to as "conditioned helplessness" (Seligman, Maier, and Geer, 1968). Maladaptive "freezing" or other stereotyped behaviors and autonomic distress may be anticipated when the organism cannot discover the contingencies that will permit escape or shock avoidance. He must have a way out that is within his capacity to grasp.

The therapist must guard against leaving open too many alternatives, as the patient could learn a response that permits him to avoid shock and yet continue the unwanted behavior. In the first case described here, failure to inhibit emesis occurred during the second treatment session, despite increasingly frequent aversive stimuli. It was soon observed that the infant had learned to curl the plantar surface of his foot (raising the shock electrodes above the skin) either coincident with or just prior to vomiting. Thus, the shock was avoided or reduced without actually discontinuing emesis. Moving the electrodes to the calf eliminated this option, and emesis inhibition was shortly reinstated. This problem of restricting alternatives is often insufficiently considered. In more sophisticated adult organisms, where new cognitive sets may significantly alter the "meaning" and impact of an intense stimulus, this problem may render aversive conditioning techniques completely impractical.

If it is assumed that the dynamic impact of the aversive stimulus is critical to the success of aversion therapies, it is important that the shock stimuli are presented abruptly, at high intensity. Low-intensity inputs will not necessarily break up a behavior sequence, and organisms more readily habituate a low-intensity stimuli or learn to accommodate intense stimuli when onset is gradual (Miller, 1960). As students of human learning discovered early in their research, moderate aversive stimuli can actually become positive counters. Thus, subjects who are shocked after correct responses will nevertheless improve their learning scores (Muenzinger, 1934). Furthermore, laboratory analogues of acquired masochism (Brown, 1965) suggest that moderate aversive stimuli, which are followed by strongly positive events, may subsequently come to be an S^D for the positive consequent and take on some positive reinforcing power themselves. Thus, an ill-considered procedure might simply make an aversive stimulus part of a chain leading to the behavior that the therapist is trying to eliminate. It is also necessary to consider that aversive stimuli tend to further arouse or activate the organism, and in that sense they will tend to energize (not suppress) any response having a high probability of occurrence. This is a further reason, if the therapist is unable to use stimuli intense enough or with sufficient temporal precision to disrupt the unwanted behavior sequence, that aversive conditioning is contraindicated.

As I have already suggested, the therapist, using aversive stimuli to remove a behavior, needs to make sure that shock is contingent only on the unwanted response. If both a useful and a maladaptive response routinely coexist, he will have difficulty setting up appropriately precise contingencies. In other words, the therapist who plans to use aversive conditioning to suppress aggression must be sure that he is not eliminating all social behavior and prompting withdrawal. In treating the ruminating infant, it was vital that aversive consequences followed reliably on vomiting, but not on sucking, feeding, or any of the other useful behaviors that surrounded the unwanted response. The electromyographic diagnostic procedures abetted the desired precision of treatment.

While the response to be deleted may be highly specific, the therapist usually aims to achieve its general suppression across a great variety of stimulus contexts. As Bucher and Lovaas (1970) point out, shock effects are quite situational, and even children quickly learn the discriminative stimuli that augur its application. Thus, in training the infant to suppress vomiting, care was taken to vary the situations in which shock occurred. Trials were conducted when he was alone on the bed, sitting on the lap of different personnel, on the floor, etc. The frequent failure of aversion therapies with adults is often attributable to the fact that a discrimination between treatment and "natural" settings is too easily acquired. The alcoholic soon learns that aversive consequences follow drinking only in the hospital, when he's been given a drug, when Dr. X is present, or when he "agrees to cooperate." Broad control of a response through aversive stimulation requires that the subject be unable to predict with high probability those instances in which aversive stimulation will *not* follow the response. While technically possible, the degree of environmental control necessary to achieve this condition becomes, with increasing age, increasingly impractical and ethically questionable.

In summary, the aversive conditioning therapy pioneered by Lovaas and his associates represents a powerful addition to the armamentarium of the clinical psychologist or psychiatrist. Used intelligently, positive rather than negative side effects are to be anticipated. In general, its greatest successes have been obtained in hospital settings, with very young children or somewhat older children with relatively limited behavioral repertoires. Failures with more sophisticated patients are to be expected because of the more limited environmental control that can be achieved with these subjects, and the ease with which they can discriminate and interpret shock vs. nonshock conditions.

While positive results have been reported with adult patients (Rachman and Teasdale, 1969), it is not clear that these effects are attributable to simple conditioning—as they appear to be for children. The aversive conditioning treatment of adults is founded on the patient's active cooperation. He must be motivated to change. He must follow treatment instructions. Directed, cognitive efforts are often required to define the context of treatment and, in some cases, even to produce the aversive stimuli. On the other hand, the course of treatment with children closely follows the pattern of aversive conditioning found in the animal laboratory.

Treatment utilizing electric shock is seldom the first choice of therapists. Responses that have been modified by aversive conditioning have also been controlled by social stimuli (either their contingent withdrawal or intervention). Aversive conditioning has usually been employed because the nature of the behavior endangered the life or health of the subject, rendering rapidity of treatment paramount, and because the habit strength of the response or the social remoteness of the subjects were such that powerful stimuli were needed to break through the pattern. In all the cases reported, disruption of the maladaptive behavior has been followed by the development of positive social responsiveness.

The following list of cautions should be kept salient in considering shock avoidance as a treatment method: (1) the aversive stimulus should be of sufficient intensity and novelty to disrupt the behavior under treatment on a single trial; (2) avoidance response alternatives compatible with the unwanted behavior must be eliminated; (3) ideally, there should be no discriminative stimuli for shock presentation other than those routinely present in the natural setting in which the treated response occurs; (4) all investigators report a relatively rapid course of treatment (failure to achieve results on early trials suggest that the procedure should be reassessed); and finally, (5) aversive conditioning should not be undertaken unless a thorough functional analysis of the response and its associated stimuli has been conducted, and these considerations as well as the severity and strength of the behavior render it the treatment of choice.

REFERENCES

Brown, J. S. A behavioral analysis of masochism. *Journal of Experimental Research in Personality,* 1965, *1,* 65–70.

BUCHER, B., and LOVAAS, O. I. Operant procedures in behavior modification with children. In D. Levis (Ed.), *Learning approaches to therapeutic behavior change.* Chicago: Aldine, 1970.

BUCHER, B., and LOVAAS, O. I. Use of aversive stimulation in behavior modification. In M. R. Jones (Ed.), *Miami symposium on the prediction of behavior 1967: aversive stimulation.* Coral Gables, Florida: University of Miami Press, 1968.

LANG, P. J., and MELAMED, B. G. Case report: avoidance conditioning therapy of an infant with chronic ruminative vomiting. *Journal of Abnormal Psychology,* 1969, 74, 1-8.

LIDDELL, H. S. The challenge of Pavlovian conditioning and experimental neuroses in animals. In Wolpe J., Salter A., and Reyna L. J. (Eds.), *The conditioning therapies.* New York: Holt, Rinehart & Winston, Inc., 1964.

LOVAAS, O. I., SCHAEFFER, B., and SIMMONS, J. Q. Experimental studies in childhood schizophrenia: building social behavior in autistic children by use of electric shock. *Journal of Experimental Research in Personality,* 1965, *1,* 99-109.

MACCULLOCH, M. J., FELDMAN, M. P., ORFORD, J. E., and MACCULLOCH, M. L. Anticipatory avoidance learning in the treatment of alcoholism: a new record of therapeutic failure. *Behavior Research and Therapy,* 1966, *4,* 187-96.

MILLER, N. E. Learning resistance to pain and fear: effects of overlearning, exposure, and rewarded exposure in context. *Journal of Experimental Psychology,* 1960, *60,* 137-45.

MUENZINGER, K. F. Motivation in learning: I. electric shock for correct responses in the visual discrimination habit. *Journal of Comparative Psychology,* 1934, *17,* 267-78.

RACHMAN, S., and TEASDALE, J. *Aversion therapy and behaviour disorders: an analysis.* Coral Gables; Florida: University of Miami Press, 1969.

RICHMOND, J. B., EDDY, E., and GREEN, M. Rumination: a psychosomatic syndrome of infancy. *Pediatrics,* 1958, *22,* 49-55.

SELIGMAN, M. E. P., MAIER, S. P., and GEER, J. H. Alleviation of learned helplessness in the dog. *Journal of Abnormal Psychology,* 1968, *73,* 256-62.

SIBINGA, M. S. St. Christopher's Hospital for Children, Philadelphia, Pa., Personal Communication, 1967.

3

Token Economy as an Illustration of Operant Conditioning Procedures with the Aged, with Youth, and with Society

LEONARD KRASNER

A historical review of operant conditioning procedures with adults would show their development from animal studies to person-to-person application via verbal conditioning (Krasner, 1958), and machine-to-person, such as early Lindsley (Lindsley, 1956). A subsequent major breakthrough in assisting individuals with problem behavior was the application of operant training procedures of living to larger units such as psychiatric wards. This paper focuses on one type of operant conditioning study in an institutional setting—the token economy, with a projection of the direction these studies will develop in the field of social planning.

In recent years there has developed an approach to the treatment of problem behaviors that has been categorized as behavior modification. The growth of these procedures, their historical antecedents, and their similarities with and differences from traditional procedures have been exten-

The studies reported in this paper were supported in part by the United States Public Health Service, National Institutes of Mental Health, Grant No. MH-11938 to the State University of New York at Stony Brook, and by the Veterans Administration Hospital, Palo Alto, California.

sively documented (Krasner and Ullmann, 1965; Ullmann and Krasner, 1964; Eysenck, 1960; Wolpe and Lazarus, 1967; Eysenck and Rachman, 1965). One specific behavioral program which can be viewed as an extension of the behavior modification procedures developed in laboratory settings and with individual clinical problems to large-scale living units is that of token economy. Such a program involves a systematic application of reinforcement contingent upon selected designated behaviors.

Three aspects define the composition of a token economy. First, there is the designation by the institutional staff of certain specific patient *behaviors* as good or desirable, hence reinforceable. Second, there is a *medium of exchange*, objects that "stand for" something else, the tokens. These may be plastic rectangles shaped like credit cards, small metallic coins, poker chips, marks on a piece of paper, or even green stamps. These are obviously important elements in the token economy, but at most represent "gimmicks." Third, there is a way for utilizing the tokens, the *back-up* reinforcers themselves. These are the good things in life, the desirable things for a given individual, and may range from food to being allowed to sit peacefully in a chair. The "economy" part of the term appropriately relates to the "supply and demand" aspects of the programs which determine changing token values.

The goals of a token program are to develop behaviors that will lead to social reinforcement from others, to enhance the skills necessary for the individual to take a responsible social role in the institution and eventually to live successfully outside the hospital. Basically the individual is trained with the techniques that he can use to control his own environment in such a way that he will elicit *positive* responses from others.

APPLICATION TO ADULT PSYCHIATRIC PATIENTS

Ayllon and Azrin (1965) report the results of the first application of a token economy to a psychiatric hospital ward. The behaviors they selected to reinforce included serving meals, cleaning floors, sorting laundry, washing dishes, and self-grooming. Reinforcement consisted of the opportunity to engage in activities that had a high level of occurrence when freely allowed. The reinforcers selected were part of the naturalistic environmental context. This is one of the unique features of behavior modification research using operant techniques, namely the use of the environment as a source of reinforcers. Ayllon and Azrin made no a priori decisions about what might be an effective reinforcer for hospitalized patients. Instead, their approach involved the observation of patients' behavior to discover what patients *actually did*. They applied the general principle expressed by Premack (1959) that any behavior with a high frequency of occurrence can be used as a reinforcer. Thus, the reinforcers included such things as having a room available for rent; selecting people with whom to dine; passes; a chance to speak to the ward physician, chaplain, or psychologist; opportunity to view TV; cigarettes; and other amenities of life. The tokens, originally of no intrinsic value themselves, serve as *acquired* reinforcers that bridge the delay between behavior and an ultimate reinforcement. The investigators placed particular emphasis on the *objective definition* and quantification of the responses and reinforcers and upon programming and recording behavior. Hence their procedures involved, to the extent possible in an institutionalized setting, a series of objective, experimental studies that allowed for replication in other settings.

Ayllon and Azrin report a series of six experiments in each of which they demonstrated that target behavior *systematically* changed as a function of the token reinforcement. One experiment is typical of the procedures developed by these investigators. The specific behavior they were interested in investigating was the selection of offward work assignments. A patient would pick a job from a list of available ones for which he would then receive tokens. After ten days he was told that he could continue working on his job but that there would be *no* tokens for the work. Of the eight patients involved in this particular study, seven immediately selected another job which had previously been "nonpreferred" by them. The eighth patient switched a few days later. Each of the patients offered socially acceptable reasons for the switch which could be summarized by the statement, "One must earn enough tokens to live." In the third phase of the experiment, the contingencies were reversed and the preferred jobs led to tokens. All eight patients immediately switched back to their previously preferred, original jobs.

The results of the six experiments demonstrated that the reinforcement procedure was effective in maintaining desired performance. In each experiment the performance fell to a near zero level when the established response-reinforcement relation was discontinued; and reintroduction of the reinforcement procedure restored performance almost immediately and maintained it at a high level.

The Aylion and Azrin token economy functioned on a ward in a midwestern state hospital with a population of long-term female patients. Another token economy program (Atthowe and Krasner, 1968; Krasner, 1965, 1966a) was set up in a Veteran's Administration Hospital in California with male patients averaging fifty-eight years of age and a median length of hospitalization of twenty-four years. Most of these patients had been labeled chronic schizophrenics, and the remaining had an organic label. As a group, their behavior was apathetic and indifferent, manifested by inactivity, dependency, and social isolation. The procedures used in the inauguration of a token economy were similar to those developed by Ayllon and Azrin. However, one of the major differences was in the amount of total environmental control exerted by the experimenters. The Atthowe and Krasner program was designed to be on an *open* ward on which patients could come and go—*if*, of course, they had the right number of tokens for the gate keeper. The ward, in fact, was changed from a "closed" ward to an "open" one. The token economy had to compete with the extra-ward economy which used dollars and cents as their tokens. In such a program many very real economic problems had to be faced. To cope with these problems, special procedures had to be developed, such as a banking system to foster savings, a monthly discount rate to cut down hoarding, and yellow tokens to prevent stealing.

Prior to the introduction of tokens, most patients refused to go to any of the activities available to them and showed little interest in their environment. The patients sat or slept on the ward during the day. In effect, their behavior represented the end point of years of shaping of compliant and apathetic institutional behavior.

The investigating team decided that there were better things in life for these people to do than to sit and waste the rest of their lives. Among the valued things were enacting the role of responsible people who are adept at self-grooming, keeping their living facilities clean, dressing neatly, holding a job, and interacting with other people. Responsibility also involved their being responsive to normal social reinforcement. Thus, each time tokens were given it was accompanied by social reinforcement such as "good," "I'm pleased," "fine job," and an explicit statement as to the contingencies involved; for example, "You received three tokens because you got a good rating from your job supervisor."

This token economy program was a significant success as measured by changes in specified behavior, observer's ratings, and reactions of hospital staff. The changes in behaviors, such as attendance at group activity, were a function of the number of tokens (value) given for the activity. Group attendance increased as more tokens were given for them, and then decreased as the "payoff" returned to its previous value.

The greatest change was in the appearance and atmosphere of the ward and in the staff expectations of what the patients were capable of. The token program had an enormous effect on the attitudes of staff throughout the hospital. The staff found that they could have a therapeutic effect on patient behavior by the kinds of acts they performed. Staff morale increased and it became a matter of prestige to work on the token ward. Finally, in the hospital where the Atthowe and Krasner program was under way, two additional wards adopted similar token economies as a way of life because of its apparent usefulness in changing patient behavior.

Schaefer and Martin (1966) in the first report of their programs in a California state hospital describe the effects of their token economy program on a specific patient behavior, that of "apathy." These authors noted that the overt behavioral pattern of apathy is a *limited* response to the environment. As the environment changes, the patient does not. To measure this lack of response, they recorded patients' behavior at half-hour intervals. A nurse would check what the patient was doing on three scales: *mutually exclusive behaviors*—walking, running, standing, sitting, lying down; *concomitant behaviors*—talking, singing, playing music, painting, reading, listening to others, listening to radio, watching TV, group activity; *idiosyncratic behaviors*—rocking, pacing, chattering. They reviewed the clinical records to designate "withdrawn," "apathetic," or disinterested patients. They found that the absence of concomitant behaviors was an excellent measure of what was generally called apathy. Having a behavioral target, the next step was to determine if this behavior could be influenced within the framework of a token economy.

Tokens plus verbal praise and more direct reinforcers (cigarettes) were used. They were given by the staff for three major areas of behavior: personal hygiene; social interactions such as polite "good mornings" and meaningful questions; adequate working performance such as emptying wastebaskets. All three types of behaviors indicate interest, "caring," and a positive interest in one's environment.

The sample was composed of forty long-term schizophrenic patients whose medical records indicated apathy. By tossing a coin, half were placed in the experimental group, half in a control group which received routine ward treatment procedures.

The patients were checked on the above three scales for five consecutive working days, every half hour from six in the morning until nine at night. The reinforcement procedure was started and twice, at the end of a month, the patients were again observed every half hour during a five-day working week. The controls improved a slight and statistically insignificant amount while the experimental group improved a significant amount. That is, the number of observations on which concomitant behaviors were not emitted decreased significantly for the experimental group. Thus the token program was successful in improving a specific target behavior.

Other successful token economy programs with adult psychiatric patients have been reported by Steffy *et al.* (1966), Marks, Schalock, and Sonoda (1967), and Garicke (1965). Token economy programs have been extended to other groups of individuals, including mental retardates, delinquents, and classroom behavior problems.

APPLICATION TO GERIATRIC PATIENTS

It might be appropriate to briefly comment on the implications of these kinds of operant programs for so-called geriatric patients. What are the characteristics for programs for older patients that are different from those previously described? The goals of the program may well differ from those of programs with younger people in many instances; the goals are to change their current behavior, to ameliorate social conditions, and to better the current lives of these individuals but *not* necessarily to get them out of the institution. The major effect on these individuals' current lives has been institutionalization and the consequences of it in terms of shaping compliant behaviors, or apathy. Thus the goal of planning for the individual to leave the institution is less pertinent; however, this brings into focus an even more serious problem: the determination of what behaviors are desirable; the value decision as to how a human being should spend the rest of his life.

The nature of the program may differ in that there are characteristics of the tokens that are specific to the goals of the program; for example, if you want to affect apathy you want the older individual to handle the token object. If he is an active person such as an adolescent delinquent, you probably don't want him to physically handle the tokens.

The nature of the behavior you are dealing with may also be different with the older individual in whom you are attempting to bring back or reinstate behaviors previously existent in his repertoire. With the younger child, the retardate, the classroom disturber, the delinquent, the desired behavior may never have been previously developed. Behavioral deficit is an apt term for them. Thus the behavior of the older person can be dealt with in larger, molar units such as attending a group meeting or dressing oneself or writing an article for a ward paper, in contrast to bits of behavior or molecular behaviors more appropriate to the retarded child.

What do these programs tell us about the behavior of older people? A hot area in recent years is that of geriatrics. Like everything else, the more we learn about an area the more clearly we see the many myths that have encompassed it. One of these has been the abandonment of the older person or the brain-damaged or the long-term institutionalized individual because his behavior is considered to be unchangeable. As in other things, the belief is determined by the theoretical model with which we work. Here we must contrast the consequence of the disease model of psychopathology against a behavioral model of human deviance. For the older person the disease model, in the first instance, implies that behavior is determined by underlying internal pathology, be it anxiety, conflict, ego-id struggles, or other internal mediating events. In contrast, the behavioral model calls for a view of behavior largely determined by consequences of behavior and by environmental events. In the first instance, change can only be brought about by a restructuring of these internal events. An elderly person having lived a long life has simply too much to talk about, too many insights to gain before his behavior can change. In contrast, the behavioral view calls for change to be brought about via the manipulation of environmental consequences, something that can be done comparatively easily in an institutional setting. Volpe and Kestenbaum (1967) introduced beer and pretzels at 2 P.M. to a group of geriatric patients who supposedly could not take care of themselves. This resulted in a changed series of behaviors of the aides toward them, eliciting and reinforcing more socially adaptive behaviors.

As is obvious, in order to introduce a token economy program into an institution in which behavioral techniques have not been extensively used, it is absolutely necessary that a considerable time be spent in training the individuals who will be working on the ward in these procedures. The experience of the author as well as other investigators in this area indicates that staff training is the most important element in the success of the token economy program. Initially there is usually strong resistance to any program that apparently threatens stability of life on the ward. Any change may represent a threat to the staff, but token programs involve in many instances a radical change in philosophy of treatment. The patient is to be approached as a *responsible* individual. He is being trained to learn new habits of behavior. He is not to be viewed as a "sick" person suffering from a mental illness and incapable of responsible behavior. The view of the mental hospital patient as an individual with "problems in living" rather than as one suffering from illness is in its present phase beginning to gain some acceptance (Szasz, 1961; Ullmann and Krasner, 1969). This is not a new concept and goes back to at least the period of moral treatment which has been recently so favorably re-evaluated (Bockover, 1963; Dain, 1964). Thus a basic element in the training procedure was to change the role concept of the patient held by the staff.

Equally important was the necessary change in the role concept of the staff, especially that of the aide and the nurse. Implicit in the token economy program is the switch of the nurse from a custodial role or from a "mental health" role with its plethora of "tender loving care" to that of a hard-nosed, scientifically oriented "behavioral engineer" (a term so aptly introduced by Ayllon and Michael, 1959).

It is obvious to any observer of behavior on hospital wards that contingency reinforcement on behalf of the nurses and aides is not a new procedure. Hospitalized patients are usually given rewards in the form of approval, cigarettes, and extra privileges for behavior that staff want. In fact, there has been a continuous shaping program to help the patient arrive at the end state of the fully institutionalized individual, apathetic and withdrawn. The difference is that the token economy programs represent the application of behavioral principles applied in a controlled, planned, systematic, and contingent manner to deliberately modify behavior.

APPLICATION TO JUVENILE DELINQUENTS

An illustration of treatment of delinquent behavior by

token economy is the program in effect at Camp Butner, North Carolina, as described by Burchard (1967). He started with the conceptualization of antisocial behavior as behavior that is "acquired, maintained, and modified by the same principles as other learned behavior." Therefore, he argued, an individual "can learn constructive, socially acceptable behavior by being placed in an environment where the behavioral consequences are programmed according to the principles of operant conditioning. Instead of administering an excess of reinforcement or punishment on an indiscriminate, noncontingent basis, behavior would be punished or reinforced systematically on a response contingent basis." The program is an experimental residential program in behavior modification for mildly retarded, delinquent adolescents. Burchard utilizes techniques based on the principles of "reinforcement, punishment, and programmed instruction." This is a standardized program involving mostly nonprofessional people that has been developed to teach the delinquent individuals the practical skills that are essential for them to adjust adequately to the community and to eliminate or markedly reduce forms of antisocial behavior. As in other types of token programs, the procedures involve the definition of the behaviors to be reinforced, selecting an effective reinforcer, and programming the reinforcement contingencies. The two criteria for the selection of the behaviors to be reinforced are, first, behaviors that produce an identifiable change in the environment that can be reliably observed and reinforced; second, behaviors that provide the individual with a behavioral repertoire that will produce reinforcement in a community environment. Behaviors that were selected were those involved in maintaining a job, staying in school, budgeting money, buying and caring for clothes, buying food and meals, and cooperating with peers and adults. Burchard used as reinforcers aluminum tokens stamped with the individual resident's number in order to reduce stealing, which was more of a problem with this group than with the psychotics previously described.

Thus the individual could utilize only those tokens stamped with his own number. The reinforcing items and privileges were those that were also available for all residents in the institution on an infrequent and *noncontingent* basis.

Most of the token programs emphasize positive reinforcement and avoid any deliberate negative consequences. In the Atthowe and Krasner study there was a system of "fines" for a few undesirable behaviors such as cursing or spitting. However, these did not seem effective. Fines really may be reformulated in the token economy as additional reinforcers for which one could pay if one "wanted" very much to perform the act. It might simply be worth five tokens to "curse out" somebody or (as in the Burchard study) to hit someone in the mouth.

Burchard made use of punishment procedures developed from laboratory operant conditioning work (Azrin and Holz, 1966). In applying these principles Burchard's aim was to develop a procedure that could be applied immediately following the response and that could be of short duration yet intense enough to decrease the frequency of response. In developing these procedures he followed the same pattern as in developing positive reinforcement procedures: defining the behaviors to be punished, selecting effective stimuli, and programming the punishment contingencies. The behaviors selected for punishment were those that typically elicit some form of punishment in a community, such as fighting, lying, stealing, cheating, physical or verbal assault, temper tantrums, or property damage.

The punishment comprised the withdrawal of positive reinforcement—that is, tokens. The punishing stimuli consisted of two verbal responses, "time out" and "seclusion." Both these responses involved the loss of tokens or the opportunity to obtain tokens. When a staff member says "time out," the resident is charged four tokens and must sit in a row of chairs to one side of the day room for three to five minutes until his behavior becomes appropriate. Seclusion is used contingent upon more serious disturbing behavior such as fights, serious property damage, or refusal to go to the time out area. Upon verbalization of "seclusion," the resident is charged fifteen tokens and taken to a nearby seclusion room, an empty room with one outside window covered with a metal screen and a drawn shade. He must stay in this room until he is quiet for thirty minutes. If the resident goes to the room and behaves in an orderly manner, staying the minimum of time, he is reinforced with five tokens on his return to the living quarters. Burchard also makes use of the concept of response cost developed by Weiner (1963). If a resident does not pay up his daily debts by the end of the day he loses what is called one behavior credit; this is his response cost. Unless a resident can maintain his maximum number of behavior credits, then all reinforcers cost additional tokens. If he does maintain his maximum number, the resident has free access to the yard area outside his unit and can also purchase the trip to town (for ninety tokens) or an hour recreation time with female residents, each hour costing fifteen tokens.

Within this general token economy context, Burchard has completed a series of specific experiments of which one will be described as illustrative. He selected a specific behavior such as sitting at a desk during workshop and school time. The design of the experiment was based on an A-B-A type of analysis with reinforcement contingent on the response during the first phase, noncontingent during the second phase, and then contingent again during the third phase, each phase lasting five consecutive days. The resident received five tokens for accumulating time while sitting at his desk and also for doing specific school tasks. In a second five days he received an equivalent amount of token reinforcement, but noncontingently. In the third period, the contingent reinforcement was resumed. There was an immediate decline in performance during the noncontingent phase and a reinstatement of performance under reinforcement during the third phase, results similar to those from other token programs.

Another illustration of the application of behavioral principles to modifying the behavior of juvenile delinquents in Project CASE (Contingencies Applicable for Social Education) at the National Training School for Boys (Cohen *et al.,* 1966). The target behavior being shaped was academic work in the form of programmed instruction. If the student completed a unit of the program with a score of at least 90 per cent, he was then eligible to take an examination that could earn him token reinforcement in the form of points, each worth one cent. These points could be used to buy items such as cokes, potato chips, or Sears Roebuck material, to gain entrance to a lounge where his friends were, to register for a new program, to rent books, to buy time in the library, or to rent a private office with a telephone. The points, unlike the tokens described in the Ayllon and Azrin, Atthowe and Krasner, and Burchard studies, were not transferable from one person to another. The only way the student could obtain points was by emitting the desired behavior, namely *studying*.

The study of Cohen *et al.* also illustrates that the systematic contingent application of reinforcement is most effective when it takes place within an environment programmed so that the likelihood of desirable behavior is enhanced and that of undesirable behavior is decreased. Thus the investigators built a special environment including classrooms, study booths, control rooms, library, store and lounge. Cohen *et al.* also used the principle of gradually incorporating newer and more relevant "payoffs." The students gradually switched from working for cokes to the more educationally relevant behavior of library time or new programs. This is a key element in token programs to keep them from stagnating and to gradually increase the complexity of expected behavior.

The results reported on the sixteen students in the project indicated that the program was enormously successful in generating desirable educational activities. There was also an accompanying change in behavior. In four and a half months there were *no* discipline problems; further, the boys did not in any way destroy or deface the facilities. The social behavior of the delinquent boys matched that of nondelinquents.

A major recent development with the token programs has been their extension into the classroom with relatively "normal" students.

The results thus far reported in a series of token economy programs with a wide range of institutionalized subjects, as represented by the above illustrations, are highly promising. Krasner and Atthowe (1968) recently reported approximately 110 reports of token economy programs in more than 50 different institutions in the United States, Canada, and Australia. These included programs with institutionalized adults, retardates, delinquents, adolescents, and emotionally disturbed children.

IMPORTANCE OF RESEARCH

However, the token economy must also be approached critically in a research context for evaluation. The problems in doing token economy research are as complex as in any other area involving human behavior change, plus more. Institutional research is particularly difficult because of the difficulty in controlling relevant variables. Most evidence from research in mental hospitals would point to the fact that some change in the behavior of patients can be brought about by almost any program involving some form of "total push." The enthusiasm, positive expectation, increased and more focused attention and interest of the staff brought about by participation in a prestigious research program all provide additional and massive amounts of social reinforcement which is likely to bring about and maintain new and desirable patient behavior. The goal of the research investigator using a token economy is to demonstrate, first, significant behavioral change, and second, that the change is a function of the specific techniques involved in the token program.

The token economy programs insofar as research techniques are concerned may be divided into the following categories:

1. Those programs that are primarily demonstrational projects; no attempt is made to control variables. Although change may be observed, it is different to attribute it to the tokens per se.

2. Those programs using base rate and own controls. Operant measurement is taken of patient behavior for a specific period of time. The token program is introduced and the same behaviors are continued to be measured. The token contingencies may be removed and again the behavior continues to be measured. Then the token contingencies are reintroduced. The Ayllon and Azrin program previously described is an illustration of this. Atthowe and Krasner approached this problem by changing the value of various activities and measuring change in rate of attendance in group activities as the rate of tokens increased from one to two and back again to one.

3. The effectiveness of the token economy procedure is tested by the use of control groups which receive either no specific treatment or a different treatment. A study by Marks, Schalock, and Sonoda (1967) illustrates this approach. They worked with twenty-two chronic schizophrenic males divided into eleven matched pairs based on rated hospital adjustment. One member of each pair was assigned to Group A called "reinforcement therapy," and the other patient of the pair was assigned to Group B called "relationship therapy." In Group A each patient

received tokens, poker chips, for individual specified behaviors. The cost of meals was ten tokens per meal. Initially the reinforced behaviors were selected by the staff. Later the goals were frequently set by the patients themselves. Selected behaviors were tailored to the individual and his progress. One man might be rewarded for simply receiving and paying tokens, another for improving his appearance, another for discussing discharge plans with a social worker, another for expressing feelings. The relationship therapy (Group B) was designed to enlarge and deepen the patient's self-understanding and self-acceptance by daily psychotherapy meetings. The nine therapists involved avoided giving social reinforcement at the appearance of specific behaviors. Each subject received both forms of treatment, approximately ten weeks of each. To assess these therapies eighteen pre-post measures were taken. Most of these measures involved work, social, and conceptual performance. The authors concluded that both therapies were effective in improving the behavior of chronic hospitalized patients. However, reinforcement therapy was more *economical* of staff time. They concluded also that "reinforcement can be used in a 'psychodynamic' way. It can be used to shape self-assertive, critical, and dominating behaviors as well as the more conforming ones. Under both therapies there are more evidences of changes in behavioral efficiency than of changes in self-regard or personality structure."

4. Performance in the token economy program is related to performance in another learning task. Panek (1966) worked with thirty-two chronic schizophrenics (from the Atthowe-Krasner ward). He conditioned common word associations (from the Kent-Rosanoff and Russell-Jenkins lists) with positive and negative contingencies of verbal and token reinforcement. The study then compared success in associate learning with total number of total ward token transactions. This latter figure was taken as a measure of the responsiveness to reinforcement; that

is, the patient who *earned* most tokens and *spent* most tokens was considered most *responsive* to the token program. The results showed a significant increase of common word associations under either positive (saying "right" and giving a fractional ward token) or negative (saying "wrong" and taking away a fractional ward token) reinforcement, but no significant differences under the two contingencies. Most important, learning rate rankings were significantly correlated with rankings of total token usage. This is one of the few studies that have demonstrated that the individual who is responsive in one conditioning task such as a token economy is also responsive in an individual verbal conditioning task. This suggests the possibility of utilizing the conditioning task as a predictor for response to token-type reinforcement programs. It also relates to a previous series of studies (Krasner, Ullmann, and Fisher, 1964; Krasner, Ullmann, and Knowles, 1965), which demonstrated that verbal conditioning of "attitudes" in one task was significantly correlated to performance in another task requiring motor performance.

SOCIAL IMPLICATIONS

An illustration of the relationship among the behavior modification programs, social planning, and ethical issues has occurred in several recent incidents in a midwestern state hospital and in a Vietnamese mental hospital. The principles involved in both incidents seem similar and are closely related to a discussion of utopian planning. In the first incident a token program was introduced on a female ward and, apparently to make the tokens more effective, traditional hospital *physical* restraints were reintroduced. Patients who could exhibit control of their behavior were given tokens with which they could eventually buy their way out of restraints. Not surprisingly, this set of procedures came to the attention of people outside the hospital, such as relatives and newspaper people. An uproar resulted in a hospital investigation, the dropping of the program, serious damage to all future behavior programs, and the probable resignation of several staff members involved.

I would certainly agree with this societal concern about the consequences of what the behavior planner is doing. I believe that the use of restraints to develop a situation from which one can use tokens to escape indicates a lack of awareness of the real purpose of token programs as we have outlined here—that is the training of staff to respect the individual and to treat him as a responsible person who is learning to cope with and control his environment.

The other incident is reported in a paper, "Operant Conditioning in a Vietnamese Mental Hospital," by an American psychiatrist in the 1967 *American Journal of Psychiatry*. Cotter, the author, having witnessed a demonstration by Lovaas, who used mild shock with autistic children, apparently decided that shock was the essential ingredient in operant conditioning and brought this form of American enlightenment with him in his two-month visit to a Vietnamese mental hospital. He was in a hurry since he had only two months, so he gave the 130 male patients a choice between the electroconvulsive therapy (ECT) three times a week and working for their living in the hospital. The rationale was that ECT "served as a negative reinforcement for the response of work for those patients who chose to work rather than to continue receiving ECT." This treatment worked well with the male patients, most of them quickly volunteering for work. He then tried it with a ward of 130 women patients with much less success, since at the end of treatment only 15 women were working. So he introduced another American procedure—work or no food. This apparently was more effective. Cotter pointed out that these were not cruel methods, but rather like giving an injection to a sick person, which may hurt a little but is for his own benefit. Besides, he observed, the Vietnamese are smaller people than the Americans and thus never had bone fractures, a not uncommon concomitant of shock in this country.

To cap off his magnificent achievements with operant conditioning, and as a contribution to our war effort in Vietnam, he worked out an arrangement with a team of American special forces, the Green Berets. He learned that the Green Berets were unsuccessful in utilizing Viet Cong prisoners to tend the crops in the headquarters area. Apparently using the same techniques, Cotter was able to supply the Green Berets with his mental patients to tend the crops. This helped the war effort and increased the self-esteem of the patients, who were not part of the team. Admittedly these ex-patients were now placed under fire of the Viet Cong but as Cotter concludes, a little stress such as a war situation is psychiatrically healthy (for example, the people in London bore up well under fire). Thus we have another successful application of operant conditioning. We must be grateful that Dr. Cotter did not read Ayllon's early papers or Dr. Cotter could have ended the war with a few tokens and a portable electric battery.

It is easy to make fun of this effort, but it seriously points up what I consider to be a basic misunderstanding of behavior modification. The aim of the program is to arrange the environment in such a way that there is an increased likelihood of the individual's learning new behavior that is more likely to elicit positive reinforcement from others in the environment. The major technique in all forms of behavior therapy in an institutional setting involves training people such as nurses' aides, psychologists, and psychiatrists so that they can react to the individual not as a sick patient but as a responsible individual who is acquiring new skills in learning to behave adequately in his environment. To introduce a procedure such as electric shock or physical restraints is to communicate denigration of the individual and thus to defeat the purpose of the training program. You cannot shape responsible behavior in an individual while at the same time treating him inhumanely. You cannot build a new social environment with any chance of enhancing human dignity based on procedures inducing indignity. Here clearly the means will distort and destroy the ends. We have deliberately avoided commenting on the goals themselves. I'm not completely sure that all therapists would consider that the final behavior of tilling soil to produce food for soldiers to kill Viet Cong is necessarily a desirable social goal, but that clearly is a value decision.

Token economy programs, because of the kinds of issues they arouse, may be compared to the development of utopian planning. At first it may sound extremely peculiar to equate a treatment program for hospitalized individuals to the setting up of an ideal society. As a starting point we would argue that the ideal place to initiate utopias is in mental hospitals. Although utopia literally means "no place," the "some place" in which planned social living programs can be carried out and tested for effectiveness is in mental hospitals. The major reason for offering this argument is that the kinds of questions that must be answered in setting up a token economy are the same ones that must be answered in the planning of the "good" society. First of all, what are to be the goals of the society, the desired behaviors that will be reinforced? Second, what would be the training or educational procedures necessary to shape or maintain these behaviors in this society? Third, how do we get from here to there; how can the current way of life be modified so that there is a fighting chance to initiate the new planned programs? Many writers from ancient to modern have had a go at this (More, 1556; Butler, 1872; Bellamy, 1888; Skinner, 1948; Huxley, 1962; Parrington, 1964).

Skinner's *Walden Two* is of special interest because it is an instance of a behavioral scientist attempting to foresee and to some extent control the consequences of his scientific endeavors. Further, the principles of token economy and Walden Two are both based upon the operant conditioning principles developed by Skinner (1938, 1953) which have also permeated the classroom via programmed learning procedures.

In fact, as one studies Walden Two it is obvious that it is a token economy. Individuals in the community work for "labor-credit." These are entries in a ledger (as previously noted, several of the token programs use the same technique, avoiding physical tokens). For whatever contribution the individual offers to the Walden Two community, he receives labor credits. The allocation of specific credits for a specific task is based on principles suggested by Bellamy in *Looking Backward* (1888). Different credit values are assigned to different kinds of work, and they are adjusted from time to time on the basis of demands. This same principle is used in several token economy programs (Ayllon and Azrin, 1965). Thus pleasant jobs have lower values and one works longer hours at them, whereas unpleasant jobs like cleaning sewers have high value, hence little work time. It is necessary for each member of the community to earn 1,200 labor credits in order to maintain his status in the community. Rather than paying tokens for specific "good" things in life, all goods and services are free. The number of labor credits to maintain oneself in the community may be changed according to the needs of the community. The aim of the society is to obtain enough work from its members so that the society can maintain itself "with a slight margin of safety."

There are six planners in Walden Two who are paid (600 credits a year, so that they must still do other work to earn their way) to plan the community, hence govern it. These positions would be analogous to the research team planning the token economy programs. It is the managers who are the specialists in charge of divisions and services in Walden Two. They serve the managerial function of the society. These managerial positions may be compared to the professional staff of the hospital. Neither the managers nor the planners are in any way elected by the rest of society. The analogy between mental hospital token economy programs and Walden Two breaks down at this point because the research investigators and the professional staff are not part of the patient community. The goal then in setting up a utopia in a mental hospital would be to train patients to the point that planners and managers can be developed from their group, so that the whole community can be autonomous. It will not be easy for professional people to permit programs that will take control of behavior out of their hands and put it in the patients' hands. But, as has been pointed out, implicit in a token economy program is that you are dealing with responsible, not "sick" people.

A conceptualization of a utopian society based on operant conditioning principles, be it a token economy in a hospital or a Walden Two, elicits considerable philosophical opposition.

An important point to note about token economy programs it that they incorporate all the principles of behavior modification. Krasner (1962) has pointed out that behavior modification involves all of the techniques derived from experimental literature on changing human behavior. Learning a new behavior may be influenced by operant and classical conditioning, modeling, placebo, or expectancy. All of these procedures may be objectively described in behavioral terms, measured and controlled. Some of the descriptions of the token programs are apt to conceptualize their programs in oversimplified reinforcement terms. Reinforcement is operating, but it is more than a simple question of a token reinforcing a behavior and increasing its likelihood of occurrence. There are many more cues in the situation. For example, in many instances in the Atthowe-Krasner program, the giving of the tokens was accompanied by social reinforcement such as verbalization of "I'm pleased," "That's very good," smiles, and head nods. The purpose of this was twofold:

to maximize a social influence process and to help develop the eventual effectiveness of social reinforcement. The deliverers of social reinforcement, aides and nurses, have been trained to expect highly effective change and are alerted to respond positively to minimal change. Whatever cues are involved in high expectancy are maximized to enhance the influence process. Demonstrations of appropriate behavior are given by aides or by other patients, thus using modeling most effectively (Bandura, 1965). In effect, whatever variables that may be involved in the placebo effect (Frank, 1961) are also involved in these programs as in all behavior modification. The evidence, however, is that just as in desensitization studies (Paul, 1966), the specific technique of token reinforcement adds something over and above all other effects. All of this discussion raises hypotheses that have to be experimentally demonstrated. These studies are still in their early stage of development.

Behavior changes only in a social context. The question is then whether behavior generalizes from one situation to another. Although laboratory studies and individual case approaches using operant procedures have to some extent attempted to approach problems of generalization (for example, changing classroom behavior and measuring changes in behavior out of the classroom), most of the token economy programs have not attempted such measures. Rather, the token programs approach outside behavior change in a somewhat different manner. The goal of institutional change usually is to bring about behavior that will enable the individual to function well in a situation outside the institution. To do that, it is necessary to first analyze the new extrainstitutionary situation to determine what behaviors are necessary in order that the individual may maximize social reinforcement for himself.

This paper has argued that the token economy programs represent the most advanced type of social engineering currently in use, and have grown out of earlier applications of learning to modify the behavior of disturbed people. Eventually there will be three types of treatment procedures when people seek help from professional healers. The first of these would be what Kanfer (1966) and Schofield (1964) call "friendship" therapy. The second would be the specific application of behavior modification to change specific disturbing behaviors. The third would be social engineering as exemplified by a token economy. It is this last direction that will involve a combination of social and economic planning. When an economist (for example, Galbraith, 1967) relates a "general theory of motivation" to the economic structure of society, he is presenting hypotheses testable in small social units such as a hospital ward via a token economy. The research potential of the application of behavioral principles to social affairs is enormous and represents the next stage of development in the application of learning to psychotherapy.

REFERENCES

ATTHOWE, J. M., JR., and KRASNER, L. Preliminary report on the application of contingent reinforcement procedures (token economy) on a "chronic" psychiatric ward. *Journal of Abnormal Psychology,* 1968, 73, *1,* 37–43.

AYLLON, T., and AZRIN, N. H. The measurement and reinforcement of behavior of psychotics. *Journal of Experimental Analysis of Behavior,* 1965, *8,* 357–83.

AYLLON, T., and MICHAEL, J. The psychiatric nurse as a behavioral engineer. *Journal of Experimental Analysis of Behavior,* 1959, *2,* 323–34.

AZRIN, N. H. and HOLZ, W. C. Punishment. In W. H. Honig (Ed.), *Operant behavior: Areas of research and application.* New York: Appleton-Century-Crofts, 1966, 383–447.

BANDURA, A. Behavior modification through modeling procedures. In L. Krasner and L. P. Ullmann (Eds.), *Research in behavior modification.* New York: Holt, Rinehart and Winston, 1965, 310–40.

BELLAMY, E. *Looking backward, 2000–1887.* Boston: Tickner & Co., 1888.

Bockover, J. S. *Moral treatment in American psychiatry.* New York: Springer, 1963.

Burchard, J. D. Systematic socialization: A programmed environment for the habilitation of antisocial retardates. *Psychological Record,* 1967, *11,* 461–76.

Butler, S. *Erehwon,* 1872.

Cohen, H. L., Filipczak, J. A., and Bis, J. S. Contingencies applicable to special education of delinquents: Establishing 24-hour control in an experimental cottage. Silver Spring, Maryland: Institute for Behavioral Research, 1966.

Cotter, L. H. Operant conditioning in a Vietnamese mental hospital. *American Journal of Psychiatry,* 1967, *124,* 23–28.

Dain, N. *Concept of insanity in the United States, 1789–1865.* New Brunswick, N.J.: Rutgers University Press, 1964.

Eysenck, H. J. *Behaviour therapy and the neuroses.* New York: Pergamon Press, 1960.

Eysenck, H. J., and Rachman, S. *The causes and cures of neuroses.* San Diego: Robert Knapp, 1965.

Frank, J. D. *Persuasion and healing.* Baltimore: Johns Hopkins Press, 1961.

Galbraith, J. K. *The new industrial state.* Boston: Houghton Mifflin, 1967.

Garicke, O. L. Practical use of operant conditioning procedures in a mental hospital. *Psychiatric Studies and Projects,* 1965, *3,* 1–10.

Huxley, A. *Island.* New York: Harper, 1962.

Kanfer, F. H. Implications of conditioning techniques for interview therapy. *Journal of Counseling Psychology,* 1966, *13,* 171–77.

Krasner, L. Studies of the conditioning of verbal behavior. *Psychological Bulletin,* 1958, *55,* 148–70.

Krasner, L. The therapist as a social reinforcement machine. In H. H. Strupp and L. Luborsky (Eds.), *Research in psychotherapy,* Vol. 2. Washington, D.C.: American Psychological Association, 1962.

Krasner, L. Operant conditioning techniques with adults from the laboratory to "real life" behavior modification. Paper presented to the American Psychological Association, Chicago, 1965.

Krasner, L. The translation of operant conditioning procedures from the experimental laboratory to the psychotherapeutic interaction. Paper presented to the American Psychological Association, New York, 1966.

KRASNER, L., and ATTHOWE, J. M., JR. Token economy bibliography. New York: State University of New York at Stony Brook, 1968.

KRASNER, L., KNOWLES, J. B., and ULLMANN, L. P. Effect of verbal conditioning of attitudes on subsequent motor performance. *Journal of Personality and Social Psychology,* 1965, *1,* 407-12.

KRASNER, L., and ULLMANN, L. P. (Eds.) *Research in behavior modification.* New York: Holt, Rinehart and Winston, 1965.

KRASNER, L., ULLMANN, L. P., and FISHER, D. Changes in performance as related to verbal conditioning of attitudes toward the examiner. *Perceptual Motor Skills,* 1964, *19,* 811-16.

LINDSLEY, O. R. Operant conditioning methods applied to research in chronic schizophrenia. *Psychiatric Research Reports,* 1956, *5,* 118-53.

MARKS, J., SCHALOCK, R., and SONODA, B. Reinforcement versus relationship therapy for schizophrenics. *Proceedings, 75th Annual Convention, American Psychiatric Association,* 1967, 237-38.

MORE, T. *Utopia,* 1556.

PANEK, D. M. Word association learning by chronic schizophrenics on a token economy ward under conditions of reward and punishment. Unpublished doctoral dissertation, Washington State University. Pullman, Washington, 1966.

PARRINGTON, V. L., JR. *American dreams: A study of American utopias.* New York: Russell & Russell, 1964.

PAUL, G. L. *Insight vs. desensitization in psychotherapy.* Stanford: Stanford University Press, 1966.

PREMACK, D. Toward empirical behavior laws: I. Positive reinforcement. *Psychological Review,* 1959, *66,* 219-33.

SCHAEFER, H. H., and MARTIN, P. L. Behavioral therapy for "apathy" of hospitalized schizophrenics. *Psychological Reports,* 1966, *19,* 1147-58.

SCHOFIELD, W. *Psychotherapy: The purchase of friendship.* New York: Prentice-Hall, 1964.

STEFFY, R. A., TORNEY, D., HART, J., CRAW, M., and MARLETT; N. An application of learning techniques to the management and rehabilitation of severely regressed, chronically ill patients: Preliminary findings. Paper presented to Ontario Psychological Association, Lakeshore Psychiatric Hospital, Ottawa, 1966.

SKINNER, B. F. *The behavior of organisms.* New York: Appleton-Century-Crofts, 1938.

SKINNER, B. F. *Science and human behavior.* New York: Macmillan, 1953.

SKINNER, B. F. *Walden two.* New York: Macmillan, 1948.

SZASZ, T. S. *The myth of mental illness.* New York: Hoeber-Harper, 1961.

ULLMANN, L. P., and KRASNER, L. (Eds.) *Case studies in behavior modification.* New York: Holt, Rinehart and Winston, 1965.

ULLMANN, L. P., and KRASNER, L. *A psychological approach to abnormal behavior.* Englewood Cliffs: Prentice-Hall, 1969.

VOLPE, A., and KESTENBAUM, R. Beer and TLC. *American Journal of Nursing,* 1967, *67,* 100–03.

WEINER, H. Response cost and the aversive control of human operant behavior. *Journal of Experimental Analysis of Behavior,* 1963, *6,* 415–21.

WOLPE, J., and LAZARUS, A. A. *Behavior therapy techniques.* New York: Pergamon Press, 1967.

Comment

THOMAS G. STAMPFL

Whenever one is asked to comment on a paper that represents a "rival" approach to behavior modification, one is tempted to emphasize the applied and theoretical weaknesses related to it. My initial impulse was to adopt a more negative attitude toward Dr. Krasner's paper than I think could be reasonably justified. Certainly, Krasner has very ably presented the main advantages of the token economy (TE) methods, while at the same time he has not overlooked many of the problems, difficulties, and disadvantages associated with it. Nor has he glossed over the formidible task of assessing its merits in terms of the rigorous standards that a truly scientific evaluation of any system of behavior modification demands.

There are some logically compelling reasons why serious consideration should be given to the behavioral techniques reviewed in Krasner's paper. First, the token economy (TE) methods are applications of operant principles of conditioning based on extensive laboratory research conducted over an appreciable period of time. Research of this nature has yielded relatively precise statements of the relationship existing between critical variables (for example, immediacy of reinforcement and schedules of reinforcements) and behavioral variables. The relatively precise statements of the relationship between critical independent variables and behavioral change makes the task of the applied practitioner a vastly simpler one. When confronted with the problem of what might be tried to modify behavior, the applied operant practitioner has a ready set of behavioral principles that furnish guidelines for the initiation of procedures in relation to the behavioral problem considered. One can hardly overemphasize the advantages that result from the knowledge and confidence provided by the basic behavioral principles established through laboratory research.

A second attractive advantage of the use of TE techniques is that many of the main principles of the system already are represented in everyday experience. Under these circumstances, behavior certainly appears to be directed and modified by the rewards and punishments established in social cultures. It is rather easy to expect that a scientific analysis of critically relevant variables derived from an intensive and prolonged experimental program would yield a sharply increased efficiency in the application of these variables to the problems of behavior control.

In this context it is not surprising that dramatic results in novel behavioral problem situations are commonly reported by those workers who systematically employ the experimentally based refinements of the common-sense principles of reward and punishment. Thus there is a strong presumptive face validity to the procedures used in TE. One can only conclude that it is an eminently plausible and reasonable approach.

A third advantage is the set of attitudes that appears to be associated with those workers applying learning principles to behavioral change, and thus to those using TE techniques. Essentially, this set of attitudes reflects a willingness to attack almost any behavioral problem on an empirical basis and to relinquish any preconceptions as to which behaviors are susceptible to change. The refusal to accept a priori conclusions based on clinical dogma is an asset of vital importance. Systematic studies of difficult behavior problems with chronic schizophrenics, autistic children, juvenile delinquents, and other diagnostic categories might never have been attempted in the absence of this attitude. It is precisely in areas of behavior where no change was thought possible that the most dramatic results appear to have been achieved.

A final advantage that must be considered in any evaluation of TE may be divided into two separate but related aspects. First, the outstanding characteristic of operant workers when dealing with applied problems of human behavior is their ingenuity in adapting operant principles to the problems encountered. Thus Krasner reports one study, for example, in which a banking system was used to foster savings, a monthly discount rate was employed to reduce hoarding, and the special use of yellow tokens was introduced to prevent stealing. In those cases where it might have been difficult to identify suitable reinforcers for special patient populations, the use of the Premack frequency principle provides another of the many possible illustrations of the ingenuity of the operant workers.

Second, the operant behavioral modifiers display a very high degree of confidence in the efficacy of their basic principles. This confidence is reflected in the high degree of persistence shown when their efforts result in initial failure. Many of the studies reported in the literature indicate that a period of time is spent applying operant principles with little effect on the behavior being modified. There is little tendency to interpret initial failure as representing deficiencies in the basic operant principles. Rather, initial failure is interpreted as a failure in technological adequacy, and workers revise the technology until success has been achieved. The refusal to accept initial failure and to attack problems with confidence and persistence tends to eventuate in unique and sophisticated use of operant principles in establishing techniques of behavior change.

From the foregoing it seems clear that the TE methods based on operant principles have many obvious advantages. It seems equally clear that they suffer from a number of weaknesses.

One obvious disadvantage related to TE is that rather close control over environmental contingencies is required. The status of the *S* whose behavior is to be modified is that of a "captive." In the absence of environmental control, it is not possible to introduce the critical contingencies. If control is present initially, but is then lost for whatever reason, the removal of the contingencies allows the altered behavior to revert in the direction of its original baseline rate. In an effort to maintain behavior when the subject has lost his status as a captive, operant conditioners have attempted to gradually alter manipulated contingencies in respect to the behavior being modified so that the changed behavior itself would tend to result in natural (intrinsic) reinforcement.

The main difficulty with this solution is that there are many patient populations (juvenile delinquents, chronic schizophrenics, and so on) that tend to be highly resistant to the usual types of natural or intrinsic reinforcement that appear to function so effectively for other "normal" populations.

Operant practitioners have overlooked a possible alternative solution to this problem. This appears to be due to a marked tendency on the part of operant workers to emphasize the reinforcing consequences that maintain behavior rather than the original conditions that led to its acquisition. The question is simply to ask why the intrinsic reinforcement that ordinarily accompanies socially desirable adaptive behavior for "normal" populations is ineffective for deviant "pathological" populations. To the extent that the past conditioning history has made socially desirable adaptive behavior aversive, one might consider the deviant maladaptive behavior as a set of avoidance responses in which the intrinsic reinforcements that accompany socially desirable behavior are not sufficient to offset the effects of the aversiveness associated with that set of adaptive behaviors. A consideration of the past conditioning history would make available an alternative strategy.

One available strategy (implosive therapy) is that of deconditioning the aversiveness of the adaptive behavior, thus permitting the intrinsic reinforcement associated with the adaptive behavior to gain ascendance in originating and maintaining that behavior. In this view, many of the contingencies thought to be critical by operant workers in maintaining the behavior of patient populations is hypothesized to be secondary rather than primary to the deviant behavior that is observed.

A related problem to the above issue is the marked tendency of operant workers to suggest that their treatment methods are superior to other more traditional techniques. This attitude may merely represent the enthusiasm of a particular group for its own methods. Nevertheless, one would expect more concern for the problems of validation in a group whose methodology depends so heavily on systematic experimentation for its fundamental principles. At the very least one would expect experimental studies that compare operant procedures with other therapeutic methods. Comparisons should be made not only with the more traditional psychodynamic approaches, but also with some of the more recent variations in treatment as represented by such techniques as Gestalt therapy, rational-emotive therapy, reality therapy, implosive therapy, sensitivity training, and so on. Furthermore, it seems likely that a combination of methods might well prove to be superior to a single method for certain classes of patients. Further experimentation seems certain to be conducted along lines that evaluate the effectiveness of different techniques and their interactions. Until this is done, there is little or no basis for judgments concerning the effectiveness and utility of a particular therapeutic method.

A final comment may be made about the attitudes of adherents to particular therapeutic systems. Typically, they have displayed much enthusiasm and conviction about the efficacy of their methods. Exponents of behavior modification techniques appear to be no exception to this rule. Nevertheless, the history of psychotherapeutic efforts abounds with instances of similar enthusiasm and conviction for treatment methods that have foundered for the lack of acceptable evidence of their validity. It seems to me that operant workers have placed too much reliance on the A-B-A design in their research. Time limitations prevent a discussion of some of the problems related to this design. However, it would be well if all those who are committed to a particular system of therapy were to view their apparent successes as comparable to the deceptions and illusions achieved by an accomplished magician's sleight-of-hand performance.

What is observed and what lies behind the observance may not be what it appears to be. It seems clear that the antidote to this possibility is simply to amass overwhelming experimental evidence of the validity of a system that will satisfy the most demanding critic. At this point, no system of therapy is close to meeting that criterion.

4

Pavlovian Conditioning Approaches

CYRIL M. FRANKS

The prevailing scene in behavior therapy is characterized by a bewildering diversity of techniques, guiding principles, and philosophical orientations, and relatively few behavior therapists would now regard themselves as Pavlovians. In defense of this position it is sometimes argued that behavior therapy has outgrown its Pavlovian origins, the techniques and principles of Pavlovian conditioning now representing but a small part of the behavior therapist's conceptual and practical armamentarium. While this is largely correct, it is nevertheless the present writer's contention that the contemporary de-emphasis of the direct contributions of Pavlovian conditioning and thinking is regrettable on both historical and practical grounds.

Much of the rejection of classical or Pavlovian conditioning stems from indifference rather than informed dismissal. But there is also much misinformation; in particular, there is the false notion that Pavlovians naively believe that conditioning somehow represents the only mechanism for understanding man's behavior and that brain function is solely a matter of conditioning. Another false notion is that classical conditioning is limited to "simple" learning and that introceptive functions, perceptual, cognitive, and other mediational factors cannot and, some would say, should not be integrated into the Pavlovian model. This again is far from the case—even if some of the early behavior therapists, in their misguided enthusiasm, would have us believe that this is so.

Inasmuch as most techniques are dependent upon the application of some form of conditioning model, virtually all behavior therapy is rooted in the Pavlovian tradition. Therefore, while recognizing the many technical and conceptual changes that have occurred since Pavlov's era, it is hoped that the present paper will help place the contribution of the classical or Pavlovian conditioning model in a more appropriate perspective with respect to present-day behavior therapy and its origins.

The threefold aims of this paper are: l. To outline and trace this Pavlovian tradition from its pre-Pavlovian origins to its many post-Pavlovian trends and ramifications, both within the Soviet Union and outside. In this section, key Pavlovian principles will be presented and appraised, with special references to psychopathology. 2. To draw attention to selected basic techniques of special relevance to the practice of clinical psychology. 3. To relate the Pavlovian scene, in both tradition and technique, to recent developments in behavior therapy.

THE DIRECT CONTRIBUTION OF PAVLOV

The basic techniques of conditioning, if not the terminology, predate Pavlov by countless centuries and the literature of the world is replete with illustrations of such mechanisms at work. For example, Benvenuto Cellini, sixteenth century author of one of the most interesting autobiographies ever written, described the process of conditioning in some detail. In more recent times, numerous distinguished scientists have made scholarly reference to the various phenomena of conditioning in language quite consistent with that employed by Pavlov. The distinguished British psychologist James Ward, writing in the 1878 edition of the *Encyclopaedia Britannica,* gave this example: "The dog's mouth waters at the *sight* of food, but the gourmand's mouth will also water at the *thought* of it." As part of his lecture series in Paris around 1855, Claude Bernard described the experimental demonstration of salivary conditioning in the horse under controlled conditions (see Rosenzweig, 1959). However, the difference between the reports of Pavlov and most of his predecessors in conditioning is crucial. Whereas virtually all earlier investigators confined their endeavors to the sporadic demonstration of already established conditional responses, Pavlov was one of the first to initiate a program of investigation that included the systematic study of the formation and extinction of new and deliberately induced conditional reflexes.

If any one scientist can be singled out for his influence upon Pavlov, it is Sechenov, the father of Russian physiology and the discoverer of the phenomenon of central inhibition (and, incidentally, a student of Bernard, whose interest in the process of conditioning has been mentioned above). Like many of his predecessors who had thought about the nature of acquired associations, Sechenov was a convinced monist and materialist. But just as Pavlov was later to continue the line of thought of earlier *observers* of conditioning, but with the key difference already noted—so Sechenov, by his practical investigations of the phenomenon of central inhibition, was among the first to replace philosophical deliberation and incidental observation with experimentation. As is well known, this course steered him into trouble with the tzarist government, culminating in a clash with the censor over the proposed title of his now famous monograph. Sechenov was forced to relinquish the more revealing—and therefore, from the censor's point of view, more dangerously "antireligious"—*An Attempt to Establish the Physiological Bases of Psychical Phenomena* in favor of the safer and more prosaic *Reflexes of the Brain,* by which title it is now known.

It must not be thought that Pavlov and Sechenov were the only reputable scientists of their day dedicated to such an approach. While it was not until the spring of 1924 that Pavlov presented what he called a "full and systematized exposition" of his researches (see Kaplan, 1966, pp. 59 ff), his colleagues and rivals were engaged in the development of alternative and related schema. In particular, one must single out the "reflexology" of Bekterev and his elaborate system for the instrumental study of the so-called "motor associated reflexes" (see Diamond, Balvin, and Diamond, 1963, pp. 201 ff). In contrast with the largely unknown writings of Pavlov, the early part of the twentieth century witnessed the translation of Bekterev's work into several Western European languages; it was not until several decades later that Pavlov achieved the position he now holds. Both Pavlov and Bekterev were intimately involved in the attempt to transform psychology—especially animal psychology—from a mentalistic series of speculations into a biologically rooted science. But it was Pavlov, above all, who did most to bring about the substitution of quantitative, objective, and permanent records of muscular and glandular activity for qualitative, subjective, and irregular imagery and ideation, and it is therefore not surprising that Pavlov eventually became the dominant world figure that he now is.

To discuss the complex and changing relationships between Pavlov and his concepts and Marxism-Leninism is not feasible in the present paper, and the reader is referred elsewhere (for example, Diamond, Balvin, and Diamond, 1963; Brozek, 1966; Franks, 1969a, 1969b; Gray, 1966; Serban, 1959). In any event, the present trend in the Soviet Union is to focus more upon the data per se and less upon their politico-philosophical ramifications (see O'Connor, 1966; Brozek, 1964). As for Pavlov and his complex relations with the Soviet government, although much has been written we will probably never know his real opinions. Extremists on both sides of the political fence tend to have opposing views about Pavlov vis-á-vis the Soviet system, ranging from the image of Pavlov as an unwilling and exploited dupe—really anti-Marxist and antimaterialist—to the official Soviet image of Pavlov, resplendent in all its Soviet-identified glory. The truth, very probably, lies in between (see Franks, 1969a, 1969b; Watson, 1963). Pavlov seems to have possessed qualities of both naiveté and sophistication, of both tender-minded concern for the individual and tough-minded scientific objectivity. Opposed to a dogma of absolute truth as then propounded by the Soviet regime, he was nevertheless a grateful and loyal Soviet citizen. Bitterly antagonistic to tzarist activities, he became increasingly sympathetic to the proclaimed goals for the new society, if not to the absolutism that was required of its members. Razran (1957), who is far better informed than most, makes it very clear that Pavlov's work and attitudes are in accord with the best traditions of Western science and democracy.

Gantt (1967a) portrays Pavlov as a man with humility, tolerance, and a sense of humor, afraid neither to acknowledge the endeavors of those who disagreed with him nor to refute himself if need be.[1] A redoubtable observer (the words "Observation, Observation and Observation!" appear in large letters outside the main building of Pavlov's laboratory at Koltushi, just outside Leningrad), a man never too old to have an inquiring mind, at eighty Pavlov made the decision to explore the field of psy-

1. Consider, for example, the following quotation from Pavlov, cited by Gantt (1967a):"Never think that you already know everything. No matter in what high esteem you are held always have the courage to say to yourself: 'I am ignorant.' " It is unfortunate that such a spirit is not voiced more often in our contemporary world of cultism and partisanship.

chiatry and see if his theories and techniques could be applied therein.

Lawrence Kubie's historical note, cited by Lebensohn (1964), concerning a meeting in Leningrad between Pavlov and Gerard in 1935, the year before Pavlov's death, provides further insight into Pavlov, the man.

> They were discussing his work on conditioning and especially the production of experimental "neuroses" in dogs by presenting them with a task of discrimination which was too difficult. To Dr. Gerard's surprise, Pavlov said with a twinkle, "Do you know that I was led to try these experiments by reading some of Freud's work?" He then proceeded to speak of his indebtedness to Freud for stimulating his thoughts and his experiments into this productive channel, and added that he anticipated that deeper understanding of behavior would come from a fusion of the concepts of the conditioned reflex and of psychoanalysis.

For Pavlov, the "conditional" reflex was a creative, emergent activity of the organism rather than a stereotyped and unchanging process (see Makarov, 1966; Gantt, 1966b). The original term, as employed by Pavlov, was intended to convey this essentially temporary nature of the connection thus formed. In this sense, Pavlov was echoing the observation of Sechenov, made back in 1856, that whenever the central hemispheres are involved in a reaction, the response to any given stimulus *must* be inconsistent and variable. With Diamond, Balvin, and Diamond (1963), one may well question whether any vertebrate reflex is so invariable that it deserves to be called unconditional.

Pavlov's first book to be translated into English, by W. H. Thompson of Trinity College, Dublin, explicitly conveyed this intent; it was only in later translations that the term "conditioned" was introduced and Gantt went along with this inaccuracy in the interests of conformity—a decision he claims to have regretted ever since (Gantt,

1966b). According to Konorski (1948), the error came about by way of the German *bedingte Reflex* (but see Mary Brazier, 1959; Diamond, Balvin, and Diamond, 1963; Hilgard and Bower, 1966 for further discussion of this interesting historical error and its implications; see also Franks, 1969a, 1969b).

Regardless of the terminology employed, it is unfortunate that Pavlov's name is associated exclusively with the conditional reflex per se. Pavlov's concern was really with the attempt to understand the principles of brain function (or higher nervous activity, to use his nomenclature). While conditioning represents the key strategem in this quest, it is to be regarded as neither an end in itself nor as somehow the basic unit of brain function. According to Pavlov the two basic processes underlying brain function are "excitation" and "inhibition," and conditioning techniques represent the means whereby these processes and their properties may be subjected to systematic study. Contemporary techniques such as the electroencephalograph and the direct electrode implant being unavailable, Pavlov had to make inferences about the properties of central processes by the conditional reflex study of more peripheral events. But always he stressed that the classical conditional reflex, like any tool that might be used, is itself governed by the same processes that control other phenomena such as "trial and error learning." This again is an important point that many contemporary conditioning therapists *and* their critics tend to overlook.

Pavlov's theory of behavior is commonly misunderstood as reducing behavior to simple unlearned stimulus-response sequences (unconditional reflexes) and acquired simple sensori-motor and sensori-secretory habits. Actually, Pavlov viewed behavior as resulting from complex interactions within the central nervous system, involving irradiation and concentration of excitatory and inhibitory processes and including both positive and negative induction effects. It is the interactions and spreading of these processes over the cortex which make up higher nervous function, normal nervous activity being characterized by Pavlov as a state of "fine balance" of these activities (see Minz, 1964).

Working primarily with dogs, he found that so-called experimental neuroses could be established in a variety of ways, all of which involved some form of collision or excessive activity of his two processes. Eventually five principle means of obtaining the breakdown were obtained (see Lynn, 1966):

1. *Intense stimuli.* The stimuli used included loud rattles, explosions, and the swinging of the dog's platform. At the conclusion of these alarming events it proved impossible to elicit any conditioned responses from the dog for a fortnight. In the Leningrad floods of 1924, the animal house was badly flooded and several of the dogs nearly drowned; and this also disrupted previous conditional behavior patterns – in some cases for several years.

2. *Delay.* A second way of obtaining neurotic breakdown was systematically to increase the time interval between the presentation of the signal and the food.

3. *Difficult discriminations.* This method involves conditioning the dog to make a reaction to one signal and not to react to a somewhat similar one. When intermediate stimuli are presented a breakdown is induced.

4. *Alternation of positive and negative stimuli.* The animal is trained in a discrimination task and the positive and negative stimuli are continually alternated.

5. *Physical stress.* The final way in which breakdown can occur is when the dog is subject to physical stresses such as disease, accident, or surgery.

Pavlov noticed that not all the dogs responded in similar fashion to seemingly similar stimuli. This led him to classify his animals according to their reactivity and, eventually, to the development of his now well-known theory of types (see Franks, 1964; Lynn, 1966; MacMillan, 1963; O'Connor, 1966; Wortis, 1962). Pavlov's first attempts at classification were exclusively in terms of excitation-inhibition *balance*. This was later extended to include two additional "dimensions," *strength* and *motility*. Drawing parallels with the ancient Hippocratic classification of temperament, Pavlov also began to order his animal-derived data in such terms and then, much later and much more speculatively, to apply this typology to man.

Another important assumption of Pavlov pertains to the concept of *protective inhibition*. Protective inhibition is a process of inhibition brought about by excessive or prolonged stimulation and its presumed function is to protect the nervous system from biological overstrain. Pavlov assumed that dogs and individuals with weak nervous systems generated protective inhibition much more readily than those with strong nervous systems. According to Pavlov, schizophrenia results from the generation of excessive protective inhibition within the cerebral cortex. This protective inhibition can be generated as a result of various kinds of shock, drugs, or physical illnesses. An important constitutional factor is also presumed to be pertinent in the etiology of schizophrenia, namely, the strength of the nervous system. By "strength of the nervous system" is meant the extent to which the nervous system is sensitive to stimulation, weak nervous systems being those that are most sensitive. A weak nervous system that is sensitive to stimulation is more likely to become overstimulated and generate protective inhibition, and hence to succumb to schizophrenia. The presence of protective inhibition in the cortex is supposed to account for the slowness and poor conditionability of schizophrenics.

According to Pavlov, the variegated symptoms of schizophrenia are determined by the effects of protective cortical inhibition on the other parts of the brain. In cases of catatonic stupor the protective inhibition has spread down to the subcortex and also affected the sympathetic nervous system. In those schizophrenic states in which violent outbursts occur, the subcortex is overexcited, due to the removal of cortical control and the operation of the law of positive induction (according to which, inhibition in one region of the brain induces excitation in other areas). Pavlov compared this latter sequence with the excited outbursts of tired children and intoxicated adults, arguing that the cerebral cortex is weakened, its control on the subcortex diminished, and hence the subcortex is freed to activate the emotional outbursts (see Lynn, 1966).

While Pavlov is not the only person to hold that hypnosis and sleep have many essentially common elements, Pavlov's theory of hypnosis is probably the first to be derived from physiological experiments—if largely with animals. Das (1958), who sifts and reviews the evidence most carefully, concludes that a good case can be made in favor of Pavlov's contention that hypnosis is a state of partial or selective inhibition. A similar rationale can be used to explain narcolepsy (for example, Levin 1961).

If psychiatric disease processes are described in terms of disruption of the normal processes of excitation and inhibition, then Pavlovian treatment must be aimed at the direct modification of this disruption. Hence the emphasis upon "sleep therapy" to protect the organism from overstimulation. For example, if necessary it can be used to strengthen protective inhibition and thus allow the cortical cells an opportunity to recover from their exhausted state. On the other hand, stimulant drugs can be given to increase the excitation process when this is indicated; and sometimes it is necessary to combine sleep and stimulant treatments.

Finally, we must mention the so-called second signal system. Pavlov recognized that the great difference between man and animal—a development, unique to man, which makes for much of his achievements, his history, learning, and communication, not to mention his tragedies—is that man's cerebral cortex has within it the unique gifts of language and speech, a second signal system in which words stand for the sights and sounds of the already described first signal system.

But the second signal system can be modified both by experience and the first signal system, and it is here that Pavlov introduced his concept of human personality types (see Lynn, 1966; MacMillan, 1963). The first and second signaling systems may be in harmony with one another (that is, developed to about the same degree) or they may be unbalanced, with one dominating the other. The type in which the first signaling system dominates the second is known as the *artistic* type. The type in which the second predominates over the first is known as the *thinking* type, and the type in which the systems are balanced is known as the *intermediate* type. Each of these three types exists on the basis of the general types; that is, the same typology which applied to animals. Consequently, the determination of human type requires both the application of the methods described by Pavlov for determination of general (animal) types and the determination of the specifically human characteristics of type.

With the exception of the weak general type, the supposed relationship between the animal typology and that applicable to man has not yet been worked out in detail. As it stands, the following personalities are covered:

1. *The weak general type in which the first and second signaling systems are in harmony.* This is supposed to correspond to the neurasthenic personality, and under stress "neurasthenia" is supposed to develop.

2. *The weak general type in which the first signaling system dominates the second (artistic).* This is supposed to correspond to the hysterical personality, and under conditions of stress, frank hysterical symptoms appear.

3. *The weak general type in which the second signaling system dominates the first (thinking).* This corresponds to the psychasthenic personality and, under conditions of stress, psychasthenic symptoms are said to develop.

In attempting to place Pavlov's system in perspective, it is desirable to separate his lifelong systematic amassing of physiological data derived from repeated observations of his laboratory animals from speculations about human disorders during the last decades of his life, a distinction which it is now safe to make within the Soviet Union as well as outside.[2] And even his experimentally based conclusions must be regarded with caution. While many of his concepts have been substantiated, others are, at best, highly questionable and, at worst, refuted. Thus, as a totality his work must be regarded as a quasineurological system rather than a firmly established body of knowledge (but see Franks, 1969a, 1969b; Hilgard and Bower, 1966; Kimble, 1967; Konorski, 1948, among others, for a further discussion of this point).

However, even if the conclusion must be that Pavlov failed to achieve his overall aim, there is no doubt that his contributions to behavior therapy as we know it today are substantial. In particular we may single out his development of classical conditioning as a viable tool, his emphasis upon objective methodology in the investigation of human activity, his consistent and rigorous scientific and materialist approach, and the impetus he gave to later Pavlovian developments both within the Soviet Union and elsewhere.

SELECTED POST-PAVLOVIAN DEVELOPMENTS

There was a time when informed and scholarly information and appraisal with respect to post-Pavlovian developments within the Soviet Union were hard to come by. But this is no longer the case; such reports are now readily available (for example, Cole and Maltzman, 1969;

2. In the words of two distinguished Soviet psychologists: "Since Pavlov's death, many new experimental methods have been discovered and many new facts that establish new laws unknown to him have been accumulated. More, we psychologists, working with people, most never forget that Pavlov worked only with dogs, and that his pronouncements on man were, as a rule, made only by analogy" (Teplov and Nebylitsyn, 1963).

Franks, 1969b), so that extensive duplication here is unnecessary.

It is important to recognize that the Pavlovian tradition, while unquestionably paramount, is not the only one within the Soviet Union. As has been pointed out on more than one occasion, there are at least three fairly distinct currents within the Soviet Union: the direct Pavlovian current (including the reflexology of Bekhterev); the Vygotsky current; and the Uznadze current (of little relevance here and therefore not to be discussed further) devoted to the theory of set and seemingly based largely upon a perceptual illusion originally reported by Fechner (see Berlyne, 1963).

The Pavlovian tradition is now being expanded and modified by such distinguished investigators as the late Teplov and his successor, Nebylitsyn, at the Institute of Psychology in Moscow. Perhaps the most noteworthy aspect of their approach is the manner in which the conventional Pavlovian emphasis upon the intensive long-term study of the too few is successfully combined with the technically and methodologically more elegant but superficial Western-type study of the too many. It is the hope of such investigators that, by such means, Pavlov's hypothetical three-dimensional classification of the nervous system can be placed upon a firm footing in terms of both measurement and possibly underlying neurophysiological basis (see Franks, 1967a, 1967b; Gray, 1964; Lynn, 1966; Teplov, 1961; Teplov and Nebylitsyn, 1966). In certain respects, the work of the Teplov-Nebylitsyn group represents a signal advance over the perhaps more internationally renowned researches of Luria and his students. For example, for Luria a process either occurs or does not occur, and little or no attempt is made to record the rate at which the activity takes place. Unlike Luria, Teplov and Nebylitsyn stress quantification, making full use of modern Western techniques of information programming in the process.

Of related importance is the attempt to develop introceptive conditioning, in which the CS or the UCS or both are delivered directly to the mucosa of some specific viscus. By such means, it is possible to integrate into the Pavlovian system biologically more meaningful conditional responses than those which the typical laboratory investigator is wont to study (see Bykov, 1957; Razran, 1961, 1965).

Of direct relevance to behavior therapists is the second stream, stemming from the work of Vygotsky, who died in 1934 at the early age of thirty-eight. For Vygotsky, social modifications are conveyed principally by language, and verbal stimuli are therefore the key to behavior control. Out of this tradition, in conjunction with Pavlovian developments with respect to the orienting reflex and semantic conditioning, or conditioning to meaning, has developed the work of such prominent psychologists as Luria, Leontiev, and Vinogradova and the attempt to develop "the word as a physiological and therapeutic factor" (Platonov, 1959).[3] Luria's interest has been in the development of the child, particularly in the development of voluntary control, and here he finds language of central importance.

These developments should not be confused with verbal conditioning, in which the attempt is simply to modify the words that a subject uses by reinforcing certain of his utterances and extinguishing others. While both can be used psychotherapeutically, the Soviet work implies rather more than conditioning of this sort. The link with classical conditioning is by way of an experiment originally designed by Ivanov-Smolensky (1927). A child is instructed to press a rubber bulb whenever a given signal comes on; this is equivalent to a UCS. Some second

3. In his book, *The Word as a Physiological and Therapeutic Factor,* Platonov combines conditioning and hypnotic suggestion as therapeutic processes. It is of parenthetic interest to note that Platonov, in treating what psychoanalysis would call "merely the symptom," finds no evidence whatsoever of symptom substitution and adopts a position consistent with that of many behavior therapists.

signal, say a colored light, is now regularly associated with the appearance of the original signal, and a conditional bulb-pressing response is made to this new CS. The usual rules about reinforcement, extinction, and discrimination apply. As Hilgard and Bower (1966, p. 66) point out, actually this experiment is transitional to instrumental conditioning, but no such recognition is made by Luria or those who work with him. For Luria, anything that is learned is conditioned, and the interest is therefore in how learning is controlled rather than the purity of the conditional reflex paradigm. What is of importance is what goes on inside the human organism as he relates to the environment. Luria points out that the laws that Pavlov discovered for the gradual development of conditional reflexes and their resistance to change are fundamental ones, but that they do not apply in full force to the human learner because of speech—the second signaling system. Speech makes possible a new information system that considerably modifies the principles according to which new responses are learned by man. For one thing, new responses in man are usually not acquired gradually; they are incorporated at once into some existing category and regulated by a rule that can be stated in words. Learned behavior is sustained by a behavior rule and no longer requires reinforcement to sustain it. Such behavior thus becomes self-regulating (see Hilgard and Bower, 1966).

Before leaving the Soviet scene a word might be said about the implications of these developments for clinical practice. While behavior therapy per se is a largely unknown concept within the borders of present-day Russia, the verbal acknowledgements paid to Pavlovian tradition, interlaced with a Marxist emphasis upon social forces, are conspicuously in evidence at all levels of the Soviet health services. While Soviet mental health facilities are in many ways outstanding, this would seem to reflect the organizational framework, the dedication of those involved, and the prevailing philosophy of social concern rather than an adherence to any psychological principles, Pavlovian or otherwise (but see the Special Section in the *American Journal of Psychiatry,* November 1968, for an extended discussion of contemporary Soviet psychiatry).

In the Western world, interest in Pavlovian concepts seems to be taking three broad but closely related directions: the recent revival of research interest in the systematic exploration of Pavlov's dimensions of central nervous function; the relatively more empirical attempts to develop techniques for the direct application of classical conditioning per se to the clinical situation; and the occasional forays into the development of therapeutic programs based on Pavlovian principles at large. Investigators such as Mangan in Australia, Gray, Eysenck, and Hume (working independently) in the United Kingdom, and the present writer in the United States express a common concern with the intrinsic complexities of Pavlovian excitation and inhibition and its three basic parameters of strength, motility, and dynamism. When the sometimes conflicting data amassed by such experimenters are appraised, it still remains unclear what the basic Pavlovian dimensions are, what are their determinants at the physiological level, and what are the relationships between, on the one hand, Pavlovian dimensions and their physiological substrates and, on the other hand, established dimensions of personality.

The debt of the behavior therapists to Pavlov is obviously great and does not need to be underscored here. Pavlovian techniques are also employed in clinical areas related only incidentally to mental health (for example, to measure hearing ability in small children, audiometrists sometimes employ what is known as the peep-show method; see Dix and Hallpike, 1959). Of the many Western investigators working within the Pavlovian framework—which implies an affinity for the model and not just the isolated application of classical conditioning procedures whenever expedient—the names of Christian Astrup, Andrew Salter, Thomas Ban, Leo Alexander, and the late Howard S. Liddell come readily to mind. But towering over all these figures is that of W. Horsley Gantt—one of the very few pupils of Pavlov still active, translator of Pavlov, founder of the Pavlovian Laboratories at Johns Hopkins University School of Medicine, first president of the Pavlovian Society of North America, and editor of the journal *Conditional Reflex.*

Gantt's unique contribution stems from his attempt to tease out the relative roles of central versus peripheral structures, with special relevance to the study of the cardiovascular system. His discovery that different systems may be conditioned by the same situation and yet extinguished at different rates is of much importance in the understanding of persisting neurotic symptoms, seemingly fragmented and unrelated to each other. The term *schizokinesis* is used by Gantt to refer to the split between general autonomic functions and a specific conditional reflex. Of all autonomic reflexes, it is the cardiovascular CR which tends to persist long after other components have been either naturally or deliberately extinguished—a situation to which both the general practitioner and the cardiac specialist will readily attest. When new relationships occur between foci of excitation in the brain without the presence of an external stimulation, then *autokinesis* is said by Gantt to occur. This can be therapeutic or pathological, depending upon the circumstances (see Gantt, 1966a).

Razran (1966) takes Gantt to task for being *plus Grec que les Grecs,* a prewar Pavlovian in a post-Pavlov Pavlovian world, a left-behind traditionalist who tends to neglect post-Pavlov developments. While there may be *some* truth in this allegation, let us also note that it was Gantt who translated the works of Bykov and Luria into English!

PAVLOVIAN CONDITIONING AND BEHAVIOR THERAPY

It is possible, and at times convenient, to make use of Pavlovian conditioning without regard for a Pavlovian model of the brain per se, and this is what many contemporary conditioning therapists tend to do. The concern can then be strictly at the empirical level, with the validity and utility of the technique regardless of the model upon which it is supposed to be based. Such a strategy offers many advantages to the practitioner, even if it is suspect to the research scientist.

The literature pertaining to classical conditioning and its many parameters is vast, complex, and—in certain areas—highly equivocal (see Franks, 1958, 1960, 1963, for more extended discussion of these matters). Many problems still await resolution—for example, the differences between so-called instrumental and classical conditioning, the relative roles of the cortex and subcortex in conditioning, the presence and nature of a general factor, or general factors, of conditioning, the nature of backward conditioning and other "artifacts." Nevertheless, much is known about such basic parameters as sex, intelligence, phylogenetic and ontogenetic differences, personality variables, brain damage, drug effects, and the influence of differential instructions with respect to specific reflexes. It is when we attempt to generalize and extrapolate that difficulties arise.

As this array of knowledge accumulates—and particularly as it relates to contemporary neurophysiology—so the traditional Pavlovian view of higher nervous activity seems increasingly antiquated, naive, and simplistic. The notion of a two-dimensional irradiation and concentration of two central processes would appear to need restatement. Pavlov's explanations (in terms of "weak" and "strong" nervous systems) of the fact that some individuals break down when confronted with a particular stress situation, whereas others do not, are too general to be very helpful to our understanding. And Western replications of presumably more sophisticated and more specific post-Pavlovian findings do not always confirm Soviet results (for example, Moss and Edwards, 1964). Nevertheless, the Pavlovian model will continue to have much to offer the clinical investigator who is prepared to recognize that much of what Pavlov proclaimed requires drastic modification. In essence, it is a matter of being students of Pavlov rather than disciples.

In principle, classical conditioning procedures can be used for both clinical diagnosis and therapy, but as yet no totally satisfactory assessment procedure would seem to have been developed. The techniques so far available tend to be ingenious but of limited value in terms of effort expended, often requiring relatively elaborate apparatus and the services of a skilled technician. For example, Gantt's (1950) battery, involving the differential abilities of psychiatric patients to form, generalize, and differentiate a variety of CR's in diverse laboratory situations, categorizes these various aspects of adaptive CR function in hierarchical terms. In ascending order, from the least to the most serious disturbance, Gantt's hierarchy is as follows:

1. Disturbance of the latent period of the CR;
2. Speed of formation of the CR;
3. Ability to form differentiated CR (that is, to positive and negative signals);
4. Disturbance of the function of generalization;
5. Ability to form spontaneous, but not integrated, CR;
6. Failure to obtain previously formed CR;
7. Inability to form any experimental CR;
8. Lack of retention of very old CR, including those to word signals, and failure of the ability to carry out orders;
9. Failure of forming some UCR, for example, the orienting reflex (seen only in severe "organic" cases).

Employing a classical galvanic skin response sound and

shock paradigm, Alexander (1962) has developed a promising technique for making the often difficult differential diagnosis between physical and psychogenic pain states. Employing an eyeblink conditioning technique, Ban and Levy (1961) have developed a sophisticated diagnostic test procedure that measures eight "physiological" patterns of conditional response behavior, the claim being that it is possible to provide "measurable evidence of change in patients exposed to any treatment regime."

The limitations of such procedures have already been noted. But they also possess the twin strengths of objectivity and anchorage to a model which is available for use if need be. There is another compelling asset which should be made explicit. Traditional psychometric tests, failing to differentiate clearly and explicitly for each sensory modality between the preservation of old learning, present learning, and the retention of new learning, tend to focus upon one or the other of these attributes but never systematically upon all three. In contrast, conditioning tests, appropriately used, make it possible to study individually and for each modality *all* of these facets of behavior. And since conditioning measures are highly sensitive to a variety of influences (pathology, drugs, psychotherapy, and so forth) it is, in principle, possible with or without commitment to a Pavlovian philosophy to develop effective assessment procedures.

The deployment of Pavlovian conditioning techniques—or, for that matter, any laboratory procedure—for the prediction of response to conditioning type therapies in the clinical situation has met with but limited success. Apart from the fact that this area of endeavor has been insufficiently explored, one formidable difficulty presents itself—the already briefly noted fact that so far, no general factor of conditioning, taking up an appreciable amount of the variance, has been demonstrated. This means that each prediction has to be specific to a particular clinical situation and formulated in such exquisitely precise terms, with respect to test and therapy parameters, that it is unlikely to be of much use to the practicing clinician having to contend with a variety of ill-defined and changing situations.

No wonder then that virtually no valid and generally useful technique exists for the prediction of success in behavior therapy. If, as the present writer believes, behavior therapy is a matter of a thoroughgoing behavioral orientation rather than, as some authors (for example, Lazarus, 1967) would have us believe, a melange of techniques; then it seems reasonable to conclude that effective prediction is more likely to be achieved in terms of this same behavioral orientation rather than by recourse to any eclectic grab-bag of tests. As Goldfried and Pomeranz (1968) make clear, it will be necessary to make a systematic and thorough criteria analysis of the relevant individual and environmental variables that seem liable to modify the patient's behavioral repertoire. While attempting to develop general laws it will also be necessary, as Paul (1967) and Goldfried and Pomeranz point out, to provide specific answers to specific questions: "*What* treatment, by *whom,* is most effective for *this* individual with that specific problem, and under *which* set of circumstances?" Such an individualized approach to assessment will surely necessitate the long-term study of the individual patient as well as the traditional acute group investigation project usually encountered in the West. Such procedures, in which the methods of experimental psychology are applied to the prediction and control of the behavior of the individual patient, seem more likely in the long run to answer questions such as those raised by Paul than any group research or conventional psychometric testing procedures (see Franks, 1967a).

By making a number of inductive and questionable leaps from our knowledge of those parameters obtaining within a specific laboratory context to those parameters presumed to be operating within the clinical situation, it is possible to set forth a number of guidelines for those who wish to embark upon some form of therapy based upon classical conditioning. For example, it is *probably* correct to conclude that anxious individuals will condition better than nonanxious, that certain forms of brain damage make it harder to form and easier to extinguish CR, that distributed trials and partial or intermittent reinforcement facilitate conditioning, that forward conditioning should be easier to bring about than trace or backward conditioning (see Franks, 1966).

These guides—and they are no more—may be used either in setting up strictly classical conditioning procedures, as in the use of aversive conditioning, or, with less justification, in the planning of a general behavior therapy program in which the stimuli are not so specifically defined. However, regardless of the setting, considerable caution is indicated. Apart from the hazards of inductive reasoning noted above, conflicting opinions occur and it is not always clear what is and what is not established. For example, it is debatable whether the phenomenon of backward conditioning (long held to be anathema to aversive conditioning therapy) occurs at all and, if so, whether forward and backward conditioning are qualitatively the same. Thus, Razran (1956) concluded that backward conditioning has a factual status, albeit a weak one, whereas Cautela (1965) is less sure. To some (for example, Champion and Jones, 1961), forward and backward conditioning are essentially the same phenomenon, whereas to others (for example, Barlow, 1956) they are qualitatively different. And according to Zeiner and Grings (1965), backward conditioning can occur, but the effect is determined in part by the way the subject perceives or structures the experimental situation.

Azrin and Holz (1966) have set up thirteen general but fairly precise rules for the optimal conduction of projects in aversion therapy based upon classical conditioning principles. On the face of it, these rules, based as they are upon experimentally derived data, would seem to provide a good working framework for the practitioner. But there are many additional parameters that are as yet little understood, and the unwary behavioral clinician who attempted to apply these rules in a mechanical fashion would soon find himself in great trouble. Some of them can actually apply "in reverse," depending upon the personality of the individual. For example, Beech (1960) found that shock as an aversive stimulus increased rather than decreased writer's cramp. The therapist familiar with Solomon and Wynne's well-known (1953) experiments on the training of dogs to avoid a traumatic shock by jumping a hurdle might have been prepared for this possibility to occur. When Solomon and Wynne tried to extinguish the jumping response by shocking the dogs for jumping, they found instead that this increased the jumping response. If, by analogy, it is argued that it is the anxiety level of the subject, together with the strength of his other drives that in part determines the success or failure of aversion therapy, then such personality differences must be taken into consideration by the conditioning therapist.

Closely related is the matter of motivation. While the role played by motivation in the application of Pavlovian conditioning principles is not as yet clearly understood, its relevance is in no doubt. It seems reasonable enough to assume that, other things being equal, the motivation for a patient to undergo aversive therapy for the treatment of an outwardly self-rewarding pattern of behavior such as smoking or drinking will be different to that of a patient willing to undergo aversive conditioning to eliminate seemingly self-punishing patterns of behavior such as hair pulling. Once again the conclusion is clear: behavior therapy principles mechanically or naively applied without recourse to the individual patient are less likely to succeed.

Of perhaps equal interest is the attempt to apply Pavlovian principles rather than classical conditioning per se.

For example, is it possible to develop a theory about old age that can be applied to the assessment and treatment of the geriatric patient? Cautela (1966) believes that it is, arguing that as part of the aging process, the efficiency of the cortical cells becomes reduced, so that these cells can be easily exhausted. If monotonous stimuli are presented, the same cortical cells are repeatedly affected. This results in an exhaustion of the excitatory substance, and inhibition occurs. Since the cortical cells have lost some efficiency due to aging, less monotonous stimulation is needed to produce inhibition than in younger individuals. Also, with old age the motility of the nervous system declines. This means that, even without the presentation of monotonous stimuli, the speed with which excitatory states are transmitted is impaired. This is seen behaviorally in the lack of ability of the aged population to adjust to change in a rapid manner.

Since the aged individual tends to have a "weak" nervous system, it is difficult for him to learn new responses. What new responses are learned are easily inhibited by distracting stimuli or very strong stimulation. As a result of the aged individual's poor inhibitory processes, it is difficult to extinguish old habits that interfere with the present adjustment of the aged to new demands brought about by reduction of physical capability and new social adjustment. For the geriatric patient who has some kind of central nervous system damage, it is even more difficult to form new CR's and more difficult again to maintain them. Also, it is more difficult to eliminate undesirable habits.

In terms of such a rationale – at present largely in the realm of speculation – it should be possible to design a threefold program for research study in the area of gerontology. Such a program might involve the development of assessment procedures; prophylaxic aimed at minimizing the effects of the aging process; and therapeutic reduction of impairments that have already occurred. While it would be naive in the extreme to imply that, somehow, Pavlovian psychology has the answer to the problem of aging, it is far from naive to suggest that such a research proposal, if carefully formulated, be given serious consideration.

In both Western and Eastern worlds evolution is taking place; in the West the trend is to place Pavlovian conditioning in its proper perspective as part of a total behavioral orientation; in the East there are the beginnings of an attempt to broaden the traditional Pavlovian approach to encompass variables hitherto condemned as either irrelevant or nonexistent.

As an example of the evolutionary process at work in the West, let us review briefly the history of the treatment of alcoholism by aversive conditioning over the past three or four decades. Both psychologically and economically, alcoholism presents a grave problem to the well-being of this country. This is as true now as it was during the period between the two World Wars when certain busy physicians, practicing clinicians confronted with the pressing problems of alcoholism but having little time to devote to them, hit upon the notion of aversive conditioning. These busy clinicians, for the most part having neither the time nor the inclination for a systematic study of Pavlovian principles, thought of using apomorphine or emetine to produce an unconditioned reaction (they would almost certainly have thought in terms of "conditioned" and "unconditioned" rather than "conditional" and "unconditional") and pairing it with alcohol as the CS.[4] But, probably for the reasons suggested, they neglected to concern themselves with details such as the delineation of consistent CS-UCS time relationships and other *known* parameters of conditioning. Had these clinicians referred to the readily available conditioning literature (including the writings of Pavlov himself) they would have recognized the need to avoid such contingencies as waiting until

4. We are simplifying matters and presenting something of a caricature in order to make the point briefly in the limited space that is available. There were, of course, certain notable exceptions (see Franks, 1966).

the patient actually felt nauseous before presenting him with the bottle, relaxing him with sedatives which also impaired the conditioning process, swallowing the alcohol (even in small doses), and so forth.

As might be expected under these circumstances, effective conditioned aversion to alcohol was rarely established and the method fell into disrepute and disuse. Some decades later the behavioral scientist came upon the scene, the expert on Pavlov, conditioning, learning theory, and the methodology of the scientist. Realizing that apomorphine could never meet the required needs for precise stimulus control, electric shock became the aversive stimulus of choice, and firmly delineated controls under theoretically optimum conditions were set up.

Making the *supposition* that it was now possible to establish an effective conditioned aversion to alcohol by such means, let us examine the probable outcome a little more closely. Unlike, say, cigarette smokers (who could be more or less relatively well adjusted except for the one undesirable behavior), most alcoholics have many problems other than the need to indulge in excessive drinking. Consequently, even if successful in its limited goal, a therapy program aimed exclusively at the setting up of a conditioned aversion to alcohol is unlikely to transform the typical alcoholic into a much better adjusted individual than he was before treatment.

It is at this stage that the contemporary behavioral clinician (or behavior therapist) emerges on the scene, with such realizations as: (*a*) that, even if one *must* restrict one's repertoire to Pavlovian conditioning, it is not necessarily desirable merely to treat the presenting complaints; this may be simplistic, unrealistic and ineffective; and (*b*) that the paradigm of classical conditioning, Aristotelian association by contiguity, is rarely sufficient even if it is often necessary – hence the development of a variety of additional behavioral techniques, especially operant conditioning. These techniques can then be applied to the broad range of problems, some of which may be unrecognized, denied, or glossed over by the patient—hence the need for behavioral assessment, clinical acumen, and the development of a broad spectrum behavioral approach.

The sophisticated behavior therapist, even while he is employing conventional conditioning procedures, recognizes the limitations of any approach that is either technique- or symptom-orientated, or both of these. Technique and symptom have to be viewed within the context of overall behavioral management. Patients with complex interpersonal problems cannot be expected to resolve them merely because one or two specific malfunctions have been eliminated.

This, then, is the Western evolution of classical conditioning as we see it, a healthy development that augurs well for the future. But, there is also a possible danger to this trend: A broad spectrum approach that allows itself to become too broad, that begins to encompass any and every variety of technique for the modification of behavior or attitudes, will eventually lose its identity as part of a biologically oriented S-R model and degenerate into yet one more example of nebulous eclecticism.

So much for the changing role of Pavlovian conditioning within the Western setting. In the USSR, Soviet "psychologists" would probably reject the more rigid type of Western behavior therapy on at least two grounds: that it is a machine-like process in which things happen to a passive organism; and that consciousness is either denied or regarded as a process beyond the realm of science. Adopting a consistently monist position which regards matter as primary and so-called psychic processes as secondary or derived—properties of matter in action—Soviet psychologists are then in a position to accept the concept of consciousness as an important property of organized matter without implying any form of mentalism or phenomenology. It is because of this property, consciousness, that the individual is able to play an active role in structuring his environment and his experiences. Unfortunately, some American psychologists still adhere tenaciously to the erroneous belief that the Pavlovian tradition encompasses a view of man as a kind of dehumanized atomistic mechanism (for example, Stafford and Combs, 1967).

The manner in which the concept of consciousness is integrated into the Soviet Marxist-behaviorist framework is of considerable interest. For example, Leontiev's 1940 doctoral dissertation, cited by Gray (1966), attempted to develop an experimental test of the hypothesis that consciousness allows organisms to respond to stimuli which, while in themselves not of crucial importance, act as signals of stimuli which do possess such importance. The ingenious method by which Leontiev tested this seemingly untestable hypothesis and the intriguing results he obtained are perhaps of less interest here than the demonstration that it is possible to investigate the concept of consciousness within a behavioral framework without any recourse to phenomenology. It would seem unnecessary either to deny that the concept serves any useful purpose or to relegate it to the realms of the beyond science, as certain Western behaviorists are inclined to do.

In their revolt against the mechanistic view of human nature which some erroneously equate with Pavlovian psychology, certain psychologists have turned to the idealistic extremes of phenomenology and humanism. As Powell (1969) points out, if we treat consciousness as a phenomenon utterly different from physical processes, then we are forced to resort to nonphysicalist explanations of mental events. At this stage of limited understanding of neurophysiology, such an invocation would seem to be, at the very least, premature.

Nothing is to be gained by speaking of a purposive act of will. It is quite feasible—and more effective—to formulate such conative concepts as purpose and other functions of consciousness in terms of reinforcement contingencies. In the concept of operant conditioning—not necessarily identical with those of stimulus-response theories – the stimulus is no more than the occasion for activity. The selection and initiation of the response are matters of probability determined by the various pertinent reinforcement contingencies. It is therefore neither necessary nor desirable to introduce purposive elements into any discussion of the components of concepts such as consciousness (see Skinner, 1963).

Current concern, for those interested in Pavlovian conditioning, should thus be with the integration of concepts such as perception, consciousness, and cognition into the overall Pavlovian model. Few behavior therapists would now dispute the relevance of cognition (once thought to be a decadent mentalistic term) for the conditioning situation. For example, Wilson (1968) produced a conditioned GSR to shock with blue stimuli as the CS and effected a conditioned discrimination by having no shock to yellow stimuli. Then he *told* his subjects that shock would henceforth follow the presentation of yellow stimuli rather than blue. In fact, no further shocks to any stimuli were given. Nevertheless, the GSR's to blue disappeared and the GSR's to yellow increased substantially, demonstrating clearly the influence of cognition upon GSR conditioning.

CONCLUDING REMARKS

Ecumenical councils seem to be in the psychological as well as the religious and political air, a sort of *Zeitgeist,* a spirit of the times. A movement toward the synthesis of classical and instrumental conditioning methods and concepts is discernable in the basic experimental literature, and Skinner was recently elected president of the Pavlovian Society of North America. In both East and West new development are based upon the premise that thinking, learning, and modification of behavior are vastly more complicated processes than traditional S-R learning theory (of any school) would suggest. In both camps it is recognized that even if classical conditioning per se is a necessary ingredient, it is far from sufficient. This does *not* mean that classical conditioning, dealing as it does with respondent behavior, can be dismissed as of little consequence. While it is true that the great bulk of behavior with which we must deal is operant behavior, it is also true that the difference between the two types of conditioning is not as clear as some individuals would have us think and that many operant situations involve more than a modicum of classical conditioning. For example, operant reinforcers such as approval, rewards, or tokens are stimuli that have been paired in classical conditioning fashion with other reinforcing stimuli.

Either directly within the Pavlovian tradition or outside it, an effective biological model which purports to account for and modify human behavior must incorporate into its schema the probability that we are dealing with a complex web in which genetic factors, individual differences, biochemical variables, and environmental influences all play complex roles. And there is little doubt that Pavlov himself would have concurred in this summing up!

REFERENCES

ALEXANDER, L. Differential diagnosis between psychogenic and physical pain. *Journal of the American Medical Association,* 1962, *181*, 855–61.

AZRIN, N. H., and HOLZ, W. C. Punishment. In W. K. Honig (Ed.), *Operant behavior: Areas of research and application.* New York: Appleton-Century-Crofts, 1966.

BAN, T. A., and LEVY, L. Physiological patterns: A diagnostic test procedure based on the conditioned reflex method. *Journal of Neuropsychiatry,* 1961, *2,* 228–31.

BARLOW, J. A. Secondary motivation through classical conditioning: A reconsideration of the nature of backward conditioning. *Psychological Review,* 1956, *63,* 406–8.

BEECH, H. R. The symptomatic treatment of writer's cramp. In

H. J. Eysenck (Ed.), *Behaviour therapy and the neuroses.* New York: Pergamon Press, 1960.

BERLYNE, D. E. Psychology in the USSR. *The Canadian Psychologist,* 1963, *4,* 1–13.

BRAZIER, M. A. B. *The central nervous system and behavior: Translations of the second conference*, Josiah Macy, Jr. Foundation, 1959.

BROZEK, J. Recent developments in Soviet psychology. *Annual Review of Psychology,* 1964, *15,* 493–594.

BROZEK, J. Contemporary Soviet psychology. In N. O'Connar (Ed.), *Present-day Russian psychology.* New York: Pergamon Press, 1966.

BYKOV, K. M. *The cerebral cortex and the internal organs,* trans. by W. H. Gantt. New York: Chemical Publishing, 1957.

CAUTELA, J. R. The problem of backward conditioning. *Journal of Psychology,* 1965, *60,* 135–44.

CAUTELA, J. R. The Pavlovian basis of old age. Paper presented to the American Gerontological Society, New York, November 5, 1966.

CHAMPION, R. A., and JONES, J. E. Forward, backward and pseudoconditioning of the GSR. *Journal of Experimental Psychology,* 1961, *62,* 58–61.

COLE, M., and MALTZMAN, I. (Eds.) *A handbook of contemporary Soviet psychology.* New York: Basic Books, 1967.

DAS, J. P. The Pavlovian theory of hypnosis: An evaluation. *Journal of Mental Science,* 1958, *104,* 82–90.

DIAMOND, S. BALVIN, R. S., and DIAMOND, S. R. *Inhibition and choice.* New York: Harper & Row, 1963.

DIX, M. R., and HALLPIKE, C. S. Peep-show audiometry. *Proceedings of the Third World Congress of the Deaf,* Wiesbaden, 1959, 77–83.

EYSENCK, H. J. *The biological basis of personality.* Springfield, Ill.: C. C. Thomas, 1967.

FRANKS, C. M. Some fundamental problems in conditioning. *Acta Psychologica,* 1958, *14,* 223–46.

FRANKS, C. M. Conditioning and abnormal behaviour. In H. J. Eysenck (Ed.), *Handbook of Abnormal Psychology.* New York: Basic Books, 1960.

FRANKS, C. M. Personality and eyeblink conditioning seven years later. *Acta Psychologica,* 1963, *21,* 295–312.

FRANKS, C. M. (Ed.) *Conditioning techniques in clinical practice and research.* New York: Springer, 1964.

FRANKS, C. M. Conditioning and conditioned aversion therapies in the treatment of the alcoholic. *International Journal of the Addictions,* 1966, *1,* 61–98.

FRANKS, C. M. A longitudinal conditional eyeblink reflex study of four adult men. *Australian Journal of Psychology,* 1967a, *19,* 125–32.

FRANKS, C. M. The use of alcohol in the investigation of drug-personality postulates. In R. Fox (Ed.), *Alcoholism-behavioral research, therapeutic approaches.* New York: Springer, 1967b.

FRANKS, C. M. Behavior therapy and its Pavlovian origins: Review and perspective. In C. M. Franks (Ed.) *Behavior therapy: Appraisal and status.* New York: McGraw-Hill, 1969a, 1–26.

FRANKS, C. M. Behavior therapy and the Pavlovian tradition. In D. Jacobs (Ed.), *Behavior therapy: New directions.* Cleveland: Western Reserve University Press, 1969b (in press).

GANTT, W. H. The conditional reflex function as an aid in the study of the psychiatric patient. In P. H. Hoch and J. Zubin (Eds.), *Relation of psychological tests to psychiatry.* New York: Grune and Stratton, 1950.

GANTT, W. H. Reflexology, schizokinesis and autokinesis. *Conditional Reflex,* 1966a, *1,* 57–68.

GANTT, W. H. Conditional or conditioned, reflex or response? *Conditional Reflex,* 1966b, *1,* 69–73.

GANTT, W. H. On humility in science. *Conditional Reflex,* 1967a, *2,* 179–83.

GANTT, W. H. Pavlovian, classical conditional reflex—a classical error? *Conditional reflex,* 1967b, *2,* 255–57.

GOLDFRIED, M. R. and POMERANZ, D. M. Role of assessment in behavior modification. *Psychological Reports,* 1968, *23,* 75–87.

GRAY, J. A., (Ed.), *Pavlov's typology: Recent theoretical and experimental developments from the laboratory of B. M. Teplov.* New York: Pergamon Press, 1964.

GRAY, J. Attention, consciousness and voluntary control of behaviour in Soviet psychology: Philosophical roots and research branches. In N. O'Connor (Ed.), *Present-day Russian psychology.* New York: Pergamon Press, 1966, 1–38.

GRAY, J. A. Strength of the nervous system, introversion-extraversion, conditionability and arousal. *Behaviour Research and Therapy,* 1967, *5,* 151-69.

HILGARD, E. R. and BOWER, G. H. *Theories of learning*. New York: Appleton-Century-Crofts, 1966.

HUME, W. I. The dimensions of central nervous arousal. Paper read to the Annual Conference of the British Psychological Society, Sheffield, April 1, 1968.

Impressions of Soviet Psychiatry. *American Journal of Psychiatry,* Nov. 1968. Special Section, *125,* 638-78.

IVANOV-SMOLENSKY, A. G. On the methods of examining the conditioned food reflexes in children and in mental disorders. *Brain,* 1927, *50,* 138-41.

KAPLAN, M. (Ed.), *Essential works of Pavlov*. New York: Bantam Books, 1966.

KIMBLE, G. A. *Foundation of conditioning and learning*. New York: Appleton-Century-Crofts. 1967.

KONORSKI, J. *Conditioned reflexes and neuron organization*. London: Cambridge University Press, 1948.

LAZARUS, A. A. In support of technical eclecticism. *Psychological Reports,* 1967, *21,* 415-16.

LEBENSOHN, Z. M. Discussion. In *Pavlovian conditioning and American psychiatry*. New York: Group for the Advancement of Psychiatry, 1964, 199-205.

LEVIN, M. Sleep, cataplexy, and fatigue as manifestations of Pavlovian inhibition. *American Journal of Psychotherapy,* 1961, *15,* 122-37.

LYNN, R. Abnormal psychology in the USSR. In N. O'Conner (Ed.), *Present-day Russian psychology.* New York: Pergamon Press, 1966.

MACMILLAN, M. Pavlov's typology. *Journal of Nervous and Mental Diseases,* 1963, *137,* 447-54.

MAKAROV, P. O. Ivan Petrovich Pavlov. *Conditional Reflex,* 1966, *1,* 288-92.

MANGAN, G. L. Studies of the relationship between neo-Pavlovian properties of higher nervous activity and Western personality dimensions: II. The relation of mobility to perceptual flexibility. *Journal of Experimental Research in Personality,* 1967a, *2,* 107-16.

MANGAN, G. L. Studies of the relationship between neo-Pavlovian properties of higher nervous activity and

Western personality dimensions: III. The relation of transformation mobility to thinking flexibility. *Journal of Experimental Research in Personality,* 1967b, *2,* 117–23.

MANGAN, G. L. Studies of the relationship between neo-Pavlovian properties of higher nervous activity and Western personality dimensions: IV. A factor analytic study of extraversion and flexibility, and the sensitivity and mobility of the nervous system. *Journal of Experimental Research in Personality,* 1967c, *2,* 124–27.

MANGAN, G. L., and FARMER, R. G. Studies of the relationship between neo-Pavlovian properties of higher nervous activity and Western personality dimensions: I. The relationship of nervous strength and sensitivity to extraversion. *Journal of Experimental Research in Personality,* 1967, *2,* 101–6.

MINZ, A., I. P. Pavlov and Soviet psychology. *I.C.R.S. Medical Reports*, 1964, *6*, 2–5.

MOSS, T., and EDWARDS, A. E. Conflict vs. conditioning: Effects upon peripheral vascular activity. *Psychosomatic Medicine,* 1964, *26,* 267–73.

O'CONNOR, N. (Ed.), *Present-day Russian psychology*. New York: Pergamon Press, 1966.

PAUL, G. L. Strategy of outcome research in psychotherapy. *Journal of Consulting Psychology,* 1967, *31,* 109–18.

PLATONOV, K. *The word as a physiological and therapeutic factor: The theory and practice of psychotherapy according to I. P. Pavlov,* trans. by D. A. Myshne. Moscow: Foreign Languages Publishing House, 1959.

POWELL, J. P. The brain and consciousness: A reply to Professor Burt. *Bulletin of the British Psychological Society,* 1969, *22,* 27–28.

RAZRAN, G. Backward conditioning. *Psychological Bulletin,* 1956, *53,* 55–69.

RAZRAN, G. Soviet psychology since 1950. *Science,* 1957, *126,* 1100–07.

RAZRAN, G. The observable unconscious and the inferable conscious in current Soviet psychophysiology: Interoceptive conditioning, semantic conditioning, and the orienting reflex. *Psychological Review,* 1961, *68,* 81–147.

RAZRAN, G. Russian physiologists' psychology and American experimental psychology: A historical and systematic collation and a look into the future. *Psychological Bulletin,* 1965, *63,* 42–64.

RAZRAN, G. The place of the conditioned reflex in psychology and psychiatry: A reply to Reese, Dykman, and Peters. *Conditional Reflex,* 1966, *1,* 80–89.

ROSENZWEIG, M. R. Salivary conditioning before Pavlov. *American Journal of Psychology,* 1959, *72,* 628–33.

SECHENOV, I. M. *Reflexes of the brain: An attempt to establish the physiological basis of psychological processes,* trans. by S. Belsky. Cambridge, Mass.: M.I.T. Press, 1965.

SERBAN, G. The psychotherapeutic approach to neurosis in the Pavlovian school. *Journal of the American Medical Association,* 1959, *170,* 1651–57.

SKINNER, B. F. Operant behavior. *American Psychologist,* 1963, *18,* 503–15.

SOLOMON, R. L. and WYNNE, L. C. Traumatic avoidance learning: The outcome of several extinction procedures with dogs. *Journal of Abnormal and Social Psychology,* 1953, *48,* 291–302.

STAFFORD, K. R., and COMBS, C. F. Radical reductionism: A possible source of inadequacy in auto-instructional techniques. *American Psychologist,* 1967, *22,* 667–69.

TEPLOV, B. M.Typological properties of the nervous system and their psychological manifestations. In N. O'Connor (Ed.), *Recent Soviet psychology.* New York: Pergamon Press, 1961.

TEPLOV, B. M., and NEBYLITSYN, V. D. The study of the basic properties of the nervous system and their significance for the psychology of individual differences. *Soviet Psychology and Psychiatry,* 1966, *4,* 80–85. (Trans. from *Voprosy Psikhologii,* 1963, *9,* 38–46.)

TEPLOV, B. M. and NEBYLITSYN, V. D. Results of experimental studies of properties of the nervous system. In A. Leontiev, A. Luria and A. Smirnov, (Eds.), *Psychological research in the U.S.S.R.* Moscow: Progress Publ., 1966, 181–98.

WATSON, R. I. *The great psychologists: From Aristotle to Freud.* Philadelphia: Lippincott, 1963.

WILSON, G. D. Reversal of differential GSR conditioning by instructions. *Journal of Experimental Psychology,* 1968, *76,* 491–93.

WORTIS, J. Pavlovianism and clinical psychiatry. In J. Wortis (Ed.), *Recent advances in biological psychiatry,* Vol. IV. New York: Plenum Press, 1962.

ZEINER, A., and GRINGS, W. W. Backward conditioning: A replication with emphasis on conceptualizations by the subject. *Journal of Experimental Psychology,* 1968, *76,* 232–35.

Comment

JULIAN B. ROTTER

Dr. Franks has presented us with a historical and thorough analysis of Pavlovian theory and has tried to examine its implications as a broad theory to account for much more than the data of classical conditioning. He describes the attempt of Soviet psychology to attack not only the problem of psychopathology and psychotherapy by revisions and extensions of Pavlovian theory, but also the problems of "perception, consciousness, cognition, and the like." Attempts to approach these problems in other ways, Franks feels, run the danger of losing the biologically oriented S-R theory which is the backbone of Pavlovian theory. It is on this aspect of his paper that I wish to comment.

Before evaluating the adequacy of extended Pavlovian theory for explaining the complex behavior of disturbed humans and their treatment, I would like to digress for a moment and briefly consider two issues that are related to such an evaluation. One issue is that of fads and swings in treatment procedures, and the second is the strategy of theory construction.

Is the current popularity of behavior therapies a fad—a temporary swing, typical of our recent history in clinical psychology? Since World War II we seem to have gone through a series of swings which might be regarded as changes from a complex, somewhat mystical approach to an overly simplified approach to therapeutic methodology. We have gone from a psychoanalytic period to a Rogerian, from a Rogerian approach to the anxiety-reduction theories of Dollard and Miller and others, and from these to existentialism. Currently, behavior therapy, perhaps as an antidote to existentialism, has become very popular. Is behavior therapy just another fad or is it a permanent beginning to a continuously growing application of sound laboratory-tested psychological principles to complex behavior?

I believe the answer to that question (atheoretical psychologists to the contrary) will lie in the development of sound general theory. The short-lived fads and swings of the past are due to the failure to develop such theory, which would allow for the continuous broadening of methods and inclusion of new data and solutions to new problems.

There seems to me to be two basic styles of theory construction, especially in the areas of personality and behavior change. One of these is to devise a model that attempts to deal with the full complexity of human behavior, not only the notion that people have consciousness and language, but also that they have what is sometimes called feelings, and that they think. Psychologists trained in animal psychology find it indeed difficult to include explanations for these phenomena in their basic formulations. However, in the absence of adequate data, broad, general theories often take on a literary quality in which the problems of measurement of variables and control are subordinated to the need to produce a picture of man which does justice to his complexity and uniqueness. The approaches of Freud, Adler, and Sullivan are typical of such theories.

The other style of theory construction is to begin at the other end and to construct only the fewest number of constructs possible which can be operationally defined and objectively and reliably measured. From a few simple but very general constructs and their relatively simple relationships, it is assumed that complex behavior can be explained. However, as such theories are actually pushed to deal with problems of predicting human behavior in life situations, they tend to construct analogues or develop analogies to the few original constructs. Often the analogues such as the use of inhibition processes to explain the problems of aging are no better operationalized than are the constructs of the literary theories. In other cases, such as the use of anxiety reduction, one construct has to account for so much that, in fact, it explains nothing. To say that neural inhibition processes increase as an individual gets older, without being able to observe and measure such processes, is no different from saying that the death instinct gets stronger as one gets older.

Both kinds of theories tend to break down after a while, except perhaps for their disciples who do not die but just fade away. The literary theorists continue to argue about their nontestable propositions but never get around to experimentally testing their adequacy. The simplistic theories stretch and bend their concepts out of shape in an attempt to avoid including new constructs; and even more seriously, they avoid the problems that are more difficult by ignoring or dismissing them. What, for example, can behavior therapy do for the college student who says he has no major long-term goals, sees no reason to struggle to achieve the culturally acceptable goals, and is experiencing feelings of alienation and vague and general dysphoria, but has no clear-cut symptoms? While I favor in general the method of developing theories by restricting oneself to only operationalized constructs and working from the most general to more specific principles, the survival of such theories depends upon their capacity to grow. If such approaches are going to persist, they will do so only because their adherents are willing, in fact eager, to add new constructs at highly generalized, middle and lower levels of abstraction, and to make their models increasingly complex.

Finally, I come back to my comments on Pavlovian theory. For me the question is not whether modified Pavlovian principles can explain everything, but rather what Pavlovian principles need to be kept and perhaps modified in order to fit into a broader and more comprehensive theory of behavior.

5

Stimulus Control, Response Control, and the Desensitization of Fear

PETER J. LANG

The 1960's have seen the development of a variety of behavior modification techniques and strategies. These methods ostensibly derive from contemporary learning theory and are direct extensions of laboratory experiments. However, the founding theories are themselves controversial, and the fundamental experiments are often conspicuously lacking, accomplished only with nonhuman subjects, conflicting in result, or incautiously interpreted. This conclusion is obvious to the most sympathetic as well as the scientifically skeptical observer.

Thus, it is not clear that the best explanation of an aversive conditioning treatment of alcoholism is the one prompted by the behavior of a dog in a shuttle box. I do not mean to suggest that the latter is necessarily irrelevant, but that it may be. We are all well aware that the presence of language, the second signal system of the Russian investigators, can profoundly affect performance

This research was supported in part by grants to the author from NIMH (MH-10993, MH-35,324) and the Wisconsin Alumni Research Foundation.

in even the simplest experimental situation. Similarly, the positive results of an operant conditioning therapy may be more a function of the feedback information provided by this routine than any positive state of affairs evoked by the M and M candies. While the operant conditioner may be indifferent to the distinction, it could be an important one to the development of a specific treatment.

Systematic desensitization has become one of the most effective new therapeutic methods. There are clinical series (Wolpe,1958; Lazarus, 1963) and laboratory experiments (Lang and Lazovik, 1963; Lang, Lazovik, and Reynolds, 1965; Paul, 1966; Davison, 1968) demonstrating its success in alleviating fear and anxiety. However, as with the other new techniques, we are uncertain as to the mechanism of change. In developing the desensitization method, Wolpe (1958) was guided by Hullian learning theory, his own conception of "reciprocal inhibition," and a series of animal experiments. Fear is held to be a primarily sympathetic, autonomic response, dimensionalized along a gradient of intensity. It is relieved by encouraging thorough muscle relaxation, responses that are incompatible with those of fear (that is, with parasympathetic activity) in the presence of the fear-evoking stimuli. So that these competitors will have maximum response strength relative to the fear response itself, desensitization is begun at the latter response's site of minimum amplitude, at the lower end of the fear gradient. Desensitization then proceeds from one item to the next highest, substituting in a progressive way relaxation responses for those of anxiety.

There are obviously many other ways of interpreting the fear reduction consequent to this method. Lader, Gelder, and Marks (1967) have recently suggested that desensitization is best understood as habituation of the fear response under conditions of low arousal. In support of this hypothesis, Lader and his associates present evidence that the effectiveness of desensitization is related to measures of the treated individual's basal, autonomic variability, and rate of glavanic skin response (GSR) habituation to simple auditory stimuli. Stampfl (1966; see Chapter 6 of this volume) argues that fear is reduced through extinction – the repeated presentation of the fear stimulus in the absence of an aversive consequent. He is thus inclined to discard relaxation training and the hierarchical form of stimulus presentation as well. Operant conditioning offers an equally likely explanation of desensitization: It is not difficult to see this treatment process as one in which progressive approach responses are "reinforced" by the therapist's positive comments or the subject's own satisfaction in success. I have discussed these and cognitive theory alternatives elsewhere (Lang, 1969), and I will not go into each hypothesis in detail here. However, it seems safe to say that at this point they all merit the Scottish verdict: unproven.

Nevertheless, it is important to consider the general orientation of theories and their implications for the study of fear modification and changes in practical treatment strategy. Fear reduction hypotheses fall into one of two broad categories: those that emphasize stimulus control and those that emphasize response control. The extinction theory of Stampfl and the habituation theory of Lader are mainly of the first type. They hold that if fear stimuli are presented at the proper intensity, with appropriate order and frequency, changes in the fear response will naturally follow. Wolpe's competing response hypothesis, operant approaches, and to some extent the cognitive explanations, are theories of the second type. While stimulus parameters are recognized to be important, the mechanics of fear change require an active effort at response manipulation; for example, one behavior substituted for another, new attitudes encouraged, or particular responses reinforced at the expense of others.

Obviously, this is a distinction of convenience, and the hypotheses, like the resulting procedures, are not so sharply dichotomized. Furthermore, in trying to research the desensitization context it is almost impossible to separately examine the effects of response control without changing stimulus topography; or on the other hand to manipulate stimuli without considering the subject's "set" to respond. Nevertheless, the distinction has proved a useful guide, and in our own laboratory we have initiated research designed to explore both concepts of the fear reduction process.

STIMULUS CONTROL

Lader's work (Lader, 1967; Lader, Gelder, and Marks, 1967) has raised interesting questions concerning the generality of habituation effects within subjects and across stimuli, and the importance of individual difference factors to treatment success. Does a subject's response to fear stimuli share common characteristics with his response to all stimuli? Can habituation rate to fear stimuli be predicted from performance in other stimulus contexts? An exploration of these issues requires that more standard fear stimuli be generated for laboratory use. The imagined scene (prompted by a descriptive statement) is uncomfortably vague and many of its characteristics are beyond experimental control. Lazarus and Opton (1966) have shown the value of filmed stimuli in studies of emotion; however, the narrative film of long duration is a somewhat unwieldy laboratory stimulus. It is often more convenient to study discrete units, which may be rearranged easily in order, frequency, or intensity. This is particularly true in studying habituation and sequence effects.

In an effort to meet this problem, we have accumulated a group of brief motion pictures of phobic objects (approximately ten seconds each). These have been scaled for fear intensity by an independent group of phobic subjects. These films are being used in some of our current experiments on the assumption that the loss of vividness or self-relevancy occasioned by these materials (relative to imagined scenes) will be compensated for by improved standardization.

A recent experiment from our laboratory (Melamed, 1969) evaluated effects of repeated stimuli (pure tones and fearful films) on autonomic activity and verbal report. Subjects were snake-phobic college students selected in a manner similar to that used in our desensitization experiments (Lang, Lazovik, and Reynolds, 1965). Following a preliminary, familiarization session, subjects were presented with two series of ten 1,000 Hertz tones – one series at high intensity (100 decibels) and one at low intensity (50 decibels). In subsequent sessions, the same subjects viewed twenty successive presentations of each of four brief motion pictures of snakes, ranked in a previous experiment as being high and low in fear intensity. Responses to both orders of presentation (high series first or low series first were examined for both the tone and the film stimuli.

In addition to recording autonomic activity and rating each film trial for fearfulness (five-point scale), subjects filled out a Snake Fear Questionnaire (SNAQ) before and after the experiment. This questionnaire had previously been shown to correlate highly with performance on the Snake Avoidance Test and verbal measures of snake phobia (Lang, Melamed, and Hart, 1969).

This same experiment also assessed the effects of cognitive set on autonomic and verbal responses to the filmed stimuli. Specifically, the experiment explored differences between a set to relax in the face of fearful materials as opposed to a set to experience fully an emotional response, as in catharsis or extinction treatments. Thus, separate groups of subjects were given three different instructions for viewing the film series: (1) catharsis – they were instructed to imagine they were actually participating in the events of the screen and to let themselves experience the full force of their emotions, (2) relaxation—they were similarly instructed to vividly experience the events but to remain relaxed (pre-film training in muscle relaxation was administered), (3) attend—subjects were just told to attend closely to the films with no particular set described.

The experimental results suggested that, when given no specific viewing set, subjects show habituation of the GSR to repeated fearful films at a rate similar to that occasioned by an intense auditory tone. As may be seen in Table 5.1 for the "attend" group, 75 per cent of the GSR habituation variance to the first high firm is accounted for by the correlation with tone. Similar, high positive

Table 5.1. Intercorrelations between GSR Habituation Rate to an Intense Auditory Tone (100 db.) and Films of Phobic Objects (Viewed under Three Different Instructional Sets).

	Instructional Set					
	Attend		Catharsis		Relaxation	
	High Fear Film	Low Fear Film	High Fear Film	Low Fear Film	High Fear Film	Low Fear Film
First 10[a]	.87**	.13	−.17	.20	.59*	.47
Second 10	.59*	.74**	.07	−.23	.17	.74**

Note: The GSR measure which provided the basis for habituation estimates was the change in log conductance from prestimulus to the first poststimulus peak. Maximum GSR change yielded similar relationships.

[a]All subjects viewed two successive series of ten film trials at each intensity.

*<.05

**<.01

relationships were found for the relaxation group while the "catharsis" group failed to generate significant correlations among intense stimuli. This latter result is not surprising, as the catharsis group was given instructions to maximize affect—that is, a set that could be construed as in competition with habituation over trials. Nevertheless, for those subjects told simply to attend or to relax while experiencing the film, individual patterns of habituation appear to be consistent for both simple, physical stimuli and more complex, subjectively fearful materials. Furthermore, high tone habituation rates of the entire sample for skin conductance measures (first conductance peak and maximum skin conductance response) correlated significantly, +.42 and +.45, respectively, with the SNAQ measure of postexperiment fear change. Thus, the present data provide indirect support for Lader's contention that subjects' individual habituation rates contribute both to the desensitization process and treatment outcome.

The different instructions also prompted differences in both autonomic responsivity and verbal report of fear. For the high intensity film series, there was a higher skin conductance level for both the relaxation and catharsis groups than for those instructed to merely attend. Heart rate appeared to be even more profoundly effected by the set condition: The catharsis group showed significantly greater heart rate activity to all films than either of the other groups (see Figure 5.l). Furthermore, this group showed no appreciable habituation with repeated presentation of the fearful films. The catharsis group also reported the highest average verbal report of fear occasioned by film presentation.

These data show that instructional set significantly effects autonomic activity and verbal report. Both groups that were told to involve themselves in the filmed materials showed more autonomic activity than the no-set "attend" subjects. Furthermore, subjects instructed to fully experience emotion, without the restraining relaxation set, showed the most fear-related behavior of all groups.

It is of interest to examine the effects of instructional set on the questionnaire measure of fear change (SNAQ). While the conditions were not intended to be explicit analogues of therapy procedures, they did have differential effects on the postexperiment questionnaire. Thus, the relationship between fear change and habituation to tone stimuli was more strongly positive for sub-

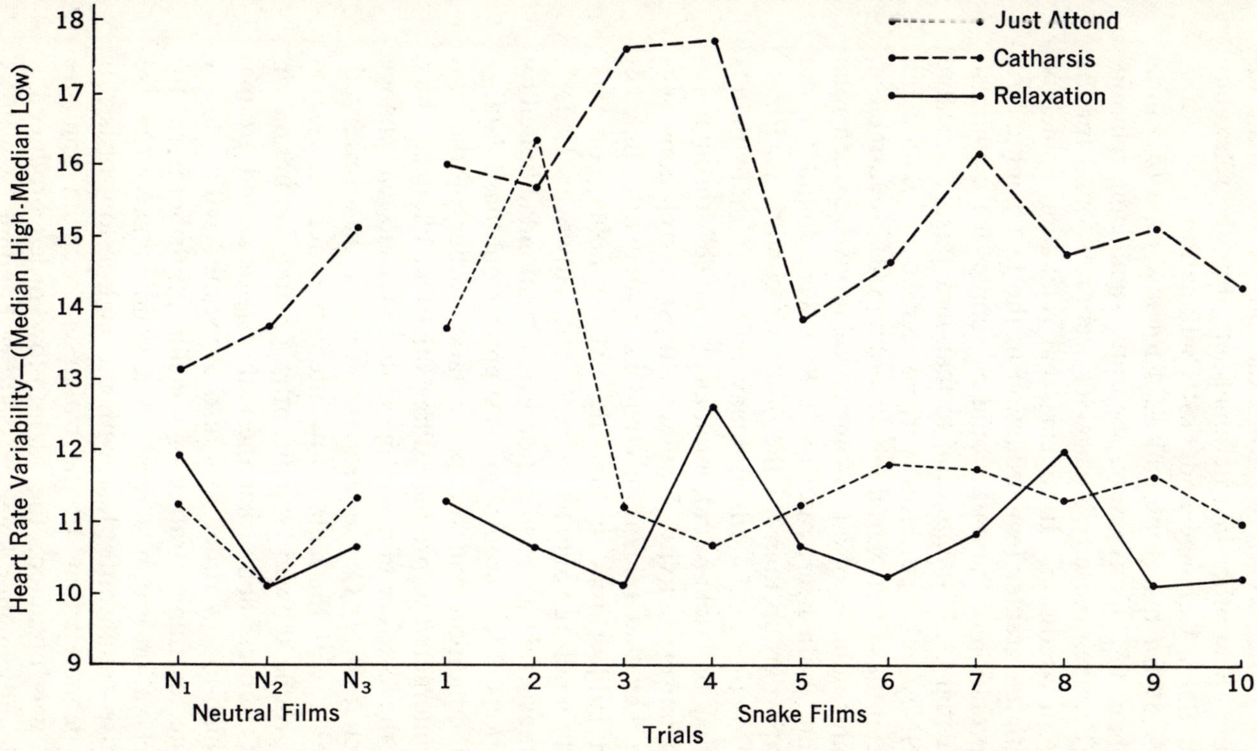

Figure 5.1. Heart Rate Variability for Instructional Set Groups across Neutral and Snake Trials for High Intensity Films

jects who had relaxed during the film series than for subjects given other instructional sets. For the relaxation group, SNAQ change and GSR habituation rate correlated +.59 for high tone and +.74 for low tone (*p* values less than .05). Conversely, separate, significant relationships between these two variables were not found for the other set conditions. It appears that relaxation somehow potentiated greater fear reduction in the fast habituators. Interpretation of the data would be simpler if I could also report that GSR habituation to fear films also correlated with SNAQ change. However, no significant relationship between these two variables was obtained. Nevertheless, a greater number of significant correlations between tone and film (both heart rate and GSR) were found for the relaxation group than for the other set conditions. Emergence of these relationships may reflect no more than a lowering of background, biological "noise" through reduced muscle activity. However, these correlations suggest a way that relaxation could be a mediating link between subject reaction in the two stimulus contexts. Clearly much remains to be explained. However, Lader's hypothesis that desensitization is habituation facilitated by conditions of low arousal gains support from these data.

Set condition and the presentation order of the two films interacted to produce differential fear change. Thus, when the low fear film was presented first, no fear change difference (SNAQ) between set groups was observed. However, with the high-to-low intensity order, the relaxation group showed significantly greater reduction in SNAQ scores than either the catharsis or attend groups. This high-to-low order was also associated with a lower average fearfulness rating of the films. Furthermore, for the relaxation group, overall skin conductance response was also significantly less with the high-to-low order. It must be noted that for the catharsis group an opposite effect was obtained: the high-to-low order produced a significantly higher level of GSR responding as well as less SNAQ change.

The results of this experiment are complex, and many relationships must run the gauntlet of cross-validation before final conclusions can be drawn. However, there are some interesting implications for the treatment context which may be developed here.

The relaxation set appears to facilitate both the habituation of autonomic responses and the reduction of verbal report of fear. Furthermore, it contributes most powerfully to these changes when high intensity stimuli are presented first. Results for the fear ratings of the films are consistent with a "contrast effect" interpretation of psychophysical judgments (Helson, 1964) and the "laws of affective equilibrium" as developed by Beebe-Center (1929) and Harris (1929). When a high intensity series is presented after a low intensity series, the high series is judged to be of greater intensity than if the two series were presented in the reverse order. The fact that the verbal judgments of fear intensity followed this rule in the present experiment can be seen in Figure 5.2. As we have already pointed out, this high-to-low order also produced lower autonomic activity to the high fear film for the relaxation subjects, while the reverse was found for the catharsis group. Thus, congruence between verbal judgment and physiological arousal was found under the relaxation set, while a dissonant relationship was obtained for the catharsis condition. Furthermore, this congruent, relaxation group showed the greater fear change following the experiment. An analogous finding was obtained in a previous study of autonomic activity during systematic desensitization (Lang, Melamed, and Hart, 1969), to be discussed later. The present result thus constitutes further evidence for the hypothesis that positive covariation between autonomic and verbal report of emotion may be fundamental to a broad change in fear behavior.

The fact that the high-to-low order facilitated fear change was unanticipated and at first glance seems inconsistent with the rationale usually given for employing an anxiety hierarchy in treatment. It is assumed by Wolpe

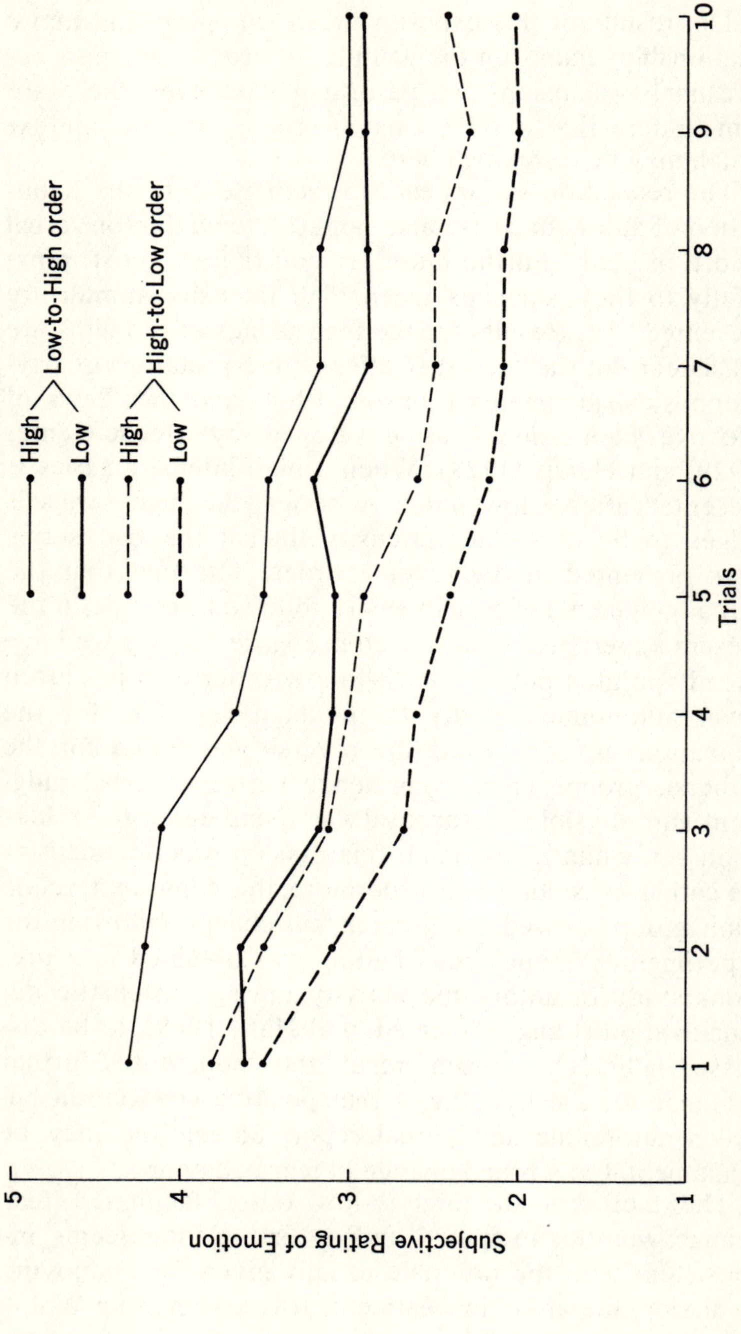

Figure 5.2. Subjective rating of emotion for high and low intensity snake films for different orders of presentation.

(1958) that forward generalization from successfully desensitized items lowers the habit strength of fear response to subsequent items. This renders these more frightening items amenable to counterconditioning or habituation. However, in the present experiment a high film series presented without preamble occasioned lower verbal reports of fear than did the same high films when preceded by a less intense series.

It will be noted from Figure 5.2 that the first film trial of the first series that was presented (whether high or low) tended to receive a rating slightly above level three. With repeated presentation, the high film tended to show habituation while the low film curve (low-to-high order) shows relatively little change over trials. Adaptation level theory predicts most of these effects: The first time a moderately intense stimulus is presented, it will be pegged somewhere near the middle of the given intensity scale (Helson, 1964). Furthermore, a reduction in intensity judgments is to be anticipated from repeated exposure. It is also no surprise that a low intensity stimulus shows a less steep habituation gradient than a high input (this phenomenon was shown for olfactory judgments, according to Osgood, 1953, p. 78). The interesting additional effect obtained here is that the habituation gradient is significantly steeper for a low stimulus, when the subject was previously exposed to high stimulation.[1] This finding was not unique to the films or to verbal judgments, and a similar significant pattern was obtained for skin conductance responses to high and low tones (Melamed, 1969).

The high-to-low order appears to have multiple

1. The 2 x 2 Latin square design confounds sequence (which condition preceded the other?) and the trial order (on what trial in a series was the condition presented?) by treatment interaction (Grant, 1949). Thus, we are not completely certain of the specific role played by these two variables in generating the present interaction. However, the general pattern of results conforms to the sequence effects found in psychophysical research, and sequence is assumed to be the primary variable in the present interpretation.

fear-reducing effects. First of all, there is the subject's tendency to judge a first stimulus to be near the middle of an established scale. Secondly, when a succeeding, lower stimulus is presented, the contrast effect drives it yet farther down the fear scale. Finally, the present results suggest that low stimuli, which normally occasion little habituation, will show progressive decrement if they are presented subsequent to a stimulus that does generate habituation. This latter result prompts the hypothesis that subjects are "learning to learn"—that is, previous experience with the stimulus context generates a *set* to show fear reduction. Thus, a variety of factors converge to produce a report that fear is less. Furthermore, these changes are not exclusively verbal. The same pattern of habituation and lowered average level of response is obtained for physiological measures. In addition, the effects obtained within the experiment apparently generalize to a fear questionnaire, which represents a very different stimulus context from the film rating situation.

We do not yet know if these phenomena extend beyond the research setting in which they were defined. However, applications to treatment are easily inferred and seem worth pursuing in the laboratory. It appears that a high-to-low order of presenting anxiety hierarchies would facilitate systematic desensitization therapy. However, two factors argue against a complete reversal of the desensitization procedure: First, the present results were obtained with filmed stimuli, which probably do not fall near the top of any absolute fear scale. Beginning treatment with extreme aversive stimuli might generate strong defensive reactions and no fear-reducing habituation (Sokolov, 1963). Evidence from the catharsis group tends to support this conjecture. These subjects attempted to maximize their fear; they showed little habituation and no post-experimental fear change.[2] Second, contrast effects

2. The present results do not invalidate extinction or cathartic procedures of

appear to depend on recency of exposure to the anchoring stimuli. It seems likely that the impetus given to fear habituation and lowered levels of autonomic responding would not persist across many sessions.

In light of these considerations, the following treatment format is proposed for experimentation: Hierarchy items should be administered in the normal order between sessions and in a reverse order within sessions. Thus, assuming a rate of four new scenes per session, a subject would start treatment with item four, hopefully finish that session with item number one, and then start the next session with item seven. Given the appropriate intensity levels, this sequence should potentiate a set to habituate within and between sessions, and thus maximize overall fear reduction. It is, of course, possible that simple alternation would be more effective, or that the reversed sequence should be extended beyond a single session. We plan to systematically explore these order effects in subsequent research on fear modification.[3]

RESPONSE CONTROL

Since a first study of desensitization (Lazovik and Lang,

the kind advocated by Stampfl (1967). In their clinical amplication, much more is often involved in these therapies than a "set" to maximize emotion and stimulus repetition. Furthermore, the present example may have included too few trials, too brief an exposure per trial, or too narrow a range of fear stimuli for significant effects to be achieved. Certainly, it was less than most cathartic therapies in all of these parameters.

3. The writer appreciates that the experimental format which generated these speculations differs in important ways from desensitization therapy. Perhaps the most significant deviation is the absence of subject control over stimulus presentation—an omission which the writer (Lang, 1969) and others (Davison, 1969) have noted in criticizing desensitization research (Folkins, Lawson, Opton, and Lazarus, 1968). However, despite invariance of stimulus selection and frequency of presentation, significant fear reduction was obtained in the present experiment. Furthermore, subjects were in control to the extent that they could terminate an excessively threatening film by signaling the experimenter (none from this sample did). Thus, it does not seem unreasonable to assume, pending validating research, that the order effects obtained here would operate in the more usual treatment setting.

1960), our laboratory has been concerned with the reduction of fear through response manipulation and control. We would like to know if the competing response formulation has any value in the treatment of fear, and if so, how we may modify existing treatment techniques or develop new ones that will take advantage of the method. Before considering our own research on this issue, I would like to indicate why I think analysis of the fear response may be necessary to effective study and treatment.

The nature of fear has been a subject of controversy ever since the advent of scientific psychology. Much early speculation was devoted to the nature of the subjective, emotional experience as a determiner of emotional behavior. James (1890) startled introspectionists by proposing that man's experience of fear was prompted by his awareness of the peripheral physiological changes generated by imminent danger or pain. Cannon (1936) demurred on objective grounds, devoting considerable research to proving that James was in error and that both cortical and autonomic events were secondary to activity in the hypothalamus. Lange (1922) identified emotion exclusively with events mediated by the autonomic nervous system. For him and more contemporary advocates of this view (Wenger, 1950), emotion *is* the blood pressure change, sweat gland activity, and tears of physiological measurement. On the other hand, students of animal behavior have usually ignored these measures, preferring to consider avoidance behavior in the shuttle box or depression in bar press rates as evidence of anxiety.

Anyone interested in assessing the effectiveness of a fear reduction method would be unwise to commit himself precipitously to one of these interpretations. If an extreme physiological view is taken, we measure only autonomic activity and ignore the verbal and motor responses in emotion. Similarly, while avoidance behavior may be maximally relevant in animal experiments, it would be unwise to overlook the language output of a human subject. Fear is a multisystem response – verbal, overt-motor, and physiological – and despite much speculation, we do not yet know precisely how these systems are integrated. In point of fact, there is a growing body of evidence that suggests these systems may be at least partially independent. In our own research on desensitization we have often noted the low correlations among basal fear measures and among fear change scores (*r*'s seldom accounting for even 50 per cent of the variance). While desensitization subjects show more change on nearly all measures than controls, individual subjects differ considerably on specific measures. Thus, one subject may show marked change in verbal behavior and almost none in avoidance, while another shows the reverse. While some of this might be ascribed to measurement error, the differences are gross, and the hypothesis of independent, parallel response systems in emotion is quite reasonable. Eriksen (1958) found evidence for partial independence in his studies of "unconscious awareness." More recently Leventhal (1967) has also found evidence for the hypothesis in social psychological research.

This possibility complicates the analysis of a competing response approach to fear reduction. The question is not just whether you can train fearful individuals to respond autonomically in ways incompatible with the responses found in fear, but also, what effect such control has on the other, overt-motor, or verbal fear responses. It is at least possible that each of these behavior systems must be dealt with in its own realm. For example, if we are to eliminate avoidance behavior, we will be most effective if we operate directly on the motor response. If the verbal report of fear is dominant in the patient (he copes, but reports intolerable degrees of "felt" anxiety), we should perhaps concentrate on manipulating verbal events. And finally, if physiological activity – tachycardia, muscle tension, and so on – dominates the symptom picture, treatment should be aimed at this response system. It may be that desensitization has proved widely effective because of a broad spectrum effect. Elements of the procedure tend to deal separately with whatever happens to be the individual subject's characteristic fear response, and the "true" explanations of success may also be legion (Lang, 1969a).

Before I carry this disintegration of the person and his treatment too far, we should consider the evidence for cross-system mediation of fear responses and also perhaps for a similar inhibitory effect. I will not dwell here on "downward" cognitive influences on autonomic responding, which have been studied extensively by many investigators (for example, Graham, Kabler, and Graham, 1962; and Lazarus and Opton, 1966), but will consider briefly some evidence for "upward" influences of autonomic events on verbal or gross motor behavior.

In studies of chronic neurophysiological preparations, Bonvallet and her collaborators (Bonvallet, Dell, and Hiebel, 1954) have shown that afferents from the pressure-sensitive baroreceptors of the carotid sinus and aortic arch have marked effects on cortical activity. Specifically, distension of the carotid, as with an increment in blood pressure, produces a decrease in cortical activity. Marked distension produced waves as low as three to five cycles per second. Other experiments by this same group have shown that such baroreceptor activity exerts a direct, neural inhibitor effect on spinal motor activity. Stimulated by this work, Lacey (1967), Birren (1963), and Calloway (1965) have presented evidence that response latency in human subjects is determined in part by heart rate, heart period, and blood pressure changes. Lacey and Lacey (1958) and Gellhorn (1964) have further suggested that afferents from autonomically mediated events and the distribution of muscle tension level may profoundly influence temperament and play a modulating role on the immediate, emotional response. While this work is not without controversy, there is good reason to believe that verbal and motor events in emotion are influenced by autonomic feedback, which may act to sustain or augment responses.

The above discussion describes some paths of interaction between response systems. However, the low intersystem correlations described earlier argue that fear is far from the coherent state suggested by experiential or drive theorists. In human subjects, fear responses appear to be loosely integrated, behavioral loops, in which somatic, verbal, and gross motor segments mutually influence each other, but are also controlled in part by separate, emotion-irrelevant events. To a considerable extent these response systems are bound to be idiosyncratic, emphasizing in their development and expression different output systems in different subjects.

In our laboratory, examination of these problems has proceeded in two directions. On the one hand, we are continuing with our laboratory dissection of the desensitization procedure; on the other, we are exploring the ability of human subjects to learn direct control of autonomically mediated responses.

In 1962 Shearn deomonstrated that human subjects could learn to accelerate briefly heart rate to avoid electric shock. Using a similar paradigm, Lisina (1958) was able to gain control of vasoconstrictive and vasodilative responses in the forearm. These data prompted us to consider the possibility that human subjects could learn autonomic responses opposite to those usually found in fear, without resorting to the uncertain medium of muscle relaxation training. We began to experiment with the presentation of various heart rate displays, while the subject was instructed to change the display in the direction of decreased or stabilized activity. In a first paper (Hnatiow and Lang, 1965), we were able to report that human subjects could significantly reduce heart rate variability when provided with continuous exteroceptive feedback. Subsequent experiments have been designed to provide data on the physiological mechanism of this control and to assess the effects of differing amounts of information about the task. Lang, Sroufe, and Hastings (1967) found that subjects receiving feedback and correctly informed about the stabilization task showed a significantly greater reduction in heart rate variability than either their non-feedback yokemates or uninformed feedback controls. A subsequent study by Sroufe (1969) indicated that these effects can be achieved independent of respiration change. Another study in our laboratory (Hnatiow, 1968) demonstrated differences in the EKG waveform of subjects when they assumed control of cardiac rate and when they were not provided with feedback. This later data prompts the hypothesis that these effects are achieved by direct neural paths, perhaps through variations in vagal activity.

The findings of other investigators have supplemented our own research on learned control of the cardiovascular system (Brenner, 1966; Engel and Hanson, 1966), and have also shown similar effects for skin resistance (Crider, Shapiro, and Tursky, 1966). In a brilliant series of experiments with animals, Miller and his colleagues (1967, 1969) demonstrated operant conditioning of heart rate, stomach motility, and peripheral vasoconstriction in curarized, artificially respirated animals. These studies provide what seems to be conclusive evidence that autonomic events can be controlled independent of striate muscular activity.

We thus have available a potentially powerful technique for clinical application, both in the areas of psychological disorder and internal medicine. Engel (1967) has already employed heart rate shaping techniques in treating various cardiac rate anomalies. Hypertension and other vascular disorders seem obvious targets for similar therapy efforts. More pertinent to our interest here, these shaping techniques provide a tool for testing the competing response formulation of fear reduction. If subjects are trained to lower cardiac rate and then exposed to a stressor, can they then maintain low heart rates? If they do, do they report less anxiety, and will we find less performance deficit? I regret that I cannot provide answers to these questions today. However, a significant part of our research effort is presently devoted to their solution.

I will conclude by briefly describing our most recent experiments on desensitization and the direction in which this work is carrying us. We have tried to greatly increase the procedural rigor of the desensitization analogue so that we might more explicitly analyze the physiological changes held to accompany the therapy process. For this purpose a Device for Automated Desensitization (DAD) was developed, which administers desensitization to the subject without necessitating the presence of an experimenter in the subject room. The apparatus consists of two tape playback decks, a simple tape search mechanism, amplifiers and earphones, and hard-wired logic for controlling the sequence and timing of auditory messages. It presents desensitization instructions in essentially the same format as in previous experiments (Lang, Lazovik, and Reynolds, 1965), with the difference that the subject signals the apparatus by pressing a microswitch rather than raising his hand for the therapist. A recent experiment comparing this method with the usual desensitization procedure (Lang, Melamed, and Hart, 1969) suggests that effectiveness is not lost by automation (see Figure 5.3). In point of fact, for one measure of fear the DAD group proved to be superior to live therapy.

Analysis of heart rate, respiration, and skin conductance recordings, taken concurrently with therapy, indicates that these measures change with treatment in a pattern to be expected by desensitization theory. Thus, the subject's signal that an item is anxiety evoking is associated with an increment in the activity of these variables. The heart beat showed a regular, significant reduction in rate with repeated presentation of the previously stressful scene. Furthermore, individual subjects who showed the most marked heart rate response and steepest

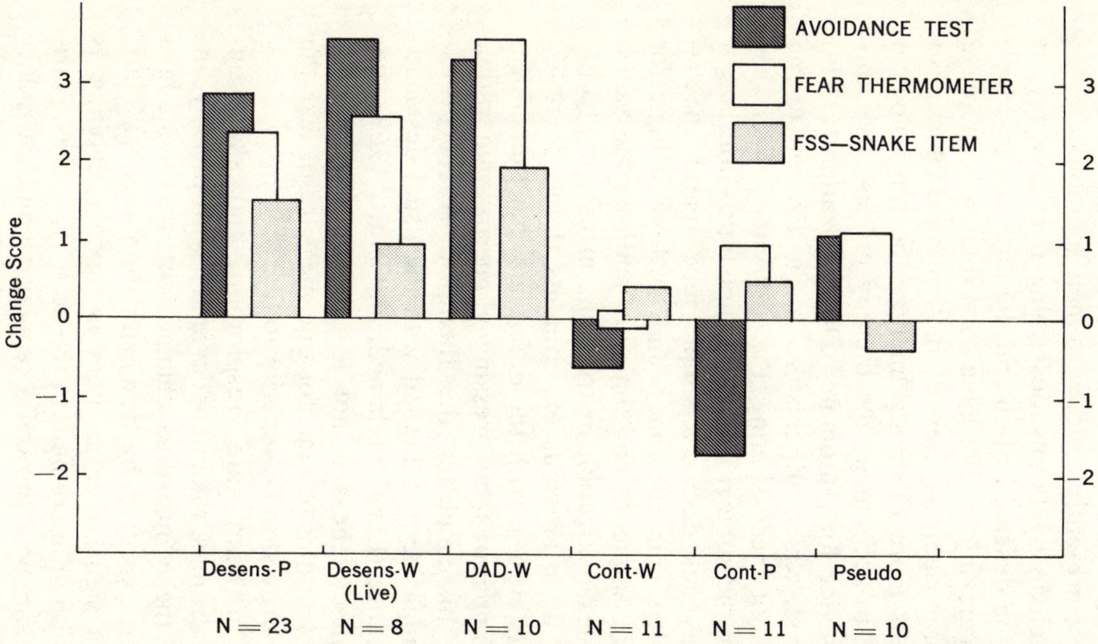

Figure 5.3

Change scores (pre-post treatment) from two verbal fear measures and the snake avoidance test (Lang & Lazovik, 1965) are presented for subjects seen at the University of Wisconsin (W) and Pittsburgh (P). Controls were untreated except for selection and fear assessment sessions. The pseudotherapy subjects participated in a placebo treatment. Statistical tests buttress the graphed data in showing that the DAD treatment reduced fear as much or more then LIVE treatment (therapist present), and was similarly superior to all control conditions (Lang, Melamed, & Hart, 1969).

habituation gradients gained the greatest profit from desensitization. Thus, as with our studies of fear films, a broad affective response to early presentations, followed by progressive habituation over trials, appears to be a reliable antecedent of successful fear reduction.

Our modest success in these experiments has encouraged us to expand the apparatus's power and flexibility (Lang, 1969b). We are now using a LINC-8, general purpose digital computer to control stimulus presentation to the subject, and we propose also to use this instrument to analyze the subject's physiological output "on line." The computer system will permit us, on the *stimulus control* side, to manipulate systematically such variables as order of presentation or length of an habituation series. Thus, we should find out how to maximize favorable contrast effects, and develop the most fear reduction with the greatest economy of stimulus presentation. Furthermore, it will provide a context in which we can analyze the effects of physiological *response control* on the fear reduction process. In one of our first experiments we propose to compare the effectiveness of desensitization as administered by our old DAD program with that achieved when the computer responds directly to the subject's physiological output. In the latter case, the subject's multichannel stress response pattern would be loaded into the computer in advance. Items would be presented only when analysis of the physiological response indicated it was absent and low arousal present. Items would be discontinued when stress indicants appeared. The length and degree of relaxation instruction or autonomic control training would be similarly determined by the subject's physiological response. If autonomic control has value in reducing fear, and autonomic events inconsistent with fear arousal do reduce other fear response components, we have hopes that this approach will provide clear evidence.

In summary, we have conjectured that both stimulus and response control elements may contribute to the success of desensitization and similar fear modification treatments. Data obtained so far appear to support this speculation and suggest directions for further research. In addition, this work points up the catalytic role of specific instructional sets in potentiating stimulus and perhaps also response control effects. Nevertheless, a host of elements remain to be explored, defined, and integrated into our concept of fear modification. Bandura and his associates (1969) have pointed to the role of social stimuli and imitation in the treatment setting; Davison (1969) has emphasized cognitive and placebo effects. Multiple factors are surely involved, and we must beware of trying to define the elephant with a single touch.

In concluding, I would like to return to the original theme of this presentation: While a wealth of possible interpretations has been offered for desensitization effects, we still have a dearth of directly relevant research. It is to be hoped that the next decade in the study of fear modification will remedy this lack.

REFERENCES

BANDURA, A., BLANCHARD, E. B., and RITTER, B. The relative efficacy of desensitization and modeling approaches for inducing behavioral, affective, and attitudinal changes. *Journal of Personality and Social Psychology,* in press.

BEEBE-CENTER, J. G. The law of affective equilibrium. *American Journal of Psychology,* 1929, *41,* 54–69.

BIRREN, J. E., CARDON, P. V., JR., and PHILLIPS, S. L. Reaction time as a function of the cardiac cycle in young adults. *Science,* 1963, *140,* 195–96.

BONVALLET, M., DELL, P., and HIEBEL, G. *Tonus sympathique et activite electrique corticale. EEG and Clinical Neurophysiology,* 1954, *6,* 119–44.

BRENNER, J. Heart rate as an avoidance response. *Psychological Record,* 1966, *16,* 329–36.

CALLOWAY, E. Response speed, the EEG alpha cycle, and the autonomic cardiovascular cycle. In A. T. Welford and J. E. Birren (Eds.), *Behavior, aging, and the nervous system.* Springfield, Illinois: C. C. Thomas, 1965.

CANNON, W. B. *Bodily changes in pain, hunger, fear and rage,* 2d ed. New York: Appleton-Century, 1936.

CRIDER, A., SHAPIRO, D., and TURSKY, B. Reinforcement of spontaneous electrodermal activity. *Journal of Comparative and Physiological Psychology,* 1966, *61,* 20–27.

DAVISON, G. C. Systematic desensitization as a counter-conditioning process. *Journal of Abnormal Psychology,* 1968, *73,* 91–99.

ENGEL, B. T. Personal communication, 1967.

ENGLE, B. T., and HANSON, S. P. Operant conditioning of heart rate slowing. *Psychophysiology,* 1966, *3,* 176–87.

ERIKSEN, C. W. Unconscious processes. In M. R. Jones (Ed.), *Nebraska Symposium on Motivation.* Lincoln: University of Nebraska Press, 1958.

FOLKINS, C. H., LAWSON, K. D., OPTON, E. M., JR., and LAZARUS, R. S. Desensitization and the experimental reduction of threat. *Journal of Abnormal Psychology,* 1968, *73,* 100–13.

GELLHORN, E. Motion and emotion: The role of proprioception in the physiology and pathology of the emotions. *Psychological Review,* 1964, *71,* 457–72.

GRAHAM, D. T., KABLER, J. D., and GRAHAM, F. K. Physiological response to the suggestion of attitudes specific for hives and hypertension. *Psychosomatic Medicine,* 1962, *24,* 159–69.

GRANT, D. A. The statistical analysis of a frequent experimental design. *The American Journal of Psychology,* 1949, *62,* 119–22.

HARRIS, A. J. An experiment on affective contrasts. *American Journal of Psychology,* 1929, *41,* 617–24.

HELSON, H. *Adaptation-level theory.* New York: Harper & Row, 1964.

HNATIOW, M. Learned control of heart rate and blood pressure. Unpublished doctoral dissertation, University of Pittsburgh, 1968.

HNATIOW, M., and LANG, P. J. Learned stabilization of cardiac rate. *Psychophysiology,* 1965, *1,* 330–36.

JAMES, W. *The principles of psychology.* New York: Henry Holt, 1890.

LACEY, J. I. Somatic response patterning and stress: Some revisions of activation theory. In M. H. Appley and R. Trumbull

(Eds.), *Psychological stress: Issues in research.* New York: Appleton-Century-Crofts, 1967, 14–37.

LACEY, J. I., and LACEY, B. C. The relationship of resting autonomic activity to motor impulsivity. Chapter V in *The brain and human behavior.* Baltimore: Williams & Wilkins Co., 1958.

LADER, M. H. Palmar skin conductance measures in anxiety and phobic states. *Journal of Psychosomatic Research,* 1967, *11,* 271–81.

LADER, M. H., GELDER, M. G., and MARKS, I. M. Palmer skin conductance measures as predictors of response to desensitization. *Journal of Psychosomatic Research,* 1967, *11,* 283–90.

LANG, P. J. The mechanics of desensitization and the laboratory study of human fear. In C. M. Franks (Ed.), *Assessment and status of the behavior therapies.* New York: McGraw-Hill, 1969a.

LANG, P. J. The on-line computer in behavior therapy research. *American Psychologist,* 1969b, *24,* 236–39.

LANG, P. J., and LAZOVIK, A. D. Experimental desensitization of a phobia. *Journal of Abnormal and Social Psychology,* 1963, *66,* 519–25.

LANG, P. J., LAZOVIK, A. D., and REYNOLDS, D. J. Desensitization, suggestibility, and pseudotherapy. *Journal of Abnormal Psychology,* 1965, *70,* 395–402.

LANG, P. J., MELAMED, B. G., and HART, J. A psychophysiological analysis of fear modification using an automated desensitization procedure. *Journal of Abnormal Psychology,* 1969, in press.

LANG, P. J., SROUFE, L. A., and HASTINGS, J. E. Effects of feedback and instructional set on the control of cardiac-rate variability. *Journal of Experimental Psychology,* 1967, *75,* 425–31.

LANGE, C. The emotions. Trans. by I. Haupt in K. Dunlap (Ed.), *The emotions.* Baltimore: Williams & Wilkins Co., 1922.

LAZARUS, A. A. The results of behavior therapy in 126 cases of severe neurosis. *Behaviour Research Therapy,* 1963, *1,* 69–79.

LAZARUS, R. S., and OPTON, E. M., JR. The study of psychological stress: A summary of theoretical formulations and experimental findings in Charles D. Spielberger (Ed.), *Anxiety and behavior*. New York: Academic Press, 1966.

LAZOVIK, A. D., and LANG, P. J. A laboratory demonstration of systematic desensitization psychotherapy. *Journal of Psychological Studies,* 1960, *11,* 238–47.

LEVENTHAL, H. Fear for your health. *Psychology Today*. September, 1967, 55–58.

LISINA, M. I. The role of orienting in the conversion of involuntary into voluntary reactions. In L. G. Voronin and others (Eds.), *The orienting reflex and exploratory behavior*. Moscow: Acad. Pedag. Sci., 1958.

MELAMED, B. G. The habituation of psychophysiological response to tones, and to filmed fear stimuli under varying conditions of instructional set. Unpublished doctoral dissertation, University of Wisconsin, 1969.

MILLER, N. E. Learning of visceral and glandular responses. *Science,* 1969, *163,* 434–45.

MILLER, N. E., and DICARA, L. V. Instrumental learning of heart rate changes in curarized rats: shaping and specificity to descriminative stimulus. *Journal of Comparative and Physiological Psychology,* 1967, *63,* 12–19.

OSGOOD, C. E. *Method and theory in experimental psychology*. New York: Oxford University, 1953.

PAUL, G. L. *Insight versus desensitization in psychotherapy*. Stanford: Stanford University Press, 1966.

SHEARN, D. W. Operant conditioning of heart rate. *Science,* 1962, *137,* 530–31.

SOKOLOV, Y. N. *Perception and the conditioned reflex*. New York: Macmillan, 1963.

SROUFE, L. A. Learned stabilization of cardiac rate with respiration experimentally controlled. *Journal of Experimental Psychology,* 1969, *81,* 391–93.

STAMPFL, T. G. Implosive therapy: The theory, the subhuman analogue, the stategy, and the technique. Pt. I: The theory. In S. G. Armitage (Ed.), *Behavior modification techniques in the treatment of emotional disorders*. Battle Creek, Michigan: V. A. Publication, 1966, 22–37.

WENGER, M. A. Emotion as visceral action: An extension of Lange's theory. In M. L. Reymert (Ed.), *Feelings and emotions*. New York: McGraw-Hill, 1950.

WOLPE, J. *Psychotherapy by reciprocal inhibition*. New York: Holt, Rinehart, & Winston, 1958.

Comment

CYRIL M. FRANKS

Systematic desensitization is undoubtedly one of the more effective of the new methods of modifying behavior. But, as Lang makes patently clear, the ensuing fear or anxiety reduction can be readily accounted for in a variety of ways. Anxiety and relaxation are supposed to be incompatible states, but the evidence for this statement is by no means as unequivocal as Wolpe contends (see Davison, 1965, 1968, 1969; Evans and Wilson, 1968; Wolpin and Raines, 1966, for extended discussions of this and related points). According to Folkins, Lawson, Opton, and Lazarus (1968), systematic desensitization is a matter not so much of relaxation and reciprocal inhibition as of "cognitive rehearsal" of the aversive scenes in the patient's imagination. There is also a study by Valins and Ray (1967) in which it is suggested that, by relaxing in the face of disturbing images, subjects reappraise the significance or cognitive meaning of these events and show a concomitant change in behavior. As Davison reminds us, Perry London put forward a similar type of cognitive reduction explanation of Wolpe's success some three years earlier.

The very assumption that conditioned anxiety or fear is the core of neurotic behavior is itself open to question, and yet, so far no one seems to have seriously questioned Wolpe's tacit acceptance of this traditionally Freudian formulation. While clinical and research experience tend to confirm the central role played by anxiety in most neuroses, there is no reason to assume that it is invariably the only one. It is possible that specialized techniques of control need to be developed for basic processes other than anxiety. Behavior therapy might do well to focus upon such lines of endeavor rather than upon a more narrow reliance upon the principle of psychotherapy by reciprocal inhibition with its superordinate emphasis upon anxiety. If "broad spectrum behavior therapy" (Lazarus, 1967) truly implies such a broadening then – provided that it does not signal a regressive return to some form of mentalism or phenomenology – it is to be welcomed.

Alternative explanations of the desensitization process so far broached seem to resolve themselves into two camps: Hullian extinction, as adapted by Wolpe (1958), and a Guthrian interfering response model, as put forward by writers such as Kimble (1961). Within the Hullian framework, it is still open to debate whether or not the efficacy of the technique of systematic desensitization can be more satisfactorily explained in terms of classical extinction than reciprocal inhibition (for example, see Lomont, 1965; Lomont and Edwards, 1967). While on the subject of extinction, it is perhaps as well to raise an issue long neglected by behavior therapists: the universality of the generally accepted rule that *"absence of reinforcement leads inevitably to extinction."* One of the most intriguing unresolved issues pertains to what has been called the Napalkov phenomenon (see Eysenck, 1967). The belief that most neurotic phobic and anxiety reactions are due to conditioning, either through single trial traumatic or many trial subtraumatic learning, is basic to behavior therapy. And repeated exposure to the conditional stimulus without reinforcement should lead to extinction (which is supposed to explain cases of spontaneous remission). But this does not always occur; sometimes repeated exposure to the conditional stimulus seems to lead to an *increase* in the severity of the response. This phenomenon has been reported in some form or another first by Pavlov himself, later by Gantt and Liddell and, more recently and more explicitly, by Napalkov. Explanations of this phenomenon are not very satisfactory but, as Eysenck suggests, it does appear as if the simple rule upon which many behavior therapists work, namely that *extinction follows repeated evocation of the conditional stimulus without reinforcement,* need not necessarily hold, at least in relation to the growth of autonomic fear reactions.

It is possible that the "arousal" model recently proposed by Lader and Matthews (1968) offers greater potential as an explanatory concept than any of those touched upon above. According to these authors, there is a critical level of arousal present in each subject that determines whether habituation will or will not take place under the circumstances then prevailing. When the level of arousal is reduced to a working minimum ("relaxation"), habituation ("desensitization") is more likely to occur.

The question of massed versus spaced practice is also of relevance. Consistent with the "interference" model is the finding of Ramsay, Barends, Breuker, and Kruseman (1966) that spaced practice is more effective than massed. Lanyon, Manosevitz, and Imber (1968) also report that spaced training produces a more effective anxiety reduction than massed in the treatment of spider phobia. But neither study appears to offer much support for the extinction model of desensitization.

In the resolution of such pertinent issues there are many formidable methodological problems to be overcome. Most of the early studies, and a not inconsiderable number of the later ones, suffer from numerous deficiencies. First, most of the data are derived from largely anecdotal reports of a handful of inadequately assessed subjects. Second, artificial problems such as "pure" snake phobias in college students are rarely as convincing as investigations of actual clinic patients, with all their "impure," less distinct, more complex and perhaps more meaningful, more encompassing, and therefore more disabling fears. Third, most of these studies have yet to come to grips with the problems of control. Both ethical and practical problems present themselves in assigning real-life patients to control groups. Perhaps the patient could serve as his own control in a series of repeated treatment variations—but this would require much careful planning.

Last, but not least, there is the problem of measurement of anxiety. Different anxiety questionnaires or indices of anxiety culled from standard personality questionnaires correlate very poorly with each other (consider, for example, the various anxiety indices devised from the Minnesota Multiphasic Personality Inventory). Many researchers employ situational measures of anxiety based upon what they can actually do (for example, with respect to touching the feared object). But, as Davison (1965) has demonstrated, there can be changes in behavior without accompanying concomitant anxiety reduction, just as changes in responses to attitudinal questionnaires need not necessarily reflect changes in behavior. At first glance, a promising approach might seem to be by way of the development of meaningful and reliable physiological indices of anxiety—but first we have to agree upon a definition of anxiety! Wolpe recommends the GSR as a competent index of anxiety, but there are many objections to such an assertion. According to Lacey (1959), the assumption that the GSR—or any physiological index, for that matter—is an appropriate measure of anxiety is totally false. Lacey's conclusion is that somatic responses to emotionally loaded verbal stimuli, being largely a function of the relationship of the individual concerned with his environment, must be interpreted within this interactional context. If this is so, it is doubtful whether physiological measures can ever be used in a one-to-one manner as validatory indices of subjective change.

Finally, I would like to discuss briefly the Pavlovian principles upon which the process of desensitization is supposed to be predicated. Many of the specific components of desensitization theory and practice fall more or less neatly into their Hullian niche, with perhaps a nod to Guthrie for good measure, but this is not the same as attempting to relate the theory of reciprocal inhibition and desensitization directly to Pavlovian psychology. The difficulty is that, while claiming lineal scientific descent from Pavlov, Wolpe's concepts nevertheless differ radically from those of Pavlov in a number of key respects. For example, according to Pavlov, if the stimulus intensities are high enough, the nerve cells concerned can experience actual physical change. But Wolpe categorically rejects the idea of physical pathology, arguing that, because neurotic responses can be unlearned, they must presumably have been established by learning in the first place. A careful examination of this statement reveals the *non-sequitur* elements. It is possible that a pathological "organic" state could be undone by learning, but it does not necessarily follow that the etiology of the maladaptive behavior has to be explained by the same principles from which the treatment is derived, no matter how successful (see Cautela, 1966).

Actually, a procedure similar to Wolpe's technique of systematic desensitization was used by Pavlov many years ago. Using food as the unconditional stimulus and electrical stimulation applied to a dog's skin as the conditioning stimulus, Pavlov gradually increased the strength of the current from one experimental session to the next until it was extremely powerful. The alimentary response, evoked by the strong electrical stimulation, remained stable for many months. While there was never any sign of a defense reaction as long as the site of the experiment remained unchanged, if the strong electrical current was applied to a *different* place on the skin, a most violent defense reaction occurred and no trace of the alimentary response remained. According to Pavlov, this phenomenon is due to the diversion of the nervous impulse from one physiological path to another.

Pavlov considers hypnosis and hypnotic-like states as being inhibitory in nature, states under which the subject, on the basis of simultaneity, can easily engage in temporary conditional connections with numerous external agents. In this state, inhibition is irradiated over much of the cortex. In the conventional desensitization situation of Wolpe, a stimulus is presented while most of the organism is in a predominantly inhibitory (or hypnotic-like) state, so that stimuli previously connected to excitatory states (for example, anxiety and fear) now become inhibitory. The inhibitory state certainly appears to be a necessary ingredient in the desensitization process, and Lang, I believe, has some experimental evidence to support this contention. It is also important to note, with Pavlov, that this irradiation occurs in both autonomic and motor components. If this were not so, it would be difficult to see how there could be any transfer from desensitization in the therapist's office to change in the real-life situation.

There are other corollaries of the Pavlovian model that are directly relevant to the theory and practice of desensitization (see Cautela, 1966). There is the firmly demonstrated Pavlovian "law of reciprocal induction," according to which a stimulus presented *immediately after* a preceding stimulus can have an effect *opposite* to that which occurs if the second stimulus is presented alone. For example, if the effect of a stimulus is usually inhibitory it can have an *excitatory* effect if presented immediately after the presentation of a stimulus which results in an inhibitory state of the organism. By this token, if desensitization is the presentation of a stimulus in an inhibitory state, the therapist should wait at least a few seconds before preceding on to the next item. This, of course, is largely speculation and further research is needed—preferably with the aid of the GSR and other accompanying psychophysiological measures.

These, then, are some of my initial reactions to Lang's excellent paper. Only through further well-designed and executed studies by experimentally trained research clinicians such as Peter Lang can the resolution of such problems be effected.

REFERENCES

CAUTELA, J. R. The Pavlovian basis of reciprocal inhibition therapy. *Conditional Reflex,* 1966, *1,* 293–300.

DAVISON, G. C. The influence of systematic desensitization, relaxation, and graded exposure to imaginal aversive stimuli on the modification of phobic behavior. Unpublished Ph.D. dissertation, Stanford University, 1965.

DAVISON, G. C. Systematic desensitization as a counter-conditioning process. *Journal of Abnormal Psychology,* 1968, *73,* 91–99.

DAVISON, G. C. A procedural critique of "desensitization and the experimental reduction of threat." *Journal of Abnormal Psychology,* 1969, *74,* 86–87.

EVANS, I., and WILSON, T. Note on the terminological confusion surrounding systematic desensitization. *Psychological Reports,* 1968, *22,* 187–91.

EYSENCK, H. J. Single-trial conditioning, neurosis and the Napalkov phenomenon. *Behaviour Research and Therapy,* 1967, *5,* 63–65.

FOLKINS, C. H., LAWSON, K. D., OPTON, E. M., JR., and LAZARUS, R. S. Desensitization and the experimental reduction of threat. *Journal of Abnormal Psychology,* 1968, *73,* 100–13.

KIMBLE, G. A. *Hilgard and Marquis' conditioning and learning.* New York: Appleton-Century-Crofts, 1961.

LACEY, J. I., Psychophysical approches to the evaluation of psychotherapeutic process and outcome. In E. A. Rubinstein and M. B. Parfoll (Eds.), *Research in Psychotherapy,* Vol. 1. Washington, D.C.: American Psychological Association, 1959.

LADER, M. H., and MATTHEWS, A. M. A physiological model of phobic anxiety and desensitization. *Behaviour Research and Therapy,* 1969 (to appear).

LANYON, R. I., MANOSEVITZ, M. and IMBER, R. R. Systematic desensitization: Distribution of practice and symptom substitution. *Behaviour Research and Therapy,* 1968 (to appear).

LAZARUS, A. A. In support of technical eclecticism. *Psychological Reports,* 1967, *21,* 415–16.

LOMONT, J. F. Reciprocal inhibition or extinction? *Behaviour Research and Therapy,* 1965, *3,* 209–20.

LOMONT, J. F., and EDWARDS, J. E. The role of relaxation in systematic desensitization. *Behaviour Research and Therapy,* 1967, *5,* 11–25.

LONDON, P. *The modes and morals of psychotherapy.* New York: Holt. Rinehart and Winston, 1964.

RAMSAY, R. W., BARENDS, J., BREUKER, J., and KRUSEMAN, A. Massed versus spaced desensitization of fear. *Behaviour Research and Therapy,* 1966, *4,* 205–07.

VALINS, S., and RAY, A. A. Effects of cognitive desensitization on avoidance behavior. *Journal of Personality and Social Psychology,* 1967, *7,* 345–50.

WOLPE, J. *Psychotherapy by reciprocal inhibition.* Stanford: Stanford University Press, 1958.

WOLPIN, M., and RAINES, J. Visual imagery, expected roles and extinction as possible factors in reducing fear and avoidance behavior. *Behaviour Research and Therapy,* 1966, *4,* 25–37.

6

Implosive Therapy: An Emphasis on Covert Stimulation

THOMAS G. STAMPFL

Implosive therapy (IT) is a behavioral therapy that has been applied to a variety of neurotic, psychotic, and other behavioral disorders (for example, character disorders). The therapy appears to be effective over a fairly wide range of behavioral deviations. Systematic experimental studies of outcome that support the effectiveness of the therapy include one with psychotic patients (Hogan, 1966), one with clinical outpatients (Levis and Carrera, 1967), and four studies with phobic college students (Barrett, 1969; Hogan and Kirchner, 1967, 1968; Kirchner and Hogan, 1966). Treatment time usually requires from one to fifteen implosive sessions with additional sessions required in some cases depending on the severity of the disturbance and other factors.

The theoretical basis of implosive therapy (IT) is derived from a two-factor model of avoidance learning (Mowrer, 1947, 1960; Schlosberg, 1937; Skinner, 1935; Tuttle, 1946). Analyses proposed by Dollard and Miller (1950), Mowrer (1939), and Shoben (1949), which relate psychotherapeutic phenomena to learning principles and reduce human deviant or maladaptive behavior to S-R mechanisms, contributed heavily to the development of specific IT techniques of treatment. In order to achieve a more explicit correspondence between the principles of two-factor theory and the clinical application of these principles to human psychopathological behavior, certain features related to the basic two-factor model required modification and extension (see Levis, 1966; Stampfl, 1960, 1961; Stampfl and Levis, 1967, 1969). These modifications and extensions depend heavily on concepts and principles drawn from systematic experimental laboratory research. In this respect, the analyses and research of other learning theorists who considered some of the problems of this translation (for example, Brown, 1961; Bugelski, 1956; Kimble, 1961; Holland and Skinner, 1961) were helpful in developing the theoretical model underlying IT.

The theory and practice of implosive therapy, however, retains to a degree certain concepts and modes of understanding emphasized in conventional psychodynamic approaches to treatment. About this Hunt and Dyrud (1968, p. 141) commented:

> Earlier writings on behavior therapy often seemed to imply that conditioning procedures and learning theory, and their application to alleviation of behavioral pathology are recent inventions and wholly owned by behavioral psychologists. This is not so. Psychoanalysis and many other dynamic personality theories assume a behavior theory not unlike contemporary two-factor learning theory. One cannot read Fenichel (1945) without being impressed by the degree to which he assumes conditioning of Type S (reinforcement correlated with a stimulus roughly equivalent to "classical" conditioning) and conditioning of Type R (reinforcement correlated with a response, roughly equivalent to "law of effect" learning) in explaining the development of defenses, fixation and regression, and the vicissitudes of development.

THE THEORETICAL MODEL

The two-process model which was adopted to account for the variety of maladaptive behaviors observed in the human patient assumes that both positive and negative affect are conditionable. When "neutral" stimuli are associated with unconditioned or conditioned positive reinforcers, positive affect is acquired. If neutral stimuli are associated with unconditioned or conditioned aversive reinforcement, negative affect is acquired. Both positive and negative affect possess motivational properties. Furthermore, the organism will behave in such a manner as to maximize those stimuli that elicit positive affect, and to minimize or eliminate those stimuli that elicit negative affect. Instrumental behavior (overt or covert) that is effective in performing these two functions will be strengthened by the consequences of the behavior in altering the level and type of affect present. Affective (emotional) responses then possess a cue function as well as a motivational one and serve as the basic mediator of overt and covert behavior.

In the remainder of this paper an attempt will be made to (1) provide a detailed examination of the role negative affect (for example, anxiety, guilt, hostility) plays in the development of symptom formation, defense mechanisms, and other deviant responses present in human psychopathology, and (2) to suggest a set of specific treatment procedures designed to modify symptomatic behavior in the human patient.

RELATION OF ANIMAL EXPERIMENTATION TO HUMAN PATHOLOGY

Typical training situations in the animal laboratory involve what is described as active avoidance learning, passive avoidance learning, and learning of a conditioned emotional response (CER). In active avoidance learning the animal is punished unless he makes some specified overt motor response such as jumping over a hurdle, running to the other half of a box, pressing a bar, turning a wheel, and so on. In passive avoidance learning the animal is punished if he makes some specified overt motor response. In the CER situation the experimental arrangement is such that ongoing learned behavior is disrupted or suppressed by a formerly neutral stimulus that has been made aversive by pairing the neutral stimulus with a noxious stimulus such as electric shock. Presumably, in the CER situation, responses incompatible with the ongoing behavior are the result of a classical conditioning process in the organism. In active avoidance the organism avoids the shock by doing something, while in passive avoidance the organism avoids the shock by not doing something. One difference in passive avoidance learning is that the neutral stimulus or conditioned stimulus is the response-correlated stimulation involved in making the response that is punished. All situations may be understood in terms of a two-factor model of learning, which asserts that a class of responses mainly autonomic in nature and labeled anxiety are classically conditioned to the neutral stimuli.

Experimental laboratory studies of active and passive avoidance learning and those pertaining to the suppression of responding obtained with the CER paradigm are assumed to be potentially relevant to the human situation. Studies that investigate the influence of other variables on this type of learning (for example, effects of electroconvulsive shock, drugs, stimulus complexity, interstimulus and intertrial intervals, time of testing following acquisition) acquire progressively greater importance in the leads they furnish for the understanding and modification of human behavior pathology. For example, let us consider the active avoidance responses of a rat (or other lower animal) shuttling to a stimulus previously paired with electric shock as an analogue of human compulsive behavior. The compulsions of the neurotic patient are then readily viewed as also being under stimulus control. Other similarities exist. An animal trained to engage in shuttling avoidance responses to a stimulus paired with shock will display little or no fear once stable avoidance responding is attained. The human compulsive usually reports little or no anxiety so long as he is able to readily engage in the compulsive behavior. Delaying or preventing the active avoidance response of the laboratory animal or the compulsions of the neurotic patient result in a marked increase in those signs which index negative affect. Equivalently, the passive avoidance behavior of the lower animal that fails to press a bar or enter a distinctive compartment may be seen as an analogue of human phobic reactions. In both cases, avoidance of the aversive stimulus situation minimizes the degree of negative affect, whereas exposure to the phobic situation maximizes it.

The basic assumption is that responses produce stimuli. This is evident in the constant change in stimulus input (visual, tactile, auditory, proprioceptive) which accompanies overt motor responses. The present model emphasizes that overt or covert responses (thinking, images, ideas) are linked associatively to the stimulus correlates of past events and classes of past events. The bodily representations (for example, neural patterns) of the past events are responses to present overt and covert responses which function as stimuli. The neural patterns reactivated by these stimuli also function as stimuli. The varying level of affect present from moment to moment corresponds to varying levels of stimulation, themselves a product of overt and covert responses.

A REINTERPRETATION OF THE DEFENSE SYSTEM

The relationship existing between traditional orientations and avoidance learning models of psychopathology is seen in the mentalistic conception of the defense system, a major explanatory concept of psychodynamic systems. The defense system is translatable into S-R mechanisms. In this translation defenses are converted into a set of instrumental avoidance responses which serve to terminate or prevent those stimuli that have been previously conditioned to generate negative affect. It is important to again emphasize that the aversive stimuli may be a product of covert as well as overt behavior. Thus, the traditional interpretation states that the defense system (set of avoidance responses) serves to bind anxiety by preventing dangerous associations (covert aversive stimuli) from surfacing to awareness. The present analysis maintains that if an individual experiences increased anxiety in a grocery store or in a large crowd or in an automobile that motivates behavior that removes these stimuli, the anxiety reaction experienced is primarily a response to the covert aversive stimuli (dangerous associations) activated by the external stimulus situation.

On the other hand, failure of the defense system leads to increased manifest emotionality. In this case the cues that elicit negative affect are not effectively avoided. The symptoms of both neurotic and psychotic patients are understandable in terms of an analysis that interprets symptoms as manifestations of avoidance or failure of avoidance. The compulsions of a neurotic or the delusion of grandeur of a psychotic may be viewed as avoidance responses that minimize negative affect, whereas the anxiety observed in a neurotic anxiety reaction or the emotionality seen in an acute schizophrenic reaction may be interpreted as a failure of avoidance.

FAILURE OF INSTRUMENTAL SYMPTOMATIC BEHAVIOR

The mentalistic treatment of covert behavior as ideas, thoughts, or images as well as impulses which are marginal or unreportable by the patient are considered in the learning translation presented here to function as stimuli or stimulus patterns that elicit the negative affective drive state. A patient may display strong avoidance behavior to crowds or to grocery stores or to flower shops. Exposure to the crowd, grocery store, or flower shop may be conceived as an external stimulus situation that correlates with increased anxiety. Central to the theoretical interpretation assumed in IT is that exposure to the external stimulus situation (crowd, grocery store, flower shop) elicits the negative drive state primarily because of its capacity to activate additional aversive stimuli which are a product of the covert behavior of the patient. Descriptively, the external situation redintegrates response-produced cues (images, thoughts, impulses) associates with covert behavior.

Thus, a patient may avoid "crowds" because exposure to the crowed elicits hostile impulses to attack those in the crowd, to be attacked by members of the crowd, to engage in sexual behavior with members of the crowd, to confess to past or current misdeeds to the crowd, and so forth. The anxiety reaction is then seen as a response to a stimulus compound made to the external stimulus situation plus the aversive stimuli related to the covert behavior that is activated. In most cases, the main function of the external stimulus is that of a mediator of covert aversive stimuli. It is hypothesized that the covert aversive stimuli carry the main weight in eliciting the anxiety reaction. In the absence of these covert aversive stimuli, little anxiety would result. The removal of the anxiety-eliciting capacity of covert stimuli, if this were possible, would lead to a very marked decrement in the anxiety reaction elicited by the external stimulus situation (for example, the crowd).

One of the problems related to learning model interpretations of psychopathology is that frequently it is difficult to establish any direct conditioning events that can plausibly account for the negative affect generated by the external stimulus situation. For example, a patient may fear crowds or snakes without apparently having experienced any negative event related to these stimuli proportional to the anxiety observed. Generally, learning theorists place heavy reliance on such principles as stimulus generalization, higher-order conditioning, and response-mediated generalization to account for this phenomenon. However, a more direct relationship between the past aversive conditioning history and the current anxiety reaction may be made if one assumes that covert aversive stimuli play an important role in the anxiety elicited. An examination of the characteristics of covert aversive stimuli bear a much closer relationship to previously punished behavior such as that related to sex and aggression.

The failure of an instrumental symptom to avoid aversive stimuli is seen as a common principle basic to a wide variety of behavior disorders. Instrumental symptomatic behavior leads to the avoidance of external stimulus situations, which minimizes the frequency of the occurrence of covert aversive stimuli. In the event that instrumental symptomatic behavior is no longer effective in achieving this anxiety-reducing function (that is, covert aversive stimuli persist in the absence of the external stimulus situation), an alternative set of instrumental behaviors (defenses) may be selected if they are effective in minimizing the anxiety experienced (for example, a shift from neurotic to psychotic defenses).

THE ROLE OF MARGINAL OR IMPOVERISHED STIMULI

In some situations, stimuli that are marginal or impoverished may be redintegrated. These stimuli appear to function below the level of verbal report. Such stimuli may also possess anxiety-eliciting strength and enter into the total compound producing the actual emotional reaction. The individual, in effect, cannot readily identify the stimuli involved, although some of them appear to be reportable if he is urged to try to remember. For example, a compulsive who failed to engage in his usual morning dressing ritual reported that he was in a state of intense anxiety driving to work that morning. The anxiety was so intense that he finally turned and drove home, where he carried out his dressing rituals and then drove to work. When asked what had been so fear inducing about driving, the patient could merely report that he felt some terrible disaster would occur, that something terrible would happen. Closer questioning revealed that some additional stimuli were correlated with the feeling of high anxiety and disaster. The patient could recall that he thought the pavement would crack wide open and that his car would plunge into the middle of the earth as in an earthquake. He said that he could feel the pavement vibrating under the wheels of his car, that he could see the cracks appearing in the road in front of him, and that the dreaded event would occur if he continued driving. He reported that the tall buildings he drove past would topple on him. It is important to emphasize that he thought he could see the buildings swaying and could hear them cracking. Again, if he continued driving he felt that the buildings would actually topple on him.

An additional assumption made is that further aversive response-produced patterns would be elicited if exposure to the reportable aversive stimuli occurred. That is, if the patient were exposed to the stimulus properties of his automobile plunging into the earth, additional stimuli involving cues related to bodily injury, suffocation, and death would be activated. The patient's avoidance responses (turning the car) terminate these aversive stimuli and prevent additional stimuli from being redintegrated. Since the patient experiences strong secondary punishment for engaging in this behavior (failing to carry out his dressing rituals), he is less likely to engage in this behavior in the future. Because he was late for work, additional punishing environmental consequences occurred. His boss was very unhappy with his coming late and told him so in unmistakable terms. Thus, exposure to chained aversive stimulus compounds is a consequence of the failure to engage in his dressing rituals, which in turn prevented subsequent segments of the chained aversive stimulus compounds from occurring.

It will be noted that the stimulus segments are initiated by the failure to engage in symptomatic behavior. The covert aversive stimuli are thought to be related to the aversive conditioning history of the patient. Frequently, the aversive conditioning events involve parental punishment for transgressive behavior.

EXPERIMENTAL EXTINCTION

It seems clear that one possible approach to the modification of symptomatic behavior would be to modify the negative affective drive state that is responsible for the symptoms. Experimental studies conducted in the laboratory with lower animals suggest procedures by which the negative emotional state can be reduced or eliminated.

A suggested procedure based on a very large number of studies differentiates the characteristics of two classes of stimuli involved in eliciting the emotional responses. One class of stimuli is assumed to elicit the negative emotional reaction as a function of an inherent (unconditioned) relationship between the stimulus and the response. For example, electric shock of sufficient intensity is conceived to be a stimulus that will elicit aversive response-produced stimuli in the absence of previous learning. The effects of aversive unconditioned stimuli are assumed to exist because they modify the internal state of the organism. The negative internal state involves features which on the human level are commonly described as physically painful. Those stimuli that bear no inherent relationship to the negative internal state are designated as neutral stimuli and comprise the other class of stimulation. Contiguity between the neutral stimuli and the internal effects of aversive unconditioned stimuli leads to the acquisition of some of the components of the negative internal aversive state to the previously neutral stimuli. This transfer of components of the aversive internal state via conditioning is thought to consist primarily of emotional components rather than the physically painful ones. The previously neutral stimuli now function as conditioned aversive stimuli by virtue of their capacity to modify the internal state of the organism. Both types of aversive stimuli, conditioned and unconditioned, possess many behavioral properties in common. Both may motivate behavior, and a reduction in the drive state elicited by either type of stimulus will reinforce instrumental behavior. The onset of the internal drive state elicited by both types of stimulus will serve as a punishment for behavior leading to it.

A major difference in the operations defining the two types of stimuli is that repetition of conditioned aversive stimuli in the absence of an unconditioned aversive stimulus (nonreinforcement) almost invariably leads to a progressive decrement in the conditioned emotional response. The repetition of unconditioned aversive stimuli, however, seldom leads to a decrement in the unconditioned response.

The basic assumption of IT is that external and covert aversive stimuli function as conditioned aversive stimuli. Repetition of these stimuli in the absence of unconditioned aversive stimuli should lead to a progressive reduction in the emotional responses that drive the symptomatic behavior of the patient. Reduction or elimination of the drive state should lead to a reduction or elimination of the patient's symptoms.

THE ANIMAL ANALOGUE OF IMPLOSIVE THERAPY

The experimenter in the typical animal study merely

arranges it so that the conditioned aversive stimulus is no longer paired with the unconditioned aversive stimulus. Since the experimenter knows the stimuli that have been conditioned, the procedure is relatively simple. After a sufficient number of nonreinforcement trials, the active or passive avoidance response, or suppression of the response in the CER situation, is eliminated.

In the human situation, however, the therapist usually does not know the conditions under which the symptoms were acquired. A more accurate but simple analogue to the therapy with the human patient would be as follows. Suppose a colleague challenges you to extinguish maladaptive behavior in an animal he has conditioned. You are to take the animal and do whatever you like with him. From time to time your colleague will privately test the animal in order to determine how successful you've been in eliminating the maladaptive behavior. Knowing the animal has been conditioned in the laboratory, one could start by exposing the animal progressively in a systematic fashion to a variety of stimuli. You could try buzzers, lights, tones, clickers, metronomes, and so on, and observe the animal to determine if any of the responses characteristic of aversive stimuli occur. If necessary, you might monitor directly a physiological response such as heart rate in order to do this. You might begin with white noise as a stimulus because you know your colleague uses white noise frequently in his laboratory for training purposes. If the hypothesized stimulus is a tone, you might introduce a 4,000-cycle tone. If a discernible emotional reaction occurs, you infer that you are proceeding in the right direction. Let's say your colleague actually did use a 1,200-cycle tone in conditioning the animal. When a 4,000-cycle tone is presented, an emotional reaction occurs by way of stimulus generalization. Here one can expect that some generalization of extinction effect should result for the 1,200-cycle tone used as the training stimulus. Following presentations with the 4,000-cycle tone it is clear that additional tone frequency values could be chosen. One could then expose the animal to 3,000-, 2,000-, 1,000-, and 100-cycle tones. Note that even if extinction trials failed to include the original 1,200-cycle tone training stimulus that your colleague used, an appreciable extinction effect might be achieved by the individual gradients of generalization of extinction set up by the use of each tone value.

However, an immediate practical difficulty arises in regard to this problem. Where will the tone presentations be given to the animal – in a Skinner box, in a shuttlebox, in his home cage, on the floor? Where? It is clear that one will have to vary context stimuli in much the same way that one varies hypothesized discrete stimuli. In this case the same procedure would be followed. That is, one would vary hypothesized training stimuli systematically in progressively different stimulus situations. Since your colleague uses Skinner boxes frequently, one might economize in regard to the procedure by presenting the hypothesized stimuli in a Skinner box. If the animal had, in fact, been conditioned in a Skinner box, note that you would not have to reproduce the contextual stimuli of the box exactly. Generalization of extinction should occur for context stimuli in the same manner that it does for discrete stimuli.

Actually, there are many difficulties related to the above analogue. For example, the organism might have been conditioned to stimulus compounds, or even to chained serial compounds. A different unconditioned aversive stimulus rather than electric shock might have been used. The conditioned stimuli might be response-correlated proprioceptive stimuli. It may not be immediately clear how these problems could be resolved on the animal level.

PROCEDURE

The procedure followed in IT is similar to the preceding analogue. In some respects it is easier to employ with human patients than with lower animals under the conditions described in the analogue. The main reason for this is that the therapist can rely on the verbal report of the human patient to help identify some of the critical aversive stimuli. The clinical experience of the therapist is also of value, since many commonalities in aversive stimuli exist within and between various classes of patients.

Usually, two standard clinical interviews are conducted with the patient. The questions the therapist seeks to answer are as follows: What is the patient avoiding? What might he be avoiding? What is he afriad of? What might he be afraid of? What are the characteristics of the patient's aversive conditioning history, and to what extent can these events be reasonably related to the aversive stimuli identified? The stimuli presumed to be aversive are listed. They may relate directly to symptomatic behavior and, in many cases, may also be related to early aversive events in the patient's history. The procedure includes the specification of internal and external stimuli and response-correlated stimulation associated with overt and covert behavior. The stimuli or cues may be classified as follows:

Symptom Contingent Cues. These cues are directly related to the external stimulus conditions under which the frequency of symptomatic behavior is maximized. Symptomatic behavior is viewed either as an increase in instrumental avoidance tendencies or as an increase in negative affect. Neurotic phobic reactions represent the clearest example of this type of cue. Proximity to the phobic object or situation maximizes avoidance tendencies. Unavoidable exposure to the phobic stimuli leads to an augmentation in negative affect. Thus, external features of the phobic object or situation represent one type of symptom-contingent cue. Any stimulus in the external environment that correlates with an increase in instrumental symptomatic behavior such as compulsive reactions would also be classified as a symptom-contingent cue. Thus, compulsive handwashing may increase when the external stimulus situation includes "dirty" objects (waste baskets, used handkerchiefs, and so on) or following certain events such as arguments with a parental figure. The failure of instrumental symptomatic behavior would be included under this classification. If a compulsive fails to engage in ritualistic behavior, the behavior itself may be considered as a change in external stimuli. Since this change leads to an increase in negative affect, the stimulus correlated with this behavior qualifies as a symptom-contingent cue.

Reportable Internally Elicited Cues. In addition to the symptom contingent cue and related to it are stimuli reportable by the patient that appear to have aversive properties. A closed space may represent a symptom-contingent cue for a claustrophobic, but the set of internal responses that refers to the patient's mentalistic description of a fear of suffocation in the closed space is interpreted in IT as a covert aversive stimulus pattern functioning as a reportable internally elicited cue. Similar reports may be obtained from patients displaying a rather wide diversity of maladaptive behavioral reactions. The compulsive handwasher may report that thoughts of dirt and a vague feeling of guilt are associated with his behavior. Frequently, the patient merely reports that he senses an impending disaster or "catastrophe." However, when the patient is questioned more closely, he very frequently is able to supply additional details that are classifiable under this category. The claustrophobic upon questioning may report that his fear of suffocation is associated with marginal thoughts that he is being punished for something.

A similar sequence of cues is present in nearly every patient. This appears to be true of psychotic disorders as well as neurotic ones.

Unreportable Cues Hypothesized to Relate to Reportable Internally Elicited Cues. Hypothesized unreportable cues may be extended at length. These cues are those that to the therapist appear to have a logical relationship to the symptom-contingent and reportable cues. Frequently, they also represent inferences made by the therapist based on aspects of the conditioning history of the patient. Sometimes they are guesses of the therapist that depend on his interpretation as to the critical features of the conditioning process. For example, much aversive conditioning may be assumed to involve tissue injury (physical punishment, falling, being cut). Stimuli immediately associated with bodily injury (for example, the sight of blood) may be assumed to be integral elements of the aversive stimulus complex, even though not reported by the patient. It may readily be inferred that the patient who fears falling from high places also fears the bodily consequences of the impact following the fall. Stimuli associated with his mangled body is a logical consequence of the aversive sequence related to his phobia—S_1 (high places), S_2 (falling), S_3 (impact), S_4 (stimuli associated with mangled body). If the patient is religiously inclined, then the implications of his death in an afterlife may be reduced to their stimulus equivalents (S_5, suffering in hell). The therapist may hypothesize that the fear of suffocation in the claustrophobic includes the fear of dying a slow agonizing death while he is completely helpless. Also, if the marginal thought is reported that suffocation in a closed space is punishment of some kind for having done something wrong, the therapist may introduce logical figures (parents, God, siblings) to apply the punishment, and also provide specific transgressive behaviors that answer the question as to why the patient is being punished. The theme of punishment for wrongdoing is very frequently related to symptomatic behavior, therefore the therapist may routinely introduce cues of this nature on a hypothetical basis. Since punishment for transgressive behavior is a common occurrence, it represents features of the inferred aversive conditioning history, whether or not it is included in the patient's report. Other common hypothesized cues are those involving sexual and aggressive stimuli. Hypothesized cues may include the stimulus characteristics of events inferred to have existed in the conditioning history or actually reported by the patient to have occurred. In all cases unreportable details of the events are supplied by the therapist. Aversive events of this type may involve dominating mothers, punative fathers, or teasing siblings.

It is difficult to adequately describe all the ramifications of the use of hypothesized cues as these apply to different types of patients. However, the basic logic of the procedure as illustrated applies to almost all types of neurotic and functional psychotic disorders.

Hypothesized Dynamic Cues. Cues included in this category are those derived from psychoanalytically based theories of personality. For the most part they can be deduced from hypothetical events in the early conditioning history. Oedipal, anal, oral, primal scene, death wish impulses, castration, and a variety of responses of a primary process type are reduced to their stimulus equivalents. Dynamic cues appear to be especially useful in the treatment of more severely disturbed patients.

Near the end of the second clinical interview, the patient is instructed to visualize imaginal scenes that include essentially neutral stimuli. Special instructions are given the patient to attend to or focus on the details of the neutral scenes that are suggested. This is done in order to establish some estimate of the patient's ability to respond to verbal instructions to imagine various scenes, and to establish the therapist as the director of the scenes.

The assumption is that imagery is a form of covert behavior that can function to represent, by approximation, stimuli related to the external environment as well as stimuli related to covert behavior.

At the beginning of the third session, the therapist may "replay" briefly the essentially neutral cues, and then introduce systematically the various aversive cues. In this procedure the cues are reduced to their imaginal equivalents. The emotional reaction that is elicited is used to determine the accuracy of the approximation. It should be noted that this procedure cannot specify with certainty the exact aversive stimuli any more than it did in the case of the hypothetical lower animal conditioned to the 1,200-cycle tone in the previously described animal analogue. Each set of cues is repeated until a reduction in anxiety appears to occur; then additional sets of cues are introduced. In the case of the lower animal the signs indexing anxiety were observed in order to determine what stimuli to use. The animal was not required to confirm the validity or accuracy of the stimuli introduced other than by his emotional behavior. A similar procedure is followed with the human patient. He is not asked to confirm the validity or accuracy of the stimuli introduced other than by his emotional behavior. He is not asked to confirm the validity of the interpretation as to what constitutes the aversive stimuli that are suggested.

The assumption is that stimuli incorporated in imaginal scenes function as approximations of conditioned aversive stimuli. Therefore, a sufficient number of nonreinforcement trials will lead to the reduction or elimination of the negative affect elicited by these stimuli. Symptomatic behavior that depends on the motivation provided by the negative affect should also be reduced or eliminated. Since the aversive stimuli cannot be established with exactness, extinction is assumed to occur by generalization.

The nature of the scenes suggested by the therapist is guided by the aversive stimuli obtained from the clinical interviews. For example, a claustrophobic may be instructed to imagine that he is entering a closed room. He remains there and is instructed to imagine that he is slowly suffocating to death, with many of the details supplied by the therapist. A scene of this type is repeated several times. The therapist may then introduce variations on this scene based on the evaluation of the patient secured from the clinical interviews. For example, scenes involving wrongdoing, with a parental figure supervising confinement to the closed space as a punishment. The parental figure might beat and scold the patient while he suffocates. Early traumatic incidents that appear to be related to the phobia may also be introduced, as represented in teasing sequences by being covered and held under blankets. If the patient appears to have been involved in a typical Oedipal situation in childhood, the therapist may suggest scenes that include sexual interaction with a mother figure followed by apprehension by a father figure, who places the patient in a closed space and castrates him. A compulsive may be instructed to visualize a failure to perform his dressing rituals. He drives to work and an earthquake occurs, buildings topple on him, the earth splits open and he plunges into the gaping crack. Trapped under the earth, he is slowly crushed to death. The cues related to bodily injury are vividly described. The possible variations of scenes for both of these patients are numerous.

The basic principle followed in all cases is simply to force exposure to the stimulus equivalents of whatever the patient is avoiding to the extent that they are thought to be related to symptomatic behavior. This is tantamount to forcing exposure to stimuli that will elicit negative affect.

In a number of cases a direct use of psychodynamic theory is made in hypothesizing the critical aversive stimuli. For example, it may be inferred that depressed patients are avoiding the behavioral expression of aggression. It may also be inferred that aggressive tendencies, in part are a product of prior events which provide for the conditioning of frustration stimuli that elicit the aggressive response. The therapist may introduce scenes incorporating frustration stimuli followed by scenes incorporating aggressive stimuli. For example, a depressed patient was exposed to the stimuli representing a series of teasing sequences by a brother figure. The patient had reported the early teasing incidents in childhood by her brother who referred to her as "mustachio." It is noteworthy that the verbal description of the past teasing incidents were not accompanied by any marked emotional reactions. However, the imaginal reproductions of being teased by the brother (with variations provided by the therapist) elicited intense negative affective reactions. The therapist continued the teasing sequences until it appeared that a partial extinction effect for the scenes had occurred. Scenes involving the expression of verbal, physical, and primary process aggression were then introduced. A very high degree of emotionality was elicited to these scenes. A continuation of the procedure which included other frustration stimuli (past and present) followed by the expression of aggression led to the progressive reduction of the anxiety associated with these stimuli. The progressive elimination of the depressive behavior was correlated with this procedure, leading to the apparent recovery of the patient.

PROBLEMS OF VALIDITY

Validation of the effectiveness of IT in modifying the symptomatic behavior of various classes of patients may be attained by appropriate experimentally controlled studies of outcome. To adequately define and control the critical variables in outcome studies is a rather formidable one. Suitable criteria of improvement must be established, and sufficient follow-up of patients over a considerable length of time is required. In addition, appropriate controls for the effects of novelty, enthusiasm of the therapist, experimenter bias, and a variety of expectation and suggestion effects must be included in the experimental design.

The question of the validity of the theoretical model of IT as it applies to the therapeutic procedure on the level of the human patient is a more difficult one. Even though adequate experimental studies suggested that IT procedures were effective in changing patient behaviors, the question would still remain as to whether the changes obtained were due to the principles of change posited in the theoretical model. It is clear that a number of alternative explanations are available that might plausibly account for any changes that might occur (for example, counterconditioning, contrast effects, protective inhibition, "flight into health" effects). A number of serious difficulties are associated with attempts to study these variables on the human level. The precise control of stimulus variables is almost impossible to achieve, and there are ethical considerations related to the inclusion of certain types of control groups with human patients. To the extent that such difficulties could be surmounted, the problem of exhausting all the possible alternatives would appear to be an endless one.

Judson Brown (1961) once suggested that we might better understand the behavior of lower animals from the vantage point of the study of human behavior. He argued that one could extrapolate from humans to lower animals as well as from lower animals to humans. The methods used in IT were originally generated from a two-factor model of learning derived principally from studies of lower animals. Application of these methods with human patients suggested certain deficiencies in two-factor theory as it was applied to animal behavior. Phenomena associated with patients undergoing implosive therapy pointed to certain critical aspects related to the learning model that would permit predictions to be made in relatively unique experiments with lower animals. To the extent that these predictions were verified, it was believed that additional validity would be conferred on the theoretical model. Thus, the main strategy in attempting to validate the theoretical model underlying IT has been along lines of experimentation with lower animals. Much of this work is still in progress.

REFERENCES

BARRETT, C. L. Systematic desensitization versus implosive therapy. *Journal of Abnormal Psychology,* 1969, *74,* 587–96.

BROWN, J. S. *The motivation of behavior.* New York: McGraw-Hill, 1961.

BUGELSKI, B. R. *The psychology of learning.* New York: Holt, Rinehart and Winston, 1956.

DOLLARD, J., and MILLER, N. E. *Personality and psychotherapy.* New York: McGraw-Hill, 1950.

FENICHEL, O. *The psychoanalytic Theory of Neurosis.* New York: W. W. Norton and Co., 1945.

HOGAN, R. A. Implosive therapy in the short term treatment of psychotics. *Psychotherapy: Theory, Research and Practice,* 1966, *3,* 25–32.

HOGAN, R. A., and KIRCHNER, J. H. Preliminary report of the extinction of learned fears via short-term implosive therapy. *Journal of Abnormal Psychology,* 1967, *72,* 106–09.

HOGAN, R. A. and KIRCHNER, J. H. A comparison of implosive, eclectic-verbal, and bibliotherapy in the treatment of snake phobias. *Behaviour Research and Therapy,* 1968, 6, 167–71.

HOLLAND, J. G., and SKINNER, B. F. *The analysis of behavior.* New York: McGraw-Hill, 1961.

HUNT, H. F. and DYRUD, J. E. Commentary: Perspective in behavior therapy. In J. M. Shlien (Ed.), *Research in psychotherapy,* Vol. 3. Washington, D.C.: American Psychological Association, 1968, 140–52.

KIMBLE, G. A. *Hilgard and Marquis' conditioning and learning.* New York: Appleton-Century-Crofts, 1961.

KIRCHNER, J. H., and HOGAN, R. A. The therapist variable in the implosion of phobias. *Psychotherapy: Theory, Research and Practice,* 1966, *3,* 102–04.

LEVIS, D. J. Effects of serial CS presentation and other characteristics of the CS on the conditioned avoidance response. *Psychological Reports,* 1966, *18,* 755–66.

LEVIS, D. J., and CARRERA, R. N. Effects of ten hours of implosive therapy in the treatment of outpatients. *Journal of Abnormal Psychology,* 1967, *72,* 504–08.

MOWRER, O. H. A stimulus response analysis of anxiety and its role as a reinforcing agent. *Psychological Review,* 1939, *46,* 553–65.

MOWRER, O. H. On the dual nature of learning—a reinterpretation of "conditioning" and "problem solving." *Harvard Educational Review,* 1947, *17,* 102–48.

MOWRER, O. H. *Learning theory and behavior.* New York: Wiley, 1960.

SCHLOSBERG, H. The relationship between success and the laws of conditioning. *Psychological Review,* 1937, *44,* 379–94.

SHOBEN, E. J. Psychotherapy as a problem in learning theory. *Psychological Bulletin,* 1949, *46,* 366–92.

SKINNER, B. F. Two types of conditioned reflex and a pseudo type. *Journal of Genetic Psychology,* 1935, *12,* 66–77.

STAMPFL, T. G. Avoidance conditioning reconsidered: An extention of Mowrerian theory. Unpublished manuscript, John Carroll University, Cleveland, 1960.

STAMPFL, T. G. Implosive therapy: A learning theory derived psychodynamic therapeutic technique. Paper presented at a colloquium of the University of Illinois, 1961.

STAMPFL, T. G., and LEVIS, D. J. The essentials of implosive therapy: A learning-theory-based psychodynamic behavioral therapy. *Journal of Abnormal Psychology,* 1967, *72,* 496–503.

STAMPFL, T. G., and LEVIS, D. J. Learning theory: An aid to dynamic therapeutic practice. In L. D. Eron and R. Callahan (Eds.), *Relation of theory to practice in psychotherapy.* Chicago: Aldine, 1969.

TUTTLE, H. S. Two kinds of learning. *Journal of Psychology,* 1946, *22,* 267–77.

Comment

LEONARD KRASNER

Dr. Stampfl obviously enjoys his work, and this crucial element is communicated to and appreciated by the patient. I would guess that one of the problems in replicating implosive therapy, in contrast to other forms of behavior therapy, is this highly idiosyncratic element of the therapist's thespian ability.

A number of other points strike me about implosive therapy. First and foremost is the ingenuity and excitement involved in moving from the laboratory to real life and back again. It's a classic example of what is taught in graduate school but which is so rarely realized in our profession: A man does basic animal work in the controlled atmosphere of the laboratory, he moves out and works with people with real problems, he develops new hypotheses, he runs back to the laboratory and tests them, and refines the techniques to use again in the clinical setting.

Secondly, many of the hypotheses Dr. Stampfl and the implosive therapists are developing could also lend themselves to being tested with investigations of desensitization such as Dr. Lang's ingenious automated apparatus. I can foresee a happy blending of these procedures under testable circumstances.

A third point is the element of *fun* for the therapist in implosive therapy. It was pointed out earlier in this conference that there is sheer, utter boredom in carrying out desensitization. Psychoanalysis is far more successful than behavior therapy in the reinforcement or gratification a therapist receives in carrying out the basic operations of his particular procedure. I suspect that one of the reasons for the introduction of mechanized desensitization is that in some instances the therapist has fallen asleep. Psychoanalysis is usually a lot more fun than behavior therapy. I think Dr. Stampfl has reintroduced an element of enjoyment for the therapist, which makes him far more effective in his work.

I'm not completely clear about all aspects of the implosive therapist's role. Dr. Stampfl described him as a *director,* but what is his role as a *reactor*? Is he reassuring, neutral, or condemning of the patient's verbalizations? Also related to techniques is the need for clarification of the differences in procedure, if any, between Rachman's "flooding" and implosive therapy as described here.

Certainly Stampfl's approach offers considerable possibilities for extending implosive therapy by going further into the reproduction of the original stimulating situation with pictures, movies, introjecting of extra characters, and going into the real environment. How far would you go in reproducing stimulus situations? Would you go into the home and ask a parent or brother for cooperation? In the case presented, would treatment have been more rapid if the brother would have been available and it were he who entered the scene at the appropriate moment yelling, "Mustachio, mustachio"?

The focus in implosive therapy is on extinction, the elimination of undesirable responses; but what about the development of new responses? How do new responses develop in this system? Dr. Stampfl was saying, "Tell him off. Call him a name." I think he was trying to elicit a new response; but, if so, is this kind of exhortation the way to do it? This is one area of concern—do the implosive therapists devote enough time and energy to the development of new responses to replace those being imploded to death?

I would like to raise one final question, which Stampfl and Levis have discussed in an article entitled "Implosive therapy—a behavioral therapy?" which appeared in *Behavior Research and Therapy* (1968, *6*, 31–36). If it is, why does it have to make use of psychodynamic concepts? Are they used as a focus for looking for cues to determinants of current behavior? Or are they used as an attempt to bridge the gap between psychoanalysis and behavior therapy? Gap-bridging has become a favorite occupation of people on both sides of the fence. I don't think that gap-bridging will be very profitable because of the "damned if you do and damned if you don't" attitude of both the behavior therapists and the psychoanalysts. I don't think that either camp is willing to accept the basic premises of the other, and he who would stand athwart the river serves as a justifiable target from each side.

7

Some Implications of a Social Learning Theory for the Practice of Psychotherapy

JULIAN B. ROTTER

The problems of psychotherapy may be viewed as problems in how to effect changes in behavior through the interaction of one person with another. That is, they are problems in human learning in a social situation or context. In spite of this, there has been until recently relatively little application of formal learning theory and of laboratory research on human learning to the techniques of psychotherapy. Where learning theory has been used at all, it frequently has been applied in one of two ways. The first of these is as a justification for therapeutic procedures developed from other theoretical approaches rather than as a basis for deriving new methods and techniques. This approach frequently fails to make use of the implications of a considerable body of knowledge regarding human learning, but rather selects particular principles to justify favorite therapeutic procedures. The second approach follows a restricted conditioning model that is limited in the kinds of problems to which it can be applied and which frequently fails to take into account much of what the individual has already learned when he comes to therapy.

It fails to recognize that the complex attitudes, goals, skills, and behaviors of the individual significantly affect what he will learn and under what conditions he will learn most efficiently. In such an approach the absence of functional content variables for stable human behavior—that is, a personality theory—often reduces the efficiency of therapy because of failure to understand the gradients of generalization of behavior changes and to understand the nature of "hidden" reinforcements that strengthen an apparent maladaptive response.

This failure to fully apply learning theory can be explained in part by the fact that many individuals involved in studying complex *human* learning as a general area of investigation are not concerned with the application of their findings to psychotherapeutic practice. A more serious barrier to application, however, is that there is too great a disparity between the kind of laboratory situations in which human learning is typically studied and the complex social interactions that characterize psychotherapy.

The gap between theory and laboratory research, and the prediction of behavior in complex social interactions is a great one and cannot be closed by a single leap. The purpose of this paper, however, is to lessen that hiatus somewhat by illustrating some implications of one social learning theory for the practice of psychotherapy, as specifically as the present state of the theory and research allows. Since no special laws are assumed that are peculiar to psychotherapeutic interactions, many of the hypotheses generated here regarding psychotherapeutic change would apply equally to effecting social change.

In order to derive either implications or predictions from a behavior theory to the problem of psychotherapy, one must have available a theory suitable to the complex phenomena concerned and sufficiently developed that at least all of the major variables and their relationships are known and measureable, so that prediction can be made or control exercised. Second, one must know the dimensions along which behaviors may be categorized, generalizations predicted, and so forth. In other words, one must have integrated with such a learning theory, a content theory (sometimes called a personality theory) that presumes to have abstracted from such social interactions the relevant aspects of behavior into functional categories (needs, traits, habit families, and so on). There must be a useful descriptive terminology to characterize the generalized aspects of behavior as well as a theory that describes the process of change.

Behavior theories vary in the degree to which they fit this ideal. The degree to which they deviate may account for the apparent minimum connection between the theories of personality and/or learning and the psychotherapeutic methods which presumably derive from them. For example, both Kelly (1955) and Rogers (1951) have in common a phenomenological theory with many points of similarity. Yet the implications each sees from theory to psychotherapeutic practice are so different that in many instances they would have to be placed at opposite ends of a set of continua used to describe therapeutic techniques. A bewildering variety of practices has been advocated by therapists who justify them as stemming from something they all refer to as "psychoanalytic theory" (Rotter, 1960). Similarly, Wolpe (1958), among learning theorists, describes a learning and neurophysiological theory of behavior of Hullian origin and goes on to advocate therapeutic practices that have only a loose connection with his theory, and appears opposed in many major ways to Dollard and Miller's (1950) application of presumably the same theory. Although awareness of this problem has led to an attempt to exercise caution in drawing implications from theory to practice in this paper, it should be stated at the outset that these implications are also loose, and although they seem logical to the author, they may well not be so perceived by others.

There is a second difficulty in the drawing of specific

implications from a personality theory for the problem of psychotherapeutic practice or of social change. An adequate theory of behavior may explain how changes take place or how to achieve the control of some behaviors, but a scientific theory does not specify what kinds of changes are good or bad from the point of view of social or ethical values. What constitutes adequate goals for psychotherapy or social change and what constitutes ethical means of achieving these goals is not a part of a scientific theory but of a value system (that is, a set of judgments dealing with what is good and what is bad). Different value systems utilizing the same theory might well lead to very different methods of practice. When one advocates a specific method of psychotherapy, one has explicitly or implicitly made a commitment to a specifiable set of values. For example, such a commitment might take the form that the therapist is ethically justified in helping the patient arrive at a better understanding of himself but should assiduously avoid affecting in any other way the kinds of changes that may take place in the patient's goals or behavior. Whether or not this is possible is a matter of controversy. However, it is clear that the methods that such a therapist would use would be quite different than those of another therapist, operating with the same theory, who explicitly states that the goal of psychotherapy is to increase the patient's capacity to love others. It is because of this latter point that it seems necessary to emphasize that the applications of social learning theory to follow have to be regarded as only one set of possible techniques.

Since social learning theory has not reached the stage where it is possible to make completely unambiguous deductions to specific complex social phenomena, it is not always possible to talk about implications at a highly specific level. The purpose of this paper is to illustrate at some middle level of generality one possible application of social learning theory to psychotherapy for a particular set of values. The intention is to apply a complex learning theory of personality as directly as possible to the problems of psychotherapy, rather than to use learning principles as post-hoc explanations of techniques derived from other points of view. The goal is to not only apply the abstract processes of learning to psychotherapy but also to take into account what the individual has already learned in order to determine what kinds of change will be most beneficial to him and under what circumstances he can learn most effectively. Before proceeding, it is necessary to indicate what value commitments are involved in the illustrative application that follows.

SOCIAL VALUES IN PSYCHOTHERAPY

Briefly stated, there are three implicit or explicit general positions that psychotherapists take in regard to the goals of treatment. Particular therapists may combine these goals in a variety of ways.

The first of these goals is one of conformity or normalcy as the ideal outcome of treatment. From this point of view, the object of treatment is to help the person change so that he is more like other people, particularly in regard to any characteristics that are considered to be detrimental to himself or others. A special case of this orientation is the disease approach, which considers that the patient's difficulty is characterized by certain symptoms. The descriptions of these illnesses are to be found in textbooks. As in medicine, the purpose of treatment is to eliminate the illness as evidenced by the reduction of symptoms.

The second general goal might be called one of subjective happiness. The purpose of treatment is to help the patient reach a state of greater happiness or comfort or pleasure. The emphasis is on internal feelings, resolution of internal conflict, acceptance of self, and so on.

The third value orientation in psychotherapy might be called the socially constructive one. Here the goals of psychotherapy are seen as helping the patient to lead a more constructive life, to contribute to society, to maximize his potential for achievement, to maximize his feeling of affection or contribution to others.

It is a combination of the last two which forms the ethical or value background for the general suggestions regarding psychotherapy which follow. Briefly and more specifically, the following value commitments are made:

1. The therapist understands that his behavior has a definite effect on the patient, in regard to not only the patient's self-understanding, but also his behaviors, his specific goals, and his ethical judgments. The therapist is willing to accept *some* of the responsibility for these changes and to attempt to direct or control them.

2. The therapist seeks to provide the patient with a greater potential for satisfaction. That is, the therapist seeks to direct the patient's behavior to goals that the patient values or that provide him with satisfaction within the limitations expressed below.

3. The therapist seeks to eliminate or to keep the patient from acquiring behaviors or goals he feels are *clearly* detrimental to others in society.

4. The therapist believes that the patient should "carry his own weight" in society, at least to the extent that he makes some contribution to the welfare of others in return for the satisfactions he receives from others.

Applying such values to the particular patient is obviously not a cut-and-dried affair, but will depend on the judgment of the therapist. It should be emphasized again that these are only the values of one person. They do not follow from social learning theory nor are they part of it, but it is necessary to have some explicit set of values before application of any theory to the practice of psychotherapy can be logically considered.

BASIC TERMS IN SOCIAL LEARNING THEORY

It is not possible to present all the theoretical concepts relevant to the problem of psychotherapy. In one way social learning theory is a far more complex personality theory than most and requires the analysis of four variables in order to make a prediction, where many theories require only one or two. In some theories explanation and prediction are based on identifying a strongest trait or internal characteristic of the individual or the conflict between two traits. It is possible in a brief paper such as this to give only a rather disjointed account, hoping that this will provide at least the flavor of a more systematic and comprehensive exposition.

Social learning theory may be briefly characterized as an expectancy learning theory that utilizes an empirical law of effect. In this theory (Rotter, 1954) the basic formula for the prediction of goal-directed behavior is as follows:

$$B.P._{x,\, s_1}\, R_a = f(E_{x,}\, R_{a,\, s_1} + RV_{a,\, s_1})$$

The formula may be read: The potential for behavior *x* to occur in situation 1 in relation to reinforcement *a* is a function of the expectancy of the occurrence of reinforcement *a* following behavior *x* in situation 1, and the value of reinforcement *a* in situation 1. It is assumed that expectancies can be measured along a continuum. Such a formula, however, is extremely limited in application, for it deals only with the potential for a given behavior to occur in relationship to a single specific reinforcement. Practical clinical application requires a more generalized concept of behavior and the formula for these broader concepts is given below:

$$B.P._{(x-n),\, s(1-n),}\, R_{(a-n)} = f(E_{(x-n),\, s(1-n),}\, R_{(a-n)} + R.V._{(a-n),\, s(1-n)})$$

This may be read: The potentiality of the functionally

related behaviors *x* to *n* to occur in the specified situations 1 to *n* in relation to potential reinforcements *a* to *n* is a function of the expectancies of these behaviors leading to these reinforcements in these situations and the values of these reinforcements in these situations. For purposes of simplicity of communication, the three basic terms in this formula have been typically referred to as need potential, freedom of movement, and need value as in the third formula below:

$$N.P. = f(F.M. + N.V.)$$

In this formula the fourth concept, that of the psychological situation, is implicit. Some of the content variables of this theory are empirically determined needs, arrived at by grouping behaviors which have some functional relationship on the basis of their leading to the same or similar reinforcements. The generality or breadth of such concepts depend on one's purpose. For example, at a very general level we may use terms such as need for recognition and status, need for love and affection, need for dependence, need for independence, need for dominance, and need for physical comfort. At a more specific level typical concepts might be need for academic recognition, need for aggression toward authority figures, need for love and affection from same sex peers, and so on. The basis for such groupings derives not from presumed instincts or drives, but is empirically determined and follows from the learning experience of the individuals of a given culture.

The variables referred to above and operations for measurement have been defined and further explicated in previous publications (Rotter, 1954, 1955, 1967a, 1967b).

SOME MAJOR HYPOTHESES AND THEIR IMPLICATIONS

In psychotherapy we are usually concerned with classes of behaviors or more general characteristics. Consequently, this paper will deal primarily with the formula that *need potential* is a function of *freedom of movement* and *need value* for a particular class of situations. A crucial part of this theory for the problem of psychotherapy is that there are specific hypotheses regarding the behavior of an individual with low freedom of movement and high need value for a particular class of satisfactions. When such an individual has low freedom of movement and places high value on some class of reinforcements, he is likely to learn behaviors to avoid the failure or punishments that he anticipates in this area and may make attempts to achieve these goals on an irreal level. The person anticipating punishment or failure may avoid situations physically or by repression, or may attempt to reach the goals through rationalization, fantasy, or symbolic means. Most of the great variety of behaviors commonly regarded as defenses or psychopathological symptoms are here referred to as avoidance or irreal behaviors. Such avoidance and irreal behaviors themselves may frequently start a vicious cycle and lead to both immediate and delayed additional negative reinforcements. Expectancies for punishment may give rise to a number of implicit behaviors, thoughts, or cognitions that can be observed only indirectly. Such implicit behaviors might include awareness of disturbed body states, fixation on the punishment, narrowing the field of attention, rehearsal of obsessive thoughts, which can seriously interfere with constructive behavior or problem solution. In other words, frequently at the bottom of a problem involving either lack of feeling of satisfaction, conflict, anticipation of punishment, irreal behavior, or lack of constructive activity, is a condition of low freedom of movement and high need value.

Low freedom of movement may result from the patient's lack of knowledge or ability to acquire adequate behaviors to reach his goals, or may be a consequence of the nature of the goal itself (such as the desire to have others take all responsibility for one's actions) which frequently results in strong punishments in a specific society. Low freedom of movement may also result from "mistaken" evaluations of the present as a consequence of early experience. For a given person sometimes the behaviors, sometimes "erroneous" expectations, and sometimes the nature of the person's goals may be considered to be the primary source of difficulty.

An important aspect of the problem of low freedom of movement concerns the concept of minimal goal level in social learning theory. In any given situation the possible outcomes of behavior can be ordered from a very high positive reinforcement or goal to a very high negative reinforcement or goal. The theoretical point at which, in this ordering, the outcome changes from one that is positive or reinforcing to negative or punishing is called the minimal goal level. Such a concept can be applied either to a series of goals that are functionally related (for example, all achievement goals) or to any combination of outcomes possible in a given situation or set of situations. An individual may have low freedom of movement although from the viewpoint of others he appears to succeed often because his reinforcements usually are below his own minimal goal level. Such internalized high minimal goals are frequently involved in problems of low freedom of movement. It should be stressed at this point that the goals referred to can be of any kind: moral, ethical, achievement, sexual, affectional, dominating, dependent. In social learning theory any functionally related set of reinforcements toward which the individual moves is considered the basis for assuming a need and for which a need potential, freedom of movement, and need value can be determined.

In order to increase the patient's freedom of movement for goals he values highly, one possible approach is to change the values of the goals themselves. This might be necessary under conditions in which the person has two or more goals of high value but of such nature that the satisfaction of one involves the frustration of the other, as in the case of individuals with strong desires for masculinity and dependency satisfactions in the same situations. Another instance would be one in which the goals of the patient, such as the desire to control and dominate others, lead to conflict with others' needs and eventuates in both immediate and delayed punishment. A third instance of changing the value of goals would involve the lowering of minimal goals when they are unrealistically high, such as in the case of an individual who regards any indication of fear in himself as proof that he is not sufficiently masculine.

To understand how minimal goal levels can be changed, one has to consider how reinforcement values, or the values attached to reinforcement, are acquired, maintained, or changed. In social learning theory, the value of reinforcement in a given situation is hypothesized to be a function of the expectancy that the reinforcement will lead to subsequent reinforcements, and the value of those subsequent reinforcements as in the formula below:

$$R.V._{a,\,s_1} = f(E_{R_a\ R_{(b-n)},\,s_1} + R.V._{(b-n),\,s_1})$$

If a child believes that when he gets an "A" in school it will lead to affection, then the value of the A is dependent upon the value of the affection and the expectancy that the affection will be forthcoming. If he feels that a B will lead to rejection, a similar analysis holds. For most goals each reinforcement is related to several consequent reinforcements rather than one.

The problem in changing minimal goals, then, or in changing the value of any goal or set of goals, is frequently one of changing expectancies for subsequent reinforcement. Adler (1939) has long emphasized the importance of discussing life goals with the patient in order to change immediate goals and behaviors. Many times the values of goals are maintained over a long period of time with the expectancy for subsequent reward relatively stable because the relationships have not been verbalized and the subject is not aware of them. In many instances delayed negative reinforcement follows from achieving an earlier reward but the subject fails to relate these to the prior goal. For example, a woman seeking to control her husband fails to recognize that the consequences of her behavior and her successful attempts at control, although bringing immediate gratification, also lead to subsequent negative reinforcements because of the hostility or rejection on the part of the husband. In other words, the value of goals can be changed sometimes by examining the early rewards with which they were associated but which may no longer be operating, and also by analysis of present and future consequences which the person has never associated directly with the goal.

One implication of such an analysis is that insight into the acquisition of particular goals may be helpful in changing their values if the subject sees that expectancies for subsequent reinforcements have changed since the time of acquisition or were mistaken in the first place. Such a conception is not different from any other insight-type of therapy. However, a further implication is that it may be of equal importance to analyze also the consequences of present behaviors and goals which are frequently delayed but nevertheless result from the behaviors the individual uses or reinforcements he seeks. It is frequently important not only to discover why it is, for example, that one seeks to demonstrate superiority over members of the opposite sex in terms of early experience, but also important to discover what are the present and long-term consequences of such goals and of the behaviors used to achieve them.

These comments deal with one method of changing freedom of movement or increasing freedom of movement by lowering minimal goals, or having the individual place greater value on alternative goals. There are other ways in which freedom of movement can be increased, and presumably as a result both personal feelings of satisfaction and more constructive behavior will be increased. As Mowrer (1948) has pointed out in his discussion of the neurotic paradox, sometimes expectancy of punishment remains high because the individual fails to learn that what he fears is no longer realistic, since he avoids the situation in which he can learn anything to the contrary. If his experience with competitive scholastic activity is such that it was negatively reinforcing as a child, he may never learn that he is capable of reaching satisfying goals in this area because he avoids involvement or competitive striving in situations involving academic or scholastic achievement. In this instance freedom of movement may be increased, sometimes by the therapist's own direct reinforcements, and by interpretation of how such an attitude came about and why it is no longer appropriate to present life situations. The emphasis here is on changing the expectancies directly and it may be possible not only to do this by the therapist's behavior and by interpretation but also by control, manipulation, or use of other environmental influences. The studies on verbal conditioning (Krasner, 1958) suggest how important the role of the therapist may be as a direct reinforcer of behavior. Changes in the attitudes and behaviors of teachers, parents, spouses, supervisors, may achieve the same effect as face-to-face therapy and in fact do so more effectively because they are not part of the temporary and artificial situation of the therapy room.

In some instances, although the patient's goals are realistic enough and appropriate enough for his social group and his expectancies are based accurately on present situations, the problem is one of having learned inadequate pathways to achieve these goals or perhaps of not having learned more effective methods of reaching his goals. Here the problem can be regarded as more pedagogical. The search for alternative ways of reaching goals must frequently be taught to the patient as a general technique of dealing with his problems and as a method of finding specific ways of achieving more satisfaction in current life situations.[1] The assumption that once the patient is free from some kind of internal disorganization, conflict, repression, he will automatically be able to find adequate ways to reach his goals, does not appear useful to this writer. It is often precisely because the patient does not have alternate pathways that he frequently holds on to his less effective behavior in spite of insight into his situation. Frequently the therapist then labels his failure to progress as due to "intellectual" but not "emotional" insight. Rather, the patient needs to know what the alternate pathways are and needs to have the experience of trying them out and finding them successful before he is willing to give up ineffective behaviors.

Although the warmth, understanding, interest, and acceptance of the therapist are important in order to have the patient verbalize his problems and express himself freely, they also result in the therapist's becoming an important source of reinforcement for the patient in his present life circumstances. It should be noted that if the therapist is a powerful reinforcer for the patient, whether he is aware of it or not, then the therapist should know a great deal about the life circumstances and the cultural milieu in which the patient lives. Only with such knowledge can he use his position as a reinforcer efficiently. To obtain this knowledge he must spend much time discussing these life situations. His independent knowledge of subcultures is an important aspect of his skill as a therapist.

Another pedagogical problem is frequently one of helping patients differentiate the nature of varied social situations. Low freedom of movement may not result so much from the use of ineffective behaviors in general as from the use of behaviors inappropriate for a given situation.

1. It can be seen here as in other discussions of implications that the value commitments described earlier are an implicit filter between theory and practice.

The kind of behavior that may be admired and respected and reinforced in a situation calling for efficiency and the solution of a specific task (for example, a combat team or a committee seeking to make some change in the community) may lead to rejection at a party or in a bedroom. Sometimes because of the distortions of parents or the limited or protective environment of childhood, a person fails to learn or to make these discriminations among social situations, which are necessary for obtaining satisfactions. When placed in these circumstances in later life he falls back on the techniques he has learned in other situations, which may in fact be quite inappropriate. Analysis of what actually transpires in social situations, how other people feel and think, what are the purposes for which particular interactions take place in a variety of life situations, may help the patient make these discriminations he has failed to make in the past. The low freedom of movement one may have in regard to a particular need, such as the desire to have others take care of one, may be a result of attempts to satisfy such needs at inappropriate times. If the individual seeks to satisfy his needs by recognizing that social situations are varied, that the needs of others change from situation to situation, and that the potential reinforcements in some conditions can be seriously limited, he may be far better able to deal satisfactorily with life problems.

This notion might give the impression of advocating the training of the patient to be a kind of chameleon who changes his personality for every situation – to be, in other words, a conformist or opportunist. This is not at all the intent. The therapeutic goal here is for the patient to recognize the real differences that exist in the purposes of people in different situations and the purposes these situations are intended to serve. For example, it is important for some patients to discover that although competitive behavior may be admired and rewarded in academic and job conditions, it is neither admired nor rewarded in many social situations. Behavior appropriate for one situation is not appropriate for another, although one may maintain the same set of consistent goals in both. Although one may always choose to value achievement in any situation, there are some circumstances in which rewards for competitive achievement are not only not possible, but attempts to gain such satisfactions are likely to lead to frustration of the patient's other goals. What the patient may wish to do in these different circumstances is his problem to work out, but the therapist can help him realize that there are differences and discover what these differences actually are. *It is usually believed that what the patient lacks most is insight into himself, but it is likely that in general what characterizes patients even more consistently is lack of insight into the reactions and motives of others.*

Another implication of social learning theory deserves brief mention. Consistent research in human learning indicates that when the subject is set to attend to the relevant aspects of a complex problem, his problem solving is much more efficient (Johnson, 1955). It appears that there is an analogue to therapy here. Frequently much time is lost in treatment because the patient is attending to the wrong (less crucial) aspects of the situation. Uncovering unconscious repressions, dreaming more interesting dreams, achieving a less inhibited freedom of expression, which were all intended as a *means* of psychotherapy, may become, for many, the *goals*. One implication of this is that therapy requires frequent and successive structuring. The therapist's as well as the patient's role in therapy needs to be discussed many times so that the patient is fully aware of why he is doing what he is doing in therapy, what his ultimate purpose is, and that there may be alternative ways of achieving the same ends. It is important that the patient does not get fixated on the means rather than the goals of psychotherapy. Too often ex-patients appear to leave therapy with behavior and characteristics learned to please the psychotherapist, and, their behavior continues to lead to a baffling kind of failure to obtain satisfactions from the significant people in their own life circumstances.

Finally, it is necessary to describe a last concept, that of broad generalized expectancies, which can be likened to the idea of higher level learning skills. These are very broad expectancies for behavior-reinforcement sequences that cut across need areas. Such expectancies are partial determinants of specific behaviors in many specific situations. Examples of some of these, of particular significance to psychotherapy, are: (1) the now popular notion of internal versus external control, or the belief that reinforcement is contingent upon one's own behavior or characteristics versus the notion that reinforcement is contingent upon chance, fate, or powerful others; (2) the expectancy that people cannot be believed or trusted to fulfill promises, which will affect the learning of delay of gratification and seriously affect the efficiency of almost any type of psychotherapy; (3) the expectancy that frustration can be overcome by seeking alternative ways of achieving goals; (4) an expectancy that reinforcement will follow from a better understanding of other people's motives; (5) an expectancy that directing attention to other people in a difficult situation will suppress distressing behaviors; and (6) a belief that many negative reinforcements can be avoided by better discrimination of situations previously regarded as the same. Clearly the learning of social skills may greatly enhance the patient's potential to deal with difficult situations on their own without requiring the intervention of a therapist.

It can be seen from these illustrations of the implications of social learning theory for the practice of psychotherapy that the therapist's behavior must depend on the nature of the problem, the nature of the resources open to him outside therapy as well as within therapy, and the kind of patient with whom he is dealing. For example, when the problem is one of reducing the patient's need for dependency and increasing the value he places on independence, the therapist's behavior would have to be considerably different from that in which the problem of the patient is one of seeking dominance satisfactions to the exclusion of almost all other needs. Similarly, a patient who seeks sympathy as an indication of social support for retreating from life's problems needs to be reacted to differently from one who is oppressed by his inability to meet successfully an unrealistic burden of responsibilities he has already accepted.

Just as highly dependent people will reject nondirective therapy, highly independent ones may reject direct reinforcement techniques. The broader needs of the patient may not be crucial in curing many cases of snake phobia, but they are in selecting a therapist and a method of treatment for a generally depressed young man who finds society a fraud, achievement meaningless, and feels that nothing is worth striving for.

It seems characteristic of this view that rather than leading to implications for a specific technique of therapist behavior, the theory itself implies that the therapist must exercise great flexibility in adjusting his own behavior to the specific needs of the patient. In fact, considering the limitations of flexibility of every therapist, there should be much more concern with matching patients and therapists and consideration of changing therapist or techniques early in therapy. Of course such a therapeutic attitude emphasizes the importance of understanding the basis for the patient's behavior as early as possible.

We have suggested five sets of content variables to provide such generalized descriptions from which gradients of generalization can be predicted: (1) behaviors leading to the same or similar reinforcements or need potentials; (2) expectancies for gratification for functionally related sets of reinforcements, or freedom of movement; (3) preference value of a group of reinforcements, or need values; (4) classes of situations functionally related on the basis of the predominant satisfaction usually obtained in them; and (5) broad generalized expectancies that cut across need areas and are related to a wide variety of behaviors and situations and have to deal with expectancies of how and under what conditions reinforcements are likely to occur. We have demonstrated in a great variety of studies that all of these variables are capable of reliable measurement.

In summary, in this view no mysterious process special to psychotherapy is assumed, nor does every therapist have to discover the same special set of ideal behaviors that will maximally facilitate this mysterious process. Rather, it is assumed that psychotherapy is a social interaction that follows the same laws and principles as other social interactions, and from which many different effects can be obtained by a variety of different conditions. It is also possible that the same effects may be obtained by a variety of different methods. The effectiveness of the changes that take place and the efficiency in arriving at them are the critieria for adequacy of method rather than for conformity to any doctrine.

IMPLICATIONS OF SOME RESEARCH FINDINGS

Thus far this paper discusses only some general implications of very broadly stated hypotheses regarding the nature of goal-directed behavior. One of the advantages of social learning theory is that it deals with constructs amenable to measurement and with hypotheses amendable to test. Under limited laboratory conditions exercising as much control as possible, a large number of studies testing some of the broader and some of the more specific hypotheses of the theory have been investigated. Many of these experiments deal with quite general propositions. A few of the studies, however, appear to have somewhat more direct analogical relationship to the type of social interaction involved in psychotherapy and to some of the specific problems encountered with particular kinds of patients. Primarily for purposes of illustration, it seems desirable to present briefly some of these and the implications they may have for more specific problems of psychotherapeutic practice.

In the course of psychotherapy the patient's own efforts need to be rewarded so that he maintains both involvement and expectation of success in this sometimes painful and slow process. If the patient experiences some positive change in himself, this may frequently serve as a starting point for a benign cycle. Relevant to this are studies by Good (1952), Castaneda (1952), and Lasko (1952). In these studies the effects of success and failure on the expectancy for future success were studied as a function of amount of experience within a particular task. All three of these experiments demonstrate that expectancies built up on the basis of many previous trials will change least with new experience. On the other hand, expectancies based on only one or two events may change dramatically with new experience. One inference from these studies for the practice of psychotherapy is the suggestion that early in therapy the therapist might well deal with more recent and less "significant" problems which may be most amenable to change. This may have the effect of encouraging the patient and reducing his resistance to change, which is usually based on his fear that without his defenses he would have no alternate ways of dealing with his problems.

Efran and Marcia (1967) conducted a "pseudo" desensitization study of snake and spider phobias. They told subjects that their fears were based on unconscious learning. In order to eliminate them, subliminal stimuli had to be presented to the subject on a screen and the fear response had to be suppressed by an unpleasant stimulus while the subject was unconsciously reacting to the stimulus. Of course, nothing was presented on the screen, and following a signal occasional shocks were given. Fake glavanic skin response improvement graphs were shown to subjects at the end of each session. Using less time than previous desensitization studies, their results compare favorably in cure and improvement measures.

What appears to have happened here is that the procedure succeeded in changing the patient's expectancies about whether or not he could be cured. Looking at fake improvement curves under convincing conditions, the subjects decided they were sufficiently cured to allow them to pick up or touch the spiders or snakes. Such an expectancy for cure may well be the basis for the start of a benign cycle allowing the patient to try, one after another, behaviors that previously have been strongly avoided. Whether conducted with relaxation or other behavior modification techniques, such procedures, used as part of a more extensive psychotherapy, may serve to start a benign cycle.

A study of Rychlak (1958) pertains to the stability of freedom of movement as a function of the number of different kinds of experiences on which it is based. Varying the number of different tasks but controlling the number and kind of reinforcements. Rychlak demonstrated that freedom of movement or generalized expectancies are more stable the greater the number of different but related kinds of events the expectancies were built upon. As an analogy, a male who has had several bad experiences with the same female would have his expectancies more likely changed after a new positive experience with another female than if he had had the same number of experiences of the same kind but with several different females. Like the studies of Good, Castaneda, and Lasko, Rychlak's experiment suggests another condition which may help identify the attitudes that can change most readily.

Phares (1964) and Schwarz (1966) have demonstrated that massed trials of success and failure experiences lead to quick changes in verbalized expectancies. Delay between trials, however, leads to a return to earlier levels of expectancy, presumably as previous experience is rehearsed by the subject during delay periods. There is a suggestion here that to achieve more stable changes, spaced therapeutic interviews or training sessions would be more efficient for most cases.

The great quantity of work on verbal conditioning has shown both how a therapist may serve as a reinforcer unwittingly and what a powerful potential the therapist has to change behavior by direct reinforcement. A study by Shaffer (1957) suggests in addition that various therapists would serve differentially as reinforcers for subjects who have identifiably different learning histories. Shaffer investigated one implication of social learning theory having to do with the potential reinforcement value of the therapist. From questionnaires given to both adjusted and maladjusted college students he determined the kind and amount of parental reinforcement during childhood. From these questionnaires he was able to predict to some extent the age and sex preferences for a therapist. Specifically, he found that female subjects who prefer a female therapist tend to have seen their mothers as more reinforcing than had females who prefer a male therapist. Males almost universally state preferences for male therapists, but those males who saw both parents as positively reinforcing tend to prefer an older therapist to a younger one. This study suggests that the utilization of such preferences significantly related to early learning experiences, by matching the patient to the therapist, may considerably increase the efficiency of psychotherapy.

Crandall, Good, and Crandall (1964) have also studied the reinforcement effects of adults on children and found that children react to no reinforcement as either positive or negative depending on the previous history of reinforcement with these same adults in the same situation. These reactions may also be predicted from generalized expectancies for positive and negative reinforcement based on earlier childhood experiences.

A therapy investigation by Strickland and Crowne (1963) had similar implications for matching patients and techniques. They found that patients with a high need for social approval dropped out of insight-type therapy prematurely. Possibly they did so because of the greater conflict engendered by the pressure to reveal their psychopathology. It is apparent that traditional insight therapy approaches would have to be modified with such patients, or other techniques used.

Two other lines of research have important implications for the practice of psychotherapy. One of these deals with the specificity of behavior in various situations. Although recognizing the generality of some behaviors, one characteristic of social learning theory is the emphasis on interaction of the individual and his meaningful environment or life space (Rotter, 1955, 1960). Like the psychology of Lewin (1951) and of Brunswik (1947), emphasis is not on abstracted traits as the basic component of personality, but rather on potentials of given classes of responses in given classes of situations.

It would be impossible here to review the many studies indicating that there are strong and significant interactions between social situations and personal characteristics. A single example from the literature on internal versus external control will have to serve to illustrate the many implications these studies have for psychotherapy practice. On separate studies, an experimenter bias study by Gore (1962) and a verbal conditioning study by Strickland (1962), it was found that internals, if they are aware of subtle attempts to influence them, are much more resistant to the influence than externals. However, if overt attempts at influence are made, internals like externals will respond positively. In general these studies simply produce additional data to support the idea that therapist, method, and patient have to be carefully matched in order to maximize the beneficial results from psychotherapy.

Another line of related research has to do with the generalization of changes in expectancies from one task to another. Studies by Crandall (1955), Jessor (1954), and Chance (1959) have all shown that a gradient of generalization is present which can be predicted on the basis of a common sense analysis of similarity along dimensions of psychological needs, goals, or reinforcements. In these studies expectancies for reinforcement were sampled in more than one situation or task, changes in expectancies in one task were then effected by experimental manipulations, and changes in the other task or tasks were measured.

The implication from both these kinds of studies is that in many instances the therapist is counting on *more* generalization of changes in behavior from the therapist in the therapeutic situation to other people in other situations than is warranted by the experimental evidence. It follows that if the therapist wishes to change attitudes and behaviors in situations outside of therapy most efficiently, then he would need to deal with these other situations, at least on a verbal basis, as much as possible in therapy. The working through and analysis of the relationship with the therapist has its value. However, these studies suggest that such behavior on the part of the therapist has its limitations in effecting changes in life situations outside of therapy or with individuals other than the therapist. When one considers how different the therapist's behavior toward the patient is from other people's and the therapeutic situation is from other life situations, this limitation takes on special significance.

Perhaps the most significant research relating to psychotherapy is the work on generalized expectancies that refers to how and under what conditions reinforcements may be expected. Investigation of generalized expectancies for internal-external control, looking for alternatives, delay of gratification, and interpersonal trust have clear implications for psychotherapy procedures.

The extensive work in internal-external control has

been reviewed by Rotter (1966) and by Lefcourt (1966). It is clear that such broad generalized expectancies exist and that patients who feel that their own behavior and characteristics have little or no influence on what happens to them can learn only inefficiently from therapy. It seems evident that if significant improvement is to take place, the patient must become more internal as therapy progresses. Gillis and Jessor (1961) have shown such changes in improved versus unimproved delinquent therapy patients. In some cases this attitude itself must be dealt with before working on other more specific problems. One suggested technique is to have the patient, early in therapy, practice different ways of behaving in some specific situation, not merely to indicate to him that he can respond a different way, but also to show him that his behavior can, in fact, change the behavior of others toward him.

Delay of reinforcement is another more specific area in which there are investigations completed. The work of Mahrer (1956) and Mischel (1958, 1961a, 1961b) indicates that the preference for immediate over delayed gratification is directly related to the degree of expectation that delayed rewards will actually occur. In these experiments children are offered the choice of obtaining a pre-established reward of lesser value (candy or a toy) immediately, or waiting a week or more for one of clearly greater value. To some extent such tendencies to delay or not to delay gratification are attached to specific social agents and to some extent they are generalized. Since the problem of therapy in many cases may be conceived of as one in which the patient must learn to give up some immediate gratification for delayed benefits, these studies have some possible implications for psychotherapy. One such implication is that the therapist himself is a social agent who must be careful not to make promises or unconsciously suggest to the patient that he is capable of "delivering the goods" in an effort to sell psychotherapy to the patient or encourage him to continue. Once he becomes an agent who does not keep his promises, his implicit or explicit attempts to get the patient to give up immediate gratifications for future benefits are not likely to be effective. Another inference from these studies is that in some cases the patient's generalization from specific figures in his past to others has led him to be overly distrustful, or to have low expectancies for reinforcements that are presumably likely to occur if he gives up his present defenses. Consequently, with such patients great emphasis must be placed on this overgeneralization and its negative consequences.

Recent work (Rotter, 1966) has supported the construct validity of a generalized expectancy for interpersonal trust defined as belief in the truthfulness of communications from others. Preliminary analysis of a study with Getter strongly suggests that attitudes of distrust impair therapeutic relationship and outcome.

Two investigations relate to the problem of teaching patients a general skill of looking for alternative solutions in problem situations. In one such study, Schroder and Rotter (1952) trained subjects on different sequences of simple concept formation problems by varying the number of *times* they were forced to find a new type of solution but keeping constant the number and type of solutions involved. They were able to demonstrate that the behavior of looking for alternatives could be rather easily learned and generalized to new problems, resulting in what is typically called flexible or nonrigid behavior. In a more direct study of therapy, Morton (1955) trained clients in a counseling center to look for alternative solutions in TAT stories they had told. Using this procedure as the primary basis for very brief psychotherapy, he was able to demonstrate a significant improvement in adjustment in comparison to matched control cases.

The generalized expectancies discussed above are only some of the important variables that describe how a person learns from experience. To find others is a task of considerable importance so that the therapist can make maximum use of what the subject has already learned in planning a therapeutic program. It is on the learning of such skills and their application to present and future life problems that the social learning therapist places reliance, rather than on the automatic generalization of changes in attitude toward the therapist.

SUMMARY OF IMPLICATIONS FOR THERAPEUTIC PRACTICE

The preceding discussion provides only a sketchy picture of the possible implications of social learning theory for psychotherapy. To summarize these comments it seems useful to point up some of the major differences between social learning theory and other points of view in the kinds of techniques the therapist might use were he to accept the same set of value commitments described earlier. It should be understood that these are frequently differences of degree, rather than of kind, or differences in relative emphasis.

1. The problem of psychotherapy is seen as a learning situation in which the function of the therapist is to help the patient accomplish planned changes in his observable behavior and thinking. Since patients come into therapy with many different motives, different values placed upon particular kinds of reinforcements, different expectancies for possible sources of gratification, different limits on skill, and different higher level learning skills, conditions for optimal learning will likewise vary considerably from patient to patient. One characteristic of therapy derived from a social learning theory point of view is that the technique must be suited to the patient. Flexibility, experimentation, marked variations in method from patient to patient might be considered characteristic of this approach. Consequently, there is no special technique which can be applied to all cases, and differences in therapists must eventually be systematically related to patient differences to obtain maximally efficient results.

2. The patient's difficulties are frequently seen from a problem solving point of view. As a result, there tends to be a greater emphasis on the development of higher level problem solving skills, such as those of looking for alternative ways of reaching goals, thinking through the consequences of behavior, looking for differences or discriminations in life situations, turning attention in social situations to the needs and attitudes of others, and recognizing that one can exercise some control over one's fate by one's own efforts.

3. In most cases the therapist perceives his role partly as guiding a learning process in which there are not only inadequate behaviors and attitudes to be weakened, but more satisfying and constructive alternatives to be learned. Consequently, the tendency is for a more active role in interpretation, suggestion, and direct reinforcement for the therapist than would be typical of traditional analytic or Rogerian therapy. In this regard there is more awareness on the part of the therapist of his role as a direct reinforcer of behavior and presumably a more deliberate use of such direct reinforcement. While the more specific behavior modification (Ullmann and Krasner, 1965) techniques are happily included in this approach, for many kinds of problems they would be used as *part* of a more comprehensive attack on the patient's problems. The therapist, however, does not consider himself merely a mechanical verbal conditioner, but rather a person whose special reinforcement value for the particular patient can be used to help the patient try out new behaviors and ways of thinking. The patient ultimately determines for himself the value of new conceptualizations and alternate ways of behaving in his experiences outside of therapy.

4. In changing unrealistic expectancies it is important to understand how particular behaviors and expectancies arose and how past experience has been misapplied or overgeneralized to present situations. Similarly, when there are conflicting goals in a situation, it is important to

know how they arose and what they are. However, such insights are considered helpful but not a necessary part of change. The use of insight as a technique varies with the patient, depending on the patient's own need and ability to use rational explanations of his current problems. Another kind of insight is of equal importance and possibly tends to differentiate a social learning approach from other methods to a greater extent: that is, insight into the long-term consequences of particular behaviors and of the values placed on particular goals. This includes an understanding not only of what consequences of behavior there are in present life situations, but also of probable consequences of current modes of behavior for the future. An individual may mold his behavior for many years in the expectancy of achieving some positive gratification (for example, a college degree), which, in fact, he has never received. He may likewise mold his behavior considerably in expectation of a negative reinforcement (for example, being left alone in one's old age), which he has not directly experienced.

5. Related to this last point is a concern for the expectations, feelings, motives, or needs of others. Long-term psychotherapy, as Otto Rank has observed, frequently encourages a patient to remain or sink deeper into his egocentric predicament through continuous emphasis on the patient's subjective reactions, past and present. However, many of the patient's problems arise from frustrations that are a result of misinterpretation of the behavior, reactions, and motives of others. From a social learning point of view, the patient's problem frequently requires considerable emphasis and discussion focused on understanding the behavior and motives of others, both past and present. In this regard learning through observation, modeling, or imitation as Bandura and Walters (1963) have pointed out, can be a source of change in expectancies for behavior reinforcement se-

quences. The use of movies, examples, books, and special groups have probably not been sufficiently exploited in psychotherapy.

6. In place of the belief that experience changes people but little once they pass infancy and that only therapy can make major changes, a major implication of social learning theory is that new experiences or different kinds of experience in life situations can be far more effective in many cases than those new experiences that occur only in the special therapy situation. While it is true that an analysis of the patient's interaction with the therapist can be an important source of learning, it is unsafe to overemphasize this as the main vehicle of treatment. Many times improvements seen by the therapist are improvements or changes that take place in relationship to the therapist or in the therapy situation, but the patient discriminates this situation from others and generalizes little to other life situations.

It is in the life situation, rather than in the psychotherapy room, that the important insights and new experiences occur. There are two implications of this view. One implication is that there should be considerable stress in treatment discussions of what is happening in the patient's present life circumstances. Questions such as What are the motives of others? What are the motives of the patient? How does the situation differ from other situations past and present? and How may the patient deal with the same situation in a way that is more satisfying and constructive? need to be discussed in detail.

The second implication is that wherever it is possible and judicious to control the patient's experience outside of therapy by the use of what is usually called environmental manipulation, such opportunities should be used maximally. Although the principal of environmental manipulation has long been accepted in the treatment of children, it is sometimes felt that this is only because the child lacks the ability to deal with his problems on a verbal or conceptual level. Environmental therapy is frequently seen only as second-best treatment. However, no such hierarchy of importance seems logical. Changes in the behavior of parents, teachers, wives, husbands, and other members of a family may frequently result in far greater changes in the patient than his direct experience with the therapist. The current trend toward behavior modification of parents fits in very well with this emphasis.

Likewise, the opportunity for the patient to make environmental changes himself, such as changes in jobs, living circumstances, and social groups, should not be overlooked or discarded in favor of a belief that all his problems lie inside himself rather than in his interactions with the meaningful environment.

Hospitalizing a patient, whether psychotic or not, thereby removing him from a destructive environment to which he must eventually return, will reinforce his avoidance symptoms. Treating him in the absence of the situations which produced his symptoms does not make much sense. It makes much better sense to keep him in his natural environment whenever possible, but to make concerted efforts to make it a more satisfying one by changing attitudes of relatives, bosses, encouraging job changes, utilizing public agencies for relief, while at the same time directly treating the patient on an outpatient basis. Similar comments can be made about the problems of delinquency.

7. At the most general level, the implications of social learning theory are that psychotherapy should be viewed as a social interaction. The therapist helps the patient achieve a more satisfying and constructive interrelationship with his social environment. The laws and principles that govern behavior in other interpersonal learning situations apply as well to the therapy situation. There is no process special to psychotherapy and there is no need, even if it were possible, for the therapist to be a shadowy figure or "catalyst." Rather, he is an active partner who

utilizes learning principles, applied to a particular individual in a particular set of circumstances, to help that person achieve a better way of dealing with the problems of life.

REFERENCES

ADLER, A. *Social interest: a challenge to mankind.* New York: Harper & Row, 1939.

BANDURA, A., and WALTERS, R. H. *Social learning and personality development.* New York: Holt, Rinehart and Winston, 1963.

BRUNSWIK, E. *Systematic and representative design of psychological experiments.* Berkeley: University of California Press, 1947.

CASTANEDA, A. A systematic investigation of the concept expectancy as conceived within Rotter's social learning theory of personality. Unpublished doctoral dissertation, Ohio State University, 1952.

CHANCE, JUNE E. Generalization of expectancies among functionally related behaviors. *Journal of Personality,* 1959, *27,* 228–38.

CRANDALL, V. An investigation of the specificity of reinforcement of induced frustration. *Journal of Social Psychology,* 1955, *41,* 311–18.

CRANDALL, VIRGINIA C., GOOD, SUZANNE, and CRANDALL, V. J. Reinforcement effects of adult reactions and nonreactions on children's achievement expectations; a replication study. *Child Development,* 1964, *35,* 485–97.

DOLLARD, J., and MILLER, N. E. *Personality and psychotherapy.* New York: McGraw-Hill, 1950.

EFRAN, J. S., and MARCIA, J. E. Treatment of fears by expectancy manipulation: An expectancy investigation. *Proceedings, 75th Annual Convention, A.P.A.,* 1967, 239.

GILLIS, J., and JESSOR, R. The effects of psychotherapy on internal-external control. Unpublished manuscript, 1961.

GOOD, R. A. The potentiality for changes of an expectancy as a function of the amount of experience. Unpublished doctoral dissertation, Ohio State University, 1952.

GORE, PEARL MAYO. Individual differences in the prediction of subject compliance to experimental bias. Unpublished doctoral dissertation, Ohio State University, 1962.

JESSOR, R. The generalization of expectancies. *Journal of Abnormal and Social Psychology,* 1954, *49,* 196–200.

JOHNSON, D. M. *The psychology of thought and judgment.* New York: Harper & Row, 1955.

KELLY, G. A. *The psychology of personal constructs,* Vols. 1 and 2. New York: W. W. Norton, 1955.

KRASNER, L. Studies of the conditioning of verbal behavior. *Psychological Bulletin,* 1958, *55,* 148–70.

LASKO, A. A. The development of expectancies under conditions of patterning and differential reinforcement. Unpublished doctoral dissertation, Ohio State University, 1952.

LEFCOURT, H. M. Internal vs. external control of reinforcement: A review. *Psychological Bulletin,* 1966, *65,* 206–20.

LEWIN, K. The nature of field theory. In M. H. Marx (Ed.), *Psychological theory.* New York: Macmillan, 1951.

MAHRER, A. R. The role of expectancy in delayed reinforcement. *Journal of Experimental Psychology,* 1956, *52,* 101–5.

MISCHEL, W. Preference for delayed reinforcement: An experimental study of a cultural observation. *Journal of Abnormal and Social Psychology,* 1958, *56,* 55–61.

MISCHEL, W. Preference for delayed reinforcement and social responsibilility. *Journal of Abnormal and Social Psychology,* 1961, *62,* 1–7.

MISCHEL, W. Father absence and delay of gratification: Cross cultural comparisons. *Journal of Abnormal and Social Psychology,* 1961, *63,* 116–24.

MORTON, R. B. An experiment in brief psychotherapy. *Psychological Monographs,* 1955, *69,* (Whole No. 1).

MOWRER, O. H. Learning theory and the neurotic paradox. *American Journal of Orthopsychiatry,* 1948, *18,* 571–610.

PHARES, E. J. Delay as a variable in expectancy changes. *Journal of Psychology,* 1964, *57,* 391–402.

ROGERS, C. R. *Client centered therapy, its current practice, implications and theory.* Boston: Houghton Mifflin, 1951.

ROTTER, J. B. *Social learning and clinical psychology.* Englewood Cliffs: Prentice-Hall, 1954.

ROTTER, J. B. The role of the psychological situation in determining the direction of human behavior. In M. R. Jones (Ed.),

Nebraska symposium on motivation. Lincoln: University of Nebraska Press, 1955.

ROTTER, J. B. Psychotherapy. In P. R. Farnsworth (Ed.) *Annual Review of Psychology,* Vol. II. Palo Alto, Calif.: Annual Reviews, Inc., 1960.

ROTTER, J. B. Generalized expectancies for internal versus external control of reinforcement. *Psychological Monographs,* 1966, *80,* No. 1 (Whole No. 609).

ROTTER, J. B. Beliefs, attitudes and behavior: A social learning analysis. In R. Jessor and S. Feshbach (Eds.), *Cognition, personality and clinical psychology.* San Francisco: Jossey-Bass, 1967a.

ROTTER, J. B. A new scale for the measurement of interpersonal trust. *Journal of Personality,* 1967b, *35,* 651-65.

RYCHLAK, J. F. Task influence and the stability of generalized expectancies. *Journal of Experimental Psychology,* 1958, *55,* 459-62.

SCHRODER, H. M., and ROTTER, J. B. Rigidity as learned behavior. *Journal of Experimental Psychology,* 1952, *44,* 141-50.

SCHWARZ, J. C. Influences upon expectancy during delay. *Journal of Experimental Research in Personality,* 1966, *1,* 211-20.

SHAFFER, J. A. Parental reinforcement, parental dominance and therapist preference. Unpublished doctoral dissertation, Ohio State University, 1957.

STRICKLAND, BONNIE R. The relationships of awareness to verbal conditioning and extinction. Unpublished doctoral dissertation, Ohio State University, 1962.

STRICKLAND, BONNIE R., and CROWNE, D. P. Need for approval and the premature termination of psychotherapy. *Journal of Consulting Psychology,* 1963, *27,* 95-101.

ULLMAN, L. P. AND KRASNER, L. *Case studies in behavior modification.* New York: Holt, Rinehart and Winston, 1965.

WOLPE, J. *Psychotherapy by reciprocal inhibition.* Stanford: Stanford University Press, 1958.

Comment

O. IVAR LOVAAS

Dr. Rotter is a pioneer in the application of learning theory principles for the treatment of clinical problems. Like many of you, I read his work while still a student, and welcomed the alternatives he offered to psychoanalytic theory. His work has had considerable impact on the clinical profession, particularly on those who have to deal with patients on a daily and more concretely behavioral basis, such as nursing personnel and educators. There are some very promising applications today, of the kinds of problems Dr. Rotter was concerned with a long time ago; for example, in the role of modeling as a therapeutic adjunct.

I do not have the time here, nor do I think it is appropriate, to attempt a detailed discussion of his research and conceptualizations. Instead, I shall limit myself to making a comment of a very general nature regarding his approach. This comment will consist of presenting a contrast, rather than discussing the many similarities between his work and that work which we see reported in much behavior therapy today. Where we do part company, and I think this is a significant departure, in the extent to which one emphasizes theoretical, as compared to more inductive, experimental-analytic approaches to the solution of psychopathology. It seems to me that Dr. Rotter is heavily concerned with relating learning models to his clinical experience, both to show the feasibility of using learning models to account for clinical phenomena, and to formulate new hypotheses about behavior, which then can be tested in subsequent experiments, usually requiring statistical tests of significance on his data. This approach is, I think, rather similar to the one employed by Miller and Dollard in their work, although the translation of psychoanalytic principles is less apparent. Dr. Rotter's approach to the problem contrasts sharply with the manner in which many of us are proceeding today from the learning model, and I think the difference is a rather substantial one. Recent work in this area has been more concerned with quite literal application of learning principles to the large classes of psychopathology that the patient brings with him to the clinic. We are also, I believe, keeping our research much closer to the actual behavior of the patient, and showing less concern with researching the theoretical implications of the patient's behavior. The emphasis is on control of the dependent variables, rather than elaborations of intervening ones. The problem in clinical practice has always been that it is difficult to formulate a concise treatment plan based on psychoanalytic constructs, and it is equally difficult to be empirically explicit after one has translated traditional clinical concerns into a learning theory framework. Perhaps we are also moving beyond the learning model, and we are open to relationships in our data that may not be explicable in what we now understand as learning principles. I am not at all certain that much of what we are doing with our patients is reduceable to learning principles, and it may be a fallacy to assume that they are. The emphasis, then, in much of current work, is on methodological rather than theoretical problems. I think this is a logical extension of the application of research and behavior theory Dr. Rotter helped to start.

8

Responses of a Nonclinician to Stimuli Provided by Behavioral Therapists

JUDSON S. BROWN

When Dr. Levis first asked me to participate in this symposium, I demurred on the ground that I was not a clinician and that psychotherapy was not an area in which I could clain even a scintilla of expertise. He insisted, however, that as a department chairman I was in fact functioning as an "allied professional" and that my own research on conflict, anxiety, and masochism indicated that I was more of a clinician than I realized. This unveiling of the clinical bent of my unconscious moved me still closer to acquiescence. Finally, Dr. Levis suggested that I could serve the useful function, as he put it, of "keeping the clinicians honest." That did it! How could any man of strong convictions decline an invitation to herd others along his own "straight" paths, regardless of how narrow they might be?

Nevertheless, in my role as the nominally toughminded watchdog of experimental psychology I have found little in this symposium at which to growl. None of the participating behavior therapists seems to require much policing and, indeed, several appear capable of giving the rest of us some pointers in scientific immaculacy. Their lack of concern with the acquisition of knowledge "for its own sweet sake" may raise the hackles of a few purists, but their success in eliminating unwanted actions and inculcating acceptable new ones can surely be credited to their account. I am reminded in this context of John B. Watson's claim, for which he was roundly castigated, that by appropriate applications of the principles of learning he could create a teacher, laborer, philosopher, musician, or whatever, from any normal child. Prescient though Watson was, were he alive today he would probably rub his eyes in disbelief at the sight of a contemporary behavior therapist transforming an autistic, apathetic, scarcely human vegetable into a nearly normal, eating, talking person. Those of us who have long believed in the efficacy of experience and the vast power of the law of effect but have done nothing about it draw great comfort from such dramatic results and applaud the courage of the action-oriented clinicians who have produced them.

From time to time during this symposium some of the participants have opined that although rewards and punishments produce spectacular changes in behavior in a seemingly automatic manner, man is nevertheless "more than mere mechanism." Dr. Franks, for example, takes some pains to explain that the Pavlovian tradition provides room for a kind of consciousness, a "derived property of matter in action" and does not view man "as a kind of dehumanized atomistic mechanism" (pp. 134-5). It is my impression that this sort of antimechanistic ploy is passé. It has the flavor of a superstitious genuflection, of a hedge against the possibility that mind or soul as a useful psychological concept, though long interred, may yet arise from its sepulcher.

Time was, obviously, when the antimechanist could chalk up points by leveling a scornful finger at the primitive machines of our grandfathers. But the incredible complexity, superhuman accomplishments, and functional beauty of such contemporary mechanisms as computers, rockets, lasers, communications satellites, and the like, have blunted the thrust of this gambit. The seemingly automatic effects upon behavior of certain contingencies and conditions no longer call for a half-embarrassed apology. Indeed, there is reason to believe that behavior therapy works precisely because its patients are treated as physical systems whose actions can be modified, ineluctably, by reaction-contingent rewards and punishments. Dr. Lovaas provided us with a striking confirmation of this point in his description of the treatment of the self-destructive behavior of a psychotic child. This patient, while immersed in a carefully programmed, merciless world of automatic rewards and punishments, not only improved dramatically and behaved almost normally, but also—and this is an astonishing fact—exhibited love and affection toward experimental gods who programmed his world. Yet when noncontingent, erringly human, tender loving care was substituted for the cold, inhuman methods of the therapist, the child's maladies reappeared and he reverted to the status of a self-destructive psychotic. Man should no longer feel demeaned either by being called a machine or by being treated as one. Were he not to react in the dependable, lawful ways we have come to expect of mechanisms, successful behavior modification would be impossible and, indeed, so would a science of behavior. Thus the work of the behavior therapist stands as a tribute to the enormous vitality of the concept of the human organism as a highly complicated physical-chemical system, the activities of which are lawfully related to the events and contingencies of the circumambient world.

The marked success of the law-of-effect methods of the behavior therapists also puts the screws to the traditional dynamic view that insight or awareness on the patient's part is a necessary condition for his improvement. The behavior therapists, after the manner of Samuel Johnson, who felt no use for the hypothesis of God, feel no need for the concepts of awareness, consciousness, or insightful understanding. This is not to say that the things people say to themselves have no affect on their behavior, but only that the therapist may attain many, perhaps even all, of his ameliorative goals without regard for what the patient is "thinking" or "feeling." Put differently, the reward-administering behavior of the therapist is contingent on the patient's overt behavior, not on the therapist's interpretations of the patient's phenomenal field. Traditionally, maladaptive behavior is viewed as a manifestation of deficiencies in cognitive structures which can be remedied, it is said, by asking the patient to verbalize, often in a more or less random manner, until the appropriate awarenesses or "corrective emotional experiences" are achieved. Once the cognitions are restructured, once the patient *understands* the dynamic significance of his symptoms, his behavior will change, surprisingly enough, *authomatically!* Since the thought is viewed as father to the deed, when thoughts change, deeds must change. Unfortunately, the details of the rules by which deeds are controlled by thoughts remain obsure, a deficiency reminiscent of Guthrie's devastating comment that Tolman's cognitive theory left the rat "buried in thought" in the maze.

The success of the behavior modifiers has highlighted other difficulties that plague the traditional dynamic approach. First and foremost is the fact that the therapist has no direct access to the phenomenal fields, thoughts, and insights of the patient. These internal events are reconstructed or inferred, usually empathically, from gestures, verbal reports, facial expressions, and the like, with which the therapist does have contact. From what the patient says about his dreams it may be asserted that he is in an anxious state and that his maladaptive behavior is due to his anxiety. The hypothetical state is defined by means of one set of (verbal) responses and is thereafter assumed to be the cause of the second set of (maladaptive) reactions, the symptoms. What cannot be ignored here is that the patient-linked empirical events with which the therapist deals, and indeed the only such events available to him for direct inspection, are sets of responses. Whenever one set of reactions is conscripted in this way to explain the vagaries of another, the inescapable result is an R-R (response-response) law.

At bottom, of course, there is nothing wrong with such a law, since it is essentially a correlation. If the correlation is high, responses to one set of test conditions can be predicted from responses to another. The hang-up with R-R relations, in the context of therapy, is that they tell us nothing about the variables of which the internal state is a function and provide no betting tips as to which therapeutic method is likely to come out the winner. Spence (1944), in a discussion of Lewin's phenomenology and the R-R laws deriving therefrom, described this defect precisely:

> A final point of no little importance is the failure of such field theories to provide us with laws which will enable us to control and manipulate the behavior-determining psychological field. Such laws are obviously a basic prerequisite to successful clinical therapy. While it may be true, as Snygg claims . . . that psychiatrists and teachers find the phenomenological approach most valuable in diagnosing behavior disorders, it is difficult to understand how the response-response laws it provides can be of much use in guiding therapeutic treatment. The latter requires a knowledge of what to do to the individual, what changes in his physical and social environment to arrange, in order to bring about the desired behavior changes. The laws telling us how to proceed in such matters are historical laws and involve as an important component of them objective variables representative of past and present factors in the physical and social environments. Psychiatrists and

> clinical psychologists who employed a purely phenomenological approach might or might not be successful at diagnosis; it is difficult to see how they could ever prescribe satisfactory reëducative procedures. [pp. 57–58]

It seems highly probably, then, that a major reason for the success of the behavior therapists is that they deal with S-R (stimulus-response) rather than with R-R relations. Their independent, manipulable variables are observable environmental events, not inferred phenomenal fields, and their dependent variables are concrete, recordable behaviors. Their successful "barside manner" rests on their ability to manipulate and control the contingencies and events of which behavior is a lawful function. They are not restricted, therefore, as are those who attribute behavior to differences in psychological environments, to after-the-fact, response-based definitions of those differences.

Whereas it is difficult to fault the practical methods of the behavior therapists, certain of their conceptualizations warrant critical scrutiny. One of these is the oft-repeated contention that they are "treating behavior directly." For example, Bucher and Lovaas in their chapter chide the traditional therapist for treating the psychosis which is assumed to underly the behavior disturbance rather than treating the speech, bizarre mannerism, or self-destruction per se. When one reflects on what might be precisely meant by "treating behavior directly," it becomes apparent that this must be an eliptical way of speaking. Consider the case, described orally by Dr. Lang in this symposium of an anorexic child who repeatedly regurgitated his food by sticking his fingers down his throat. The successful treatment involved the administration of an electric shock to the bottom of the boy's foot at the exact instant when a peristaltic movement was about to be initiated. Since the foot was not misbehaving, one wonders why it was being punished and how shock to the foot could ever be construed as a "direct treatment" either for jamming one's fingers into the throat or for vomiting. In this, and in similar cases, it would make more sense to say that is is the organism that is being treated, and that changes (or lack thereof) in overt behavior serve to weathercock the therapeutic winds. The traditional therapist performs his exorcismal rites *and* something may happen; the behavior therapist performs his *until* something happens.

I would contend, therefore, that the behavior therapists, regardless of what they say they are doing, do not treat behavior directly in a literal sense. Unlike sore muscles, bad behavior cannot be cured by massage. If the patient swears in mixed company, the therapist does not have to shock the patient's tongue. Instead, he may give the patient candy whenever he stops swearing and withhold candy when swearing reappears. But in this case it looks as though the stomach, rather than the swearing, is being "treated." Evidently, there is no requirement that the palliative poultice must be applied directly to the miscreant peripheral reaction system. An enormous variety of behaviors of vastly different topographies can be strengthened by candy in the mouth and weakened by shock anywhere on the skin. The treatment is thus not specific to the malady, but cures a wide variety of disorders if applied or withheld at the proper times.

Behavior therapists have also lashed out against the medical model, after which the currently most popular formulations of maladaptive behavior have been patterned. A clear statement of the issues involved is provided by Ullmann and Krasner's (1966) excellent introduction to the conceptions and procedures of the behavior-modification buffs. While many of their critical shafts are well aimed, it is possible that some have missed the mark and that a minor reformulation of learning theory concepts would permit them to speak in acceptable ways about those aspects of the medical model that they strongly reject. Thus, such concepts as that of an underlying disease entity, symptom formation, and symptom substitution can be reinterpreted by a learning model and whatever residual value they may possess for psychotherapy can be conserved. Let me speak to this point.

Considering first the concept of an underlying disease entity and its psychological twin, a neurosis, it is of interest to consider some of the possible reasons for the original introduction of such a concept into the realm of maladaptive behavior. One may surmise that medical practitioners, when faced initially with the problems of insanity, searched first for more of the same sorts of physiological disease entities with which they were already familiar. Their readily available diagnostic instruments were specifically tuned to detect germs, poisons, lesions, and the like. But when no correlated disease entities could be found, the next step was to postulate, and to look for evidence of, some sort of condition or state which, though not obviously physiological nor yet clearly mental, was nevertheless as chronic as though it were a persistent focus of infection. The failure of the medically oriented student of behavior lay not in his choice of an organic model over a mental one, but in his failure to see that *maladaptive behavior may be situation-specific rather than chronic*. Both physiological diseases and maladaptive behavior are physical phenomena with physical causes, but only the aberrant reactions appear and disappear upon the presentation and removal of external stimuli. The medical model failed not because of its organic, physicalistic aspects but because of its chronicity. Medical practitioners were trained neither to think in terms of reinforcement histories and habits nor to spot the kinds of learning experiences that lead to maladaptive behavior. The conceptual outcome, etched in the image of a focus of infection, was the neurotic state—the chronic incubus with which the patient was burdened at every step and which controlled his behavior more or less independently of the external situation.

Once the centralized neurosis became reified, it was easy to view it as "the real disorder" and to differentiate it from its overt manifestations, which were therefore not disorders. The behavior therapists, among others, have criticized this view, though their own insistence on the possibility that behavior can be treated directly seems to be consistent with such a dualistic view. Within the field of behavior, however, it makes little sense to attempt to distinguish between a "true" disorder and its manifestations. Maladaptive action, as an empirical event, is itself a disorder in the sense that it alerts society to the patient's need for help. Were there no visible maladaptive behaviors of any kind, there would be no neuroses. But if it is meaningful to say that behavior is disordered, or is a disorder, then every one of its antecedents, whether immanent or remote, also qualifies as a disorder. Overt responses and their muscular, neural, and glandular accompaniments constitute such an inseparable complex that no one part can be called a disorder without implicating other parts. Disordered behavior, unlike a malfunctioning light bulb, cannot be "unscrewed" from its antecedents and repaired or replaced. On each occasion, when behavior changes, one must look for changes in causally related precursors.

As has been suggested above, some of the difficulties spawned by the chronic rather than the organic properties of the medical model and by the behavior therapist's overreactions to that model can perhaps be sidestepped by minor modifications of learning theory as applied to psychotherapy. Something along the following lines might offer promise.

First, since the prevalence of maladaptive reactions and the absence of appropriate ones is attributable, in part, to a patient's history of rewards and punishments, the relative prominence of the two classes of responses can be modified by changing the contingencies. This is the fundamental assumption of the behavior therapist and needs no elaboration. Second, the response-reward contingencies affect behavior indirectly by changing some underlying plexus of associations or habit strengths or predispositions. The pellets in the behavior therapist's black bag of medicaments are effective only because they alter the associative substrate of behavior. This network of associations, which is the repository, so to speak, of the effects of rewards and punishments, is not a psychic *ignis fatuus* but a physical-chemical-neural reality. Third, to have acquired sets of responses that society describes as "sick" or "maladaptive" means that a patient has accumulated corresponding sets of "sick" or "maladaptive" predispositions to respond in those ways. Behind every "sick" response there lies a functionally isomorphic reactive tendency which in some sense, therefore is also "sick."

Presumably, then, overt behavior is related to its underlying reactive propensity in much the same way that the traditional symptom is related to its underlying disease entity. It is difficult to see how this way of speaking of symptoms and disease entities within a learning theory model would offend even the most rabid behavior therapist. The interpretation proposed here does differ, however, from the traditional disease model in one important respect: the learning model gives central prominence to a population of habits, each with its specific response, in place of a single, general-purpose evil spirit. The conventional concept of a monolithic disease entity or neurotic state with its multiple symptomatic manifestations is replaced by the concept of multiple habits each of which is the determinant of its own unique behavioral manifestation.

This theoretical approach also permits us to resolve the troublesome issue of symptom substitution without undue strain. Dr. Franks, among others, has expressed his apprehension over the possibility that whenever the behavior therapist gets rid of some unwanted act, the alleged focal neurosis will reappear in some other symptomatic form. This fear that two bad habits will spring up, hydra-like, for each one that has been eradicated follows from the misconception that peripheral behavior can be modified without changing anything else and that the true disorder is distinguishable from its nondisordered manifestations. I have already tried to dispose of both of these notions. Whatever residuum of truth remains in the symptom substitution notion can be handled by several well-established learning theory principles in the following ways.

First, of course, if an unwanted response is extinguished by nonreinforcement, spontaneous recovery may take place after a period of no further training. Presumably, a number of instances of alleged symptom-substitution as well as examples of recidivism would be consonant with this interpretation. Second, the apparent eruption of new symptoms of an old disorder may be due to new learning or to the evocation of previously acquired responses during encounters with appropriate, but infrequent, stimuli. Third, it has commonly been assumed by learning theorists (for example, Thorndike, Hull, Spence) that the multitudinous habits acquired through social and other reinforcements can be arranged in a hierarchy according to the probability that they will become manifest in overt behavior. If the dominant response is weakened through a process of nonreinforcement, reactions lower in the hierarchy will automatically appear. The patient with many maladaptive responses may be seen as possessed of an underlying matrix of reaction potentials of differing strengths that are symptomatic of past learning and stand ready to be revealed under appropriate circumstances. The dominant response may be thought of as symptomatic of the conditions that developed the strongest associative tendency, and after its elimination the appearance of a different, but weaker reaction is likewise symptomatic of the patient's reinforcement history. If all members of the hierarchy are socially undesirable, all will presumably be eliminated in the end. The process of elimination becomes progressively simpler as the members get weaker and as the extinction effects generalize among the hierarchical population. The successive appearance of new responses in this manner seems to constitute a phenomenon strongly resembling the common description of symptom substitution, and the attendant learning theory has the merit of not involving such concepts as the struggle of unconscious impulses for gratification. Finally, the fact that the literature of behavior therapy contains few reports of symptom return or symptom substitution following treatment need not concern us here. This may be a tribute to the breadth and depth of the extinction procedures that have been used or an indication that insufficient attention has been paid to the frequency with which spontaneous recovery occurs and to the appearance of responses low in the acquired hierarchy.

REFERENCES

SPENCE, K. W. The nature of theory construction in contemporary psychology. *Psychological Review,* 1944, *51,* 47–68.

ULLMANN, L. P., and KRASNER, L. Case studies in behavior modification. New York: Holt, Rinehart and Winston, 1966.

Ackerknecht, E. H., 3, 30
Adler, A., 145, 218, 239
Albrondo, H. F., 3, 30
Alexander, F., 7, 30
Alexander, L., 124, 127, 137
Allen, K. E., 43, 57, 62-3
Angyal, A., 17, 30
Appley, M. H., 171
Armitage, S. G., 35, 173
Astrup, C., 124
Atthowe, J. M., Jr., 77, 85, 87-9, 96, 98, 100
Ayllon, T., 75-7, 83, 87, 89, 93, 95,
Azrin, N. H., 75-7, 85, 87, 89, 95, 98, 129, 137

Baer, D. M., 51, 62, 64
Bagby, E., 12, 30
Balvin, R. S.,111, 113-4, 138
Ban, T. A., 19, 30, 124, 127, 137
Bandura, A., 14, 30, 97-8, 170, 236, 239
Barends, J., 176, 181
Barlow, J. A., 129, 137
Barrett, C. L., 182, 203
Becker, W. C., 46, 64
Beebe-Center, J. G., 157, 170
Beech, H. R., 130, 137
Bekhterev, V. M., 15, 30, 120
Bellamy, E., 94-5, 99
Belsky, S., 142
Berlyne, D. E., 120, 138
Bernard, C., 110
Bijou, S. W., 64
Birren, J. E., 164, 170
Birnbrauer, J. S., 43, 50, 62, 64
Bis, J. S., 87, 99
Blanchard, E. B., 170
Bockover, J. S., 83, 99
Bonvallet, M., 164, 170
Bower, G. H., 114, 119, 122, 140
Brazier, M., 114
Breger, L., 6-7, 26, 31
Brenner, J., 166, 170
Breuker, J., 176, 181
Brousseau, K., 12, 31
Brown, J. S., 15, 31, 70, 72, 183, 202-3
Browning, R. M., 46, 62
Brozek, J., 111-2, 138
Brunswick, E., 230, 239
Burchard, J. D., 84-7, 99
Bucher, B., 18, 45, 62, 65, 67-8, 70, 73, 250
Buell, J. S., 43, 57, 62-3
Bugelski, B. R., 183, 203
Bunker, H. A., 32
Burt, 141
Butler, S., 94, 99
Bykov, K. M., 121, 124, 138
Byrne, D., 31, 33

Callahan, R., 204
Calloway, E., 164, 170
Campbell, N., 17, 31
Cannon, W. B., 162, 171
Cardon, P. V., Jr., 170
Carrera, R. N., 182, 203
Castaneda, A., 227-8, 239
Cautela, J. R., 14, 31, 129, 131, 138, 178-80
Cellini, B., 109
Champion, R. A., 129, 138
Chance, J. E., 231, 239
Cohen, H. L., 87, 99
Cole, H. L., 99
Cole, M., 119, 138
Combs, C. F., 135, 142
Cotter, L. H., 92-3, 99
Crandall, V., 229, 231, 239
Crandall, V. C., 229, 239
Craw, M., 80, 101
Crider, A., 166, 171
Crowne, D. P., 230, 241

Dain, N., 83, 99
Das, J. P., 117, 138
Davison, G. C., 149, 161, 170-1, 174, 177, 180
Dean, R. L., 3, 30
Dell, P., 164, 170
Diamond, S., and S. R., 111, 113-4, 138
DiCara, L. V., 166, 173
Dix, M. R., 123, 138
Dollard, J., 12-13, 25, 31, 145, 182, 203, 210, 239, 243
Dunham, H. W., 5, 31
Dunlap, K., 172
Dykman, 142
Dyrud, J. E., 183, 203

Eddy, E., 68, 73
Edwards, A. E., 126, 141
Edwards, J. E., 175, 181
Efran, J. S., 227, 239
Elkes, C., 3, 34
Engle, B. T., 166, 171
Eriksen, C. W., 163, 171
Eron, L. D., 204

Etzel, B. C., 58, 62
Evans, I., 174, 180
Eysenck, H. J., 2-3, 7-8, 12-13, 23, 31, 34, 63, 75, 99, 123, 138, 175-6, 180

Farber, I. E., 8, 31
Farmer, R. G., 141
Farnsworth, P. R., 241
Feldman, M. P., 65, 73
Fenichel, 183
Ferster, C. B., 15, 31
Feshbach, S., 241
Filipczak, J. A., 87, 99
Fisher, D., 91, 100
Flint, A. A., 3, 34
Folkins, C. H., 161, 171, 174, 180
Ford, D. H., 6, 10, 32
Fox, R., 139
Frank, J. D., 97, 99
Franks, C. M., 10, 20, 32, 111-2, 114-5, 119-20, 125, 128-9, 132, 138-9, 172
Freud, S., 5, 32, 145

Galbraith, J. K., 98-9
Gantt, W. H., 112-4, 124, 126, 138-9, 176
Gardner, J. E., 44, 62
Garicke, O. L., 80, 99
Geer, J. H., 69, 73
Gelder, M. G., 149, 151, 172
Gelfand, D. M., 36, 63
Gellhorn, E., 164, 171
Gerard, 113
Getter, 233
Gewirtz, J. L., 58, 62
Gillis, J., 232, 239
Goldfried, M. R., 128, 139
Good, R. A., 227-8, 239
Good, S., 229, 239
Gore, P. M., 230, 239
Graham, D. T., and F. K., 164, 171
Grant, D. A., 159, 171
Gray, J. A., 111, 120, 123, 135, 139
Green, M., 68, 73
Greenspoon, J., 6, 32
Grings, W. W., 129, 143
Guthrie, E. R., 12, 32, 34, 178

Hall, C., 16, 32
Hallpike, C. S., 123, 138
Hanson, S. P., 166, 171
Harris, A. J., 157, 171
Harris, F. R., 43, 57, 62, 63
Hart, B. M., 43, 57, 62, 63
Hart, J., 80, 101, 152, 157, 167, 172
Hartmann, D. P., 36, 63
Hastings, J. E., 166, 172
Haupt, I., 172
Helson, H., 156, 159, 171
Hering, E., 19
Hewett, F. M., 52, 63
Hiebel, G., 164, 170
Hilgard, E. R., 32, 114, 119, 122, 140, 180, 203
Hnatiow, M., 165-6, 171
Hobbs, N., 5, 32
Hoch, P. H., 139
Hogan, R. A., 182, 203
Holland, J. G., 183, 203
Holz, W. C., 85, 98, 129, 137
Honig, W. K., 15, 32, 98, 137
Hull, C. L., 14, 18, 20-3, 26, 32, 255
Hume, W. I., 123, 140
Humphrey, G., 12, 32
Hunt, H. F., 28, 32, 183, 203
Huxley, A., 94, 99

Imber, R. R., 176, 181
Ivan-Smolensky, A. G., 121, 140

Jacobs, D., 139
Jacobson, E., 23, 32
James, W., 162, 171
Jessor, R., 231, 232, 239, 240-1
Johnson, D. M., 223, 240
Johnson, I., 248
Jones, H. G., 49, 63
Jones, J. E., 129, 138
Jones, M. C., 12, 32
Jones, M. R., 32, 33, 62, 73, 171, 240-1

Kabler, J. D., 164, 171
Kalish, H. I., 11, 32
Kanfer, F. H., 98-9
Kaplan, M., 111, 140
Kelly, G. A., 210, 240
Kerr, N., 49, 63
Kestenbaum, R., 82, 101
Kidder, J. D., 50, 62
Kimble, G. A., 7, 15-16, 19, 32, 119, 140, 175, 180, 183, 203
Kirchner, J. H., 182, 203
Knowles, J. B., 91, 100
Koch, S., 28, 33
Konorski, J., 15, 33, 114, 119, 140
Krasner, L. J., 18, 64, 74-5, 77, 83, 85, 87-9, 91, 96, 98-102,

104, 220, 235, 240–1, 251, 256
Kruseman, A., 176, 181
Kubie, L., 113

Lacey, B. C., 164, 172
Lacey, J. I., 164, 171–2, 177, 180
Lader, M. H., 149–51, 156, 172, 176, 181
Lang, P. J., 23, 59, 63, 66, 73, 149–50, 152, 157, 161–2, 164–7, 169, 171–4, 179, 206, 250
Lange, C., 162, 172
Lanyon, R. I., 176, 181
Lasko, A. A., 227–8, 240
Lawler, J., 43, 64
Lawson, K. D., 161, 171, 174, 180
Lazarus, A. A., 75, 101, 128, 149, 172, 175, 181
Lazarus, R. S., 151, 161, 164, 171–2, 174, 180
Lazovik, A. D., 59, 63, 149, 152, 161–2, 167, 172–3
Lebensohn, Z. M., 113, 140
Lefcourt, H. M., 232, 240
Leontiev, A., 121, 135, 142
Leventhal, H., 163, 173
Levin, M., 117, 140
Levis, D. J., 14, 24, 35, 73, 182–3, 203–4, 207, 245
Levy, L. H., 3, 33, 127, 137
Lewin, K., 26, 230, 240, 249
Liddell, H. S., 28, 73, 124, 176
Lindsley, O. R., 12, 33, 74, 100
Lindzey, G., 16, 32
Lisina, M. I., 165, 173
Lomont, J. F., 174, 181
London, P., 174, 181
Lovaas, O. I., 18, 40, 45, 52–3, 62–3 65, 67–8, 70–1, 73, 92, 247, 250
Lovibond, S. H., 49, 63
Luborsky, L., 99
Luria, A., 120–2, 124, 142
Lynn, R., 115, 117–18, 120, 140

MacCulloch, M. J., and M. L., 65, 73
MacMillan, M., 115–16, 118, 140
Maher, A. R., 232, 240
Maier, N. R. F., 28, 33
Maier, S. P., 69, 73
Makarov, P. O., 113, 140
Maltzman, I., 119, 138
Mangan, G. L., 123, 140, 141
Manosevitz, M., 176, 181
Marcia, J. E., 227, 239
Marks, I. M., 149, 151, 172
Marks, J., 80, 89, 100
Marlett, N., 80, 101
Marquis, 32, 180, 203
Martin, P. L., 79, 100
Marwell, G., 47, 63
Marx, M. H., 240
Masserman, J. H., 28, 33
Matthews, A. M., 176, 180
McGaugh, J. L., 6–7, 26, 31
Mees, H., 45, 64
Melamed, B. G., 66, 73, 152, 157, 159, 167, 172–3
Metz, J. R., 52, 63
Meyerson, L., 49, 63
Michael, J. L., 49, 83, 98
Miller, N. E., 8, 12–13, 20, 25, 28, 31, 73, 145, 166, 173, 182, 203, 210, 239, 243
Minz, A., 115, 141
Mischel, W., 232, 240
More, T., 94, 100
Morton, R. B., 233, 240
Moss, F. A., 35
Moss, T. A., 126, 141
Mostofsky, D. I., 16, 33
Mowrer, O. H., 12, 14, 18, 23–5, 33, 182, 204, 220, 240
Mowrer, W. M., 12, 33
Muenzinger, K. F., 69, 73
Murphy, E., 30
Murphy, W., 30
Myshne, D. A., 141

Napalkov, 175–6
Nebylitsyn, V. D., 119–20, 142
Newman, R. G., 3, 34

O'Connor, N.. 112. 116, 138–42
O'Leary, K. D., 46, 64
Opton, E. M., Jr., 151, 161, 164, 171–2, 174, 180
Orford, J. E., 65, 73
Osgood, C. E., 159, 173

Panek, D. M., 90, 100
Parfoll, M. B., 181
Parrington, V. L., Jr., 94, 100
Paul, G. L., 11, 33, 59, 64, 97, 100, 128, 141, 149, 173
Pavlov, I. P., 11, 14–15, 18–20, 28, 33, 108–147

Peters, 142
Phares, E. J., 228, 240
Phillips, S. L., 170
Pinel, 5
Platonov, K., 121, 141
Pomeranz, D. M., 128, 139
Powell, J. P., 135, 141
Premack, D., 76, 100, 104
Prokasy, W. F., 16, 33-4

Rachman, S., 7, 31, 34, 36, 64, 71, 73, 75, 99
Raines, J., 174, 181
Ramsay, R. W., 176, 181
Rank, O., 236
Ray, A. A., 174, 181
Rayner, R., 12, 35
Razran, G., 112, 121, 124, 129, 141-2
Reese, 142
Rescorla, R. A., 24, 34
Reymert, M. L., 173
Reyna, L. J., 34, 73
Reynolds, D. J., 59, 63, 149, 152, 167, 172
Richmond, J. B., 68, 73
Rioch, M. J., 3, 34
Risley, T. R., 45, 52-3, 56, 64
Ritter, B., 170
Rogers, C. R., 210, 240
Rosenthal, R., 3, 34
Rosenzweig, M. R., 110, 142
Rotter, J. B., 26-7, 34, 210, 214-15, 230, 232-3, 239-44
Rubinstein, E. A., 181
Rychlak, J. F., 228, 241

Salter, A., 19, 34, 73, 124
Schaefer, H. H., 79, 100
Schaeffer, B., 40, 63, 67, 73
Schalock, R., 80, 89, 100
Schlosberg, H., 182, 204
Schmitt, D. R., 47, 63
Schofield, W., 98, 100
Schroder, H. M., 233, 241
Schwarz, J. C., 228, 241
Sechenov, I. M., 110-11, 142
Seligman, M. E. P., 69, 73
Serban, G., 111, 142
Shaffer, J. A., 229, 241
Shapiro, D., 166, 171
Shaw, F. J., 12, 34
Shearn, D. W., 165, 173
Sherman, J. A., 51, 62
Sherrington, C. S., 19, 22, 34
Shlien, J. M., 203
Shoben, E. J., 12, 21, 34, 182, 204
Sibinga, M. S., 68, 73
Silber, E., 3, 34
Simmons, J. Q., 40, 45, 63, 67, 73
Skinner, B. F., 8, 15, 17, 31, 34, 94-6, 101, 136, 142, 182-3, 194, 203-4
Smirnov, A., 142
Smith, S., 12, 34
Snygg, 249
Sokolov, Y. N., 160, 173
Solomon, R. L., 24, 34, 130, 142
Sonoda, B., 80, 89, 100
Spence, K. W., 16, 34, 249-50, 255-6
Spielberger, C. D., 172
Sroufe, L. A., 166, 172-3
Stafford, K. R., 135, 142
Stampfl, T. G., 14, 24-5, 35, 150, 161, 173, 183, 204-7
Starkweather, J. A., 3, 30
Steffy, R. A., 80, 101
Stone, C. P., 34
Strickland, B. R., 230, 241
Strupp, H. H., 3, 35, 99
Sullivan, 145
Szasz, T. S., 83, 101

Tague, C. E., 50, 62
Teasdale, J., 71, 73
Teplov, B. M., 119-20, 139, 142
Thompson, W. H., 113
Thorndike, E. L., 15, 20, 35, 255
Tolman, E. C., 14, 18, 25-7, 35
Torney, D., 80, 100, 101
Tourney, G., 3, 5, 35
Tuttle, H. S., 182, 204
Trumbull, R., 171
Turner, R. K., 49, 64
Turskey, B., 166, 171

Ullman, L. P., 3, 35, 64, 75, 83, 91, 98, 100-1, 235, 241, 251, 256
Urban, H. B., 6, 10, 32
Usdansky, B. S., 3, 34
Uznadze, 120

Valins, S., 174, 181
Vinogradova, 121
Volpe, A., 82, 101
Voronin, L. G., 173
Vygotsky, 120-1

Walters, R. H., 236, 239

Ward, J., 110
Watson, J. B., 11-12, 35, 246
Watson, R. I., 112, 142
Weiner, H., 86, 101
Weitzman, B., 14, 35
Welford, A. T., 170
Wenger, M. A., 162, 173
Wike, E. L., 16, 35
Williams, C. D., 42, 64
Williams, T., 43, 64
Wilson, G. D., 136, 142
Wilson, T., 174, 180
Wing, J., 63
Wolf, M. M., 43, 45, 50, 52-3, 62-4
Wolman, B., 32
Wolpe, J., 12, 19, 21-3, 34-5, 73, 75, 101, 149-50, 157-9, 173-5, 178-9, 181, 210, 241
Wolpin, M., 174, 181
Worschel, P., 31, 33
Wortis, J., 116, 143
Wynne, L. C., 130, 142

Young, G. C., 49, 64

Zeiner, A., 129, 143
Zubin, J., 139

Subject Index

Aggression, 38, 46-7, 184, 200
Alcoholism, 132-3, 148
Animal experimentation, 5, 10, 27-29, 115, 130, 178-9, 184-6, 192-4
Anxiety
  conditioning of, 14, 148-81, 184
  measurement, 177-8
Apathy, 79
Assertive response, 19, 22
Autism, 56-7

Behavior
  daily, 48-50, 76-7, 84
  school, 47-8, 80, 87
  self-destructive, 44-5, 53-4, 70
Behavior therapy
  assets, 6-14, 102-7, 245-56
  assessment, 7, 9-10, 55-62, 71, 128, 134, 201-2
  avoidance conditioning, 22, 66, 72
  conditioned reflex, 19-20
  history, 11-14, 125-36
  limitations, 6, 175, 208-12
  research, 9-10, 58-60, 160, 226-34
Bodily injury, 190, 197
Brain damage, 44

Catharsis, 153
Claustrophobia, 197, 199
Clinical training programs, 3-5
Cognitions, 26, 36, 145, 164, 170, 174
Communication, 2
Community mental health, 5
Conditioning
  avoidance, 20, 23, 152, 165, 184-6, 216, 220
  autonomic, 150, 152, 154, 162, 164-169, 179
  counter, 14, 21, 23, 49, 159, 202
  difference between animal and human, 38, 148, 192-4
  galvanic skin response (GSR), 136, 150, 153, 156, 180
  of sequential cues, 185-6, 196-201
  paradigm, 14-16, 132, 184-6
  principles, 14-16, 132, 178, 191-2, 232
  verbal, 229, 235, 249
Consciousness, 136, 145, 246, 248
Covert cues, 13-14, 25, 109, 121, 189-91, 196-201
Crying, 42-4, 47

Device for automated desensitization (DAD), 167, 169
Death, 190, 197
Defense mechanism, 186-9, 216
Delinquency, 80
Diagnosis, 126-7
Discriminative stimulus (SD), 14, 39-40, 46-7, 52
Dynamic cues, 25, 198-201

Enuresis, 48-9
Existentialism, 1, 145
Expectancy, 26-7, 214, 224-33, 235
Experimental neurosis, 11-12, 115
Extinction, 14, 18, 20-1, 24-5, 150, 191-2

Films, 151-160
Freedom of movement, 215-17, 219, 222, 228

Generalization, 10, 14, 225, 231-3
  stimulus, 55

Geriatrics, 131-2
Guilt, 184

Habituation, 150, 152, 156, 169, 176
Helplessness, 197
Hierarchy, 149, 161, 196-201, 255-6

Imitative, 38, 51
Implosive therapy, 14, 25, 106, 182-215
  animal analogue, 192-4
Insight, 219-20, 236-7, 247-8

Learning
  animal, 5, 10, 27-9, 38, 115, 148
  human, 10, 38, 165, 208-9, 223
  language, 10
  model, 7, 38
  principles, 14-27, 115
  social, 3, 14, 26-7, 40-3, 208
  theory, 7-9, 14-27, 37

Masochism, 245
Medical model, 249-53
Muscle relaxation, 22-3, 153, 157, 174

Need potential, 215-16
Need value, 215-16

Operant treatment procedures, 12, 17 36-73, 150, 247
  children, 36-73
  adult, 74-107

Pavlovian conditioning approaches, 19-20, 108-147, 178-80, 246
Personality, 11, 209-11, 214
Phenomenology, 135, 210, 248-9
Professional organization, 2-3
Protective inhibition, 116
Psychoanalysis, 1, 210
Psychosis, 40, 54, 89
Psychotherapy, 1-4, 183, 208-9, 211-13, 223-4, 226-7, 232, 235, 248
  research, 1, 4-5, 49, 226-234, 249-50
  schools, 4

Reciprocal inhibition, 22, 149, 175
Reinforcement, 18-27, 39, 218, 222, 225, 229, 232, 235, 246-7
  negative, 22, 24, 40-1, 52, 85, 92-4, 216-17, 219-20
  positive, 24, 47, 52, 75-83, 217
Research
  design, 59-62, 88-91, 102-7
  outcome, 2, 142, 201-2
Response control, 161-70
Retardation, 50-1, 80, 84
Rogerian therapy, 1, 210, 235

Schizophrenia, 16
Second signal system, 118, 148
Sleep therapy, 117
Social values, 212-13
Stimulus
  conditioned (CS), 14-15, 18
  control, 151-61
unconditioned (UCS), 14-15, 18
Symptom contingent cues, 195-6
Symptom substitution, 254-6
Systematic desensitization, 12, 23, 148-81

Theory
  construction, 8-9, 14-27, 38, 145-7
  critics, 17-18, 45
Hull's monistic reinforcement theory, 20-3, 175, 178, 210
Mowrer's two-factor theory, 23-5, 182, 184
Pavlov's physiological theory of the cerebral cortex, 18-20, 108-47
Tolman's sign learning theory, 27, 208-43
Rotter's social learning theory, 27, 208-43
Therapists
  ethics of, 2, 4, 211
  experience, 3, 213, 234
  housewife, 3
  humanitarian, 4, 135
  interactions, 3, 22, 38, 213, 220-1, 237
  professional, 2-3
  skill, 3, 40, 213, 223-5, 235, 248
Token economy, 47, 50, 74-107
  adults, 75-83
  children, 47, 50
  geriatric patients, 80-3
  juvenile delinquents, 83-91
  social implications, 91-8
  training, 82-3, 92-5

Vomiting, 44, 65-8, 250

Walden Two, 94-6